"This lively, readable, and sometimes provocative book is a masterful approach to reading Revelation as a witness to God's mission in the world and as an instrument of that mission. In conversation with many others, Dean Flemming—a leading voice in reading Scripture missionally—offers us a much-needed, eye-opening thematic interpretation of Revelation that is both from and for the global church. Highly recommended!"

Michael J. Gorman, Raymond E. Brown Professor of Biblical Studies and Theology at St. Mary's Seminary and University, Baltimore

"Dean Flemming invites readers to listen afresh to Revelation apart from the speculative and often trivializing interpretations based on the flawed premise that this book is primarily a road map for the future. He offers instead a reading of Revelation both richly informed by consideration of its word to and impact on John's first-century congregations, and highly relevant to twenty-first-century congregations eager to learn how to speak and live that witness to which John passionately calls Christians in every age. Flemming's application of a missional hermeneutic to Revelation provides proof positive of the value of this lens for our engagement with all the texts within the canon."

David A. deSilva, Trustees' Distinguished Professor of New Testament and Greek at Ashland Theological Seminary

"Two common and problematic reactions to the book of Revelation are repulsion (Why is God so wrathful?) and unhealthy fascination (What is God's eschatological schedule?). Dean Flemming proposes a missional approach to Revelation that focuses on God's gospel mission, the grace and power of Jesus Christ, and the opportunity for the church to be faithful and resilient witnesses to the good work of God that can triumph over evil in our world. Flemming approaches this theology of Revelation with clarity, humility, wisdom, and hope. If you have ever put Revelation at a distance because of its oddness, Flemming just might turn this into one of your favorite biblical books after all."

Nijay K. Gupta, professor of New Testament at Northern Seminary

"Few things matter more for the recovery of the church's prophetic missional encounter with culture than that biblical believers remember the story we are in, whose story it is, who controls the narrative, how it achieves its goal, and where it all leads. The book of Revelation climactically tells us all of these, but in a way that is so easily misused or ignored. Dean Flemming provides a brilliantly straightforward guide, enabling us to grasp the big picture and its sharply relevant themes, and challenging us, as followers of the Lamb, to recognize and resist the idolatries of our culture and our churches."

Christopher J. H. Wright, Langham Partnership

"Revelation is a book that defies easy explanation. It often engenders fear and wildly imaginative readings. Enter Dean Flemming and his compelling companion to this intriguing New Testament book. Flemming's writing is clear and compelling. His insights are deeply theological and immensely practical. He illumines the beauty of Revelation's vision of God on mission and the way of the Lamb, all the while not shying away from addressing its often-violent imagery. In the end, his goal meets that of the Apocalypse—to encourage the church be a winsome community of worship and mission for the sake of God's entire creation."

Jeannine Brown, professor of New Testament at Bethel Seminary, St. Paul, Minnesota

"The book of Revelation is perhaps the richest theological book of the New Testament and has an urgent message for the church today—that is, if it is read faithfully along its missional grain. Dean Flemming offers a rich reading of this book that listens carefully to the original message in its first context and to the missional calling of the church today. The book is characterized by what we have come to expect from Flemming—careful scholarship that yields rich, contemporary pastoral and missional insight. We need the book of Revelation today, and we need books like this to open up its powerful message."

Michael Goheen, professor of missional theology at Covenant Theological Seminary, St. Louis, and director of theological education at the Missional Training Center, Phoenix

DEAN
FLEMMING

FORETASTE

of the

FUTURE

READING
REVELATION
IN LIGHT OF GOD'S
MISSION

ĩvp
Academic
An imprint of InterVarsity Press
Downers Grove, Illinois

InterVarsity Press
P.O. Box 1400 | Downers Grove, IL 60515-1426
ivpress.com | email@ivpress.com

InterVarsity Press® is the publishing division of InterVarsity Christian Fellowship/USA®.
For more information, visit intervarsity.org.

Scripture quotations, unless otherwise noted, are from the New Revised Standard Version Bible,
copyright © 1989 National Council of the Churches of Christ in the United States of America. Used by permission.
All rights reserved worldwide.

The publisher cannot verify the accuracy or functionality of website URLs used in this book beyond
the date of publication.

Cover design and image composite: David Fassett
Interior design: Daniel van Loon

ISBN 978-1-5140-0156-1 (print) | ISBN 978-1-5140-0157-8 (digital)

Printed in the United States of America ∞

Library of Congress Cataloging-in-Publication Data
A catalog record for this book is available from the Library of Congress.

29 28 27 26 25 24 23 22 | 8 7 6 5 4 3 2 1

To my students at Asia-Pacific Nazarene Theological Seminary,

European Nazarene College, and MidAmerica Nazarene University,

who, over the years, have inspired me to read

and teach Scripture more faithfully.

CONTENTS

ACKNOWLEDGMENTS

WRITING THIS BOOK has turned out to be a joyful journey. In part, that has to do with the subject, the mind-blowing book of Revelation. But it also stems from the rich input of conversation partners along the way. Above all, I want to thank three dear friends, Andy Johnson, Darrell Ranum, and Chris Lindenmeyer, for carefully reading the full manuscript. Each has offered astute suggestions and welcome encouragement from their distinctive perspectives. Others have read and commented on significant parts of the book, including Corlis McGee, Tim Isbell, and Robert Menzies, and I am grateful.

My deep thanks also goes to Anna Gissing, my editor at IVP Academic, for her guidance and encouragement throughout the life of the project, as well as to Rebecca Carhart and others at InterVarsity Press who have helped shepherd the book into publication. In addition, I want to express appreciation to the following publications and editors: *Missiology* and its editor Richard Starcher, along with Sage Publications, for permission to use revised material from an article that appeared in the April 2020 edition of the journal and Claremont Press, and Thomas E. Phillips for permission to adapt material from the essay "Divine Judgment and the *Missio Dei* in the Book of Revelation," which appears in the 2020 volume *Listening Again to the Text: New Testament Studies in Honor of George Lyons*, edited by Richard P. Thompson.

Finally, I give glory to God for the Spirit's strength, insight, and motivation, without which this book would not be possible. "Praise and glory and wisdom and thanks and honor and power and strength be to our God for ever and ever" (Rev 7:12 NIV).

REIMAGINING REVELATION

He who was seated on the throne said, "I am making everything new!"

REVELATION 21:5 (NIV)

LIKE MANY OF YOU, I've had a love/hate relationship with the book of Revelation. Frankly, Revelation and I got off to a rocky start! I grew up in an American evangelical church culture that read the visions in Revelation as a kind of screenplay for the end times. Prophecy experts came to my church and with the aid of their impressive charts explained step by step how the future would play out. My youth group watched a movie that vividly portrayed the horror of what it would be like to be left behind on earth during the Great Tribulation, after true believers had been "raptured" to heaven. It really scared me! As a college student I read Hal Lindsey's *The Late Great Planet Earth*, which tried to cross-reference the images in Revelation with then-current events, especially in the Middle East, speculating that the events leading up to the end of the world might occur during the 1980s.[1] It's worth noting that some interpreters of Revelation still follow this method of deciphering Revelation's message. As I write these words, well-meaning Christian bloggers speculate on whether the coronavirus pandemic unlocks the meaning of Revelation's symbol of a pale horseman unleashing lethal pestilence on the earth (Rev 6:8). Although I largely bought into this

---

[1]Hal Lindsey, *The Late Great Planet Earth* (Grand Rapids, MI: Zondervan, 1970).

"script-of-the-end-times" approach to interpreting Revelation (it was the only one I knew), I struggled to fathom how the "prophecy experts" could be so certain that "this means *this*."

All of this left me with two fundamental responses to Revelation: confusion and fear. Not surprisingly, I see the same reactions to the Apocalypse in my students today. Some of them have come under the influence of the wildly popular Left Behind series of Christian fiction books and the four action movies that they spawned. Others know little about Revelation, except that is it supposed to predict the future. One student pictured Revelation as "the elephant in the room" in his Christian life. Like the proverbial elephant, it's *there*. It's uncomfortable. But we ignore it. Even as a pastor and later a teacher of the Bible, I largely avoided the book of Revelation. It was too violent, too depressing, too hard to understand. Instead, I left it mainly to the "experts" to try to figure out the meaning of this baffling book. In effect, I did what many Christians do when confronted with the complexities of the Apocalypse. Revelation became the "ugly stepsister" in my personal canon of Scripture, strangely disconnected from the Jesus of the Gospels and the practical theology of the New Testament Letters.

I wasn't alone. For centuries Christians have wrestled with what to do with this mysterious book of visions. The reformer Martin Luther struggled with whether it should be included in the New Testament canon. For John Calvin, it was virtually the only New Testament book on which he did *not* write a commentary. Methodist founder John Wesley, after "utterly despairing of understanding" much of Revelation, "subcontracted" his explanatory notes on it, relying mainly on the comments of the earlier scholar Bengel.[2] At least I was in good company.

But then my relationship with Revelation changed—dramatically. It happened quite unintentionally. While teaching New Testament in Germany, I was asked to write an essay on Revelation for a book honoring one of my former professors. The reason the editors of the volume enlisted me for this assignment had absolutely nothing to do with my brilliance as a

---

[2]John Wesley, *Explanatory Notes upon the New Testament*, repr. (Salem, OH: Schmul, 1976), 650.

Revelation scholar. They simply couldn't find anyone else willing to do it! I reluctantly—and perhaps foolishly—agreed to write the essay, not because I felt in the least qualified but out of respect for my former teacher. You might say that I backed into the study of Revelation. In the early stages of my research, however, I came across Richard Bauckham's *The Theology of the Book of Revelation*, a book that altered my perspective on the Apocalypse.[3] Bauckham helped me to read Revelation not as a play-by-play script for the end times or as a collection of incomprehensible visions but rather as the culmination of God's entire loving purpose for the world. I began to read Revelation *theologically* and *missionally*. And that changed *everything*.

Studying for that initial essay sparked within me what has fanned into a deep passion for the book. I am passionate about Revelation not because I think I have figured it all out but because I am convinced that this often-neglected, misunderstood, and intimidating book carries a message that we cannot ignore. Revelation stands as one of the richest, although untapped, veins in Scripture for understanding *both* God's sweeping mission to make everything new *and* how the church is caught up in that renewing mission. If like me you've ever felt uncertain, ignorant, fearful, or put off when it comes to Revelation, this book is for you.

In a nutshell, this book tries to show that *Revelation is not about scripting future events but revealing God's great purpose to redeem and restore the whole creation, including people, through the mission of the slain Lamb. At the same time, Revelation seeks to shape and equip Christian communities to participate in God's saving purpose by living as a foretaste of God's coming new creation now, through their lips and through their lives.*

Why This Book?

I wrote this book in part because I believe Revelation has so much more to say to the church and its role in the world today than we normally expect. Too often a deep disconnection operates in the minds of students, preachers, and church members between the Bible's final book and the everyday life and mission of the church. This gap between Revelation and real life isn't

---

[3]Richard Bauckham, *The Theology of the Book of Revelation* (Cambridge: Cambridge University Press, 1993).

surprising. Many popular readings of Revelation focus almost entirely on how events will unfold in the *future*; consequently, it has little to say about what God is doing in the world *now*. For some Christians, Revelation offers a kind of picture guide to their future home in heaven, especially the throne room scene in chapters 4–5 and John's vision of New Jerusalem in Revelation 21–22. But this leaves most of the book with little connection to everyday life. "Because we're bound for heaven," N. T. Wright observes, "the rantings and ragings of bestial powers on earth are interesting, but largely irrelevant to us."[4]

For many other Christians, Revelation unveils a *way out* of this world. This literal "left behind" approach (technically "dispensationalism") has dominated evangelical interpretations of Revelation in North America over the past century and has been widely exported to other parts of the global church. Many such readings of Revelation claim that genuine believers in Jesus are secretly "raptured" to heaven at the beginning of chapter 4 when the risen Christ says to John, "Come up here" (Rev 4:1). In such a scenario not just unbelievers but *the church's entire mission in the world* is left behind. This amounts to an *escape* from any role for the church in God's mission to a rebellious world. Beyond that, if Revelation is simply a coded prophecy of end-time events (at least after chapter 3), what could it possibly have meant to the people to whom John originally wrote?

> *"There's no time to change your mind*
> *The Son has come and you've been left behind."*[5]
>
> LARRY NORMAN

Perhaps in reaction to such futuristic "pie-in-the-sky" approaches, other interpreters read Revelation's symbols and visions exclusively in their first-century historical and political context in the Roman Empire. But they

---

[4]N. T. Wright, "Revelation and Christian Hope: Political Implications of the Revelation to John," in *Revelation and the Politics of Apocalyptic Interpretation*, ed. Richard B. Hays and Stefan Alkier (Waco, TX: Baylor University Press, 2012), 105.

[5]Larry Norman, "I Wish We'd All Been Ready," Beechwood Music Corp./J. C. Love Pub. Co, 1969.

struggle to build any kind of bridge between John's first-century world and that of the present life and mission of God's people. The chasm between Revelation and the church today remains.

Is there a way to read Revelation without confining its message either to the events of a frozen past, the prophecies of a distant (or not so distant) future, or at best an individualistic warning to be ready for Jesus' return? Absolutely! I propose that a *missional* reading of Revelation will lead us to read this "weird and wonderful exclamation point on the Christian canon" in a more faithful and responsible way.[6] But before I explain what I mean by a missional reading, I need to tell you another reason that motivates me to write this book.

For more than thirty years I've had the privilege of teaching and learning from people in global settings outside of my own North American context. I spent most of that time in Asia and Europe, but more recently I had the opportunity to engage doctoral students in Africa. Although I have fulfilled the role of a Bible *teacher*, my interpretation of Scripture has been shaped through interacting with students, church leaders, and parishioners in those different cultural settings. It troubles me that too often theologians and interpreters of the Bible in the West seem to assume that their (mostly White male) interpretations are the only ones that matter. We too easily forget that the center of gravity of world Christianity has shifted dramatically from West to East and from North to South.[7] The phrase *Majority World*—the world outside of the West—represents more than politically correct language. It describes the reality of global Christianity. Consequently, Western Christians must listen to voices unlike their own. This also includes the insights of people living in the West who are not part of the dominant culture. As I explore a missional reading of Revelation in this book, I will seek to include perspectives from people representing various cultures and contexts. Such an approach, in fact, rings true to Revelation itself, where those from every tribe, language, and nation make up the people of God (Rev 7:9).

---

[6]Dean Flemming, *Why Mission?* (Nashville, TN: Abingdon, 2015), 110.
[7]See Philip Jenkins, *The New Christendom: The Coming of Global Christianity* (Oxford: Oxford University Press, 2002).

What Is a Missional Reading of Revelation?

The most important reason for writing this book is that I believe a missional reading of Revelation enables us to read the last book of the Bible more *faithfully*; that is, in a way that's more in sync with Scripture's character and purpose. Bible scholars, theologians, and missiologists alike increasingly have come to recognize that the whole of Scripture tells, as Christopher Wright puts it, "the story of God's mission through God's people in their engagement with God's world for the sake of the whole of God's creation."[8] A missional reading of Scripture, then, rests on three important assumptions:[9]

- God is a missional God; therefore, God is engaged in a loving mission to bring salvation to all people and to restore the whole creation.

- Scripture bears witness to God's mission in the world.

- God has called the church to participate in the divine mission, and Scripture seeks to equip God's people to do so within their specific life settings.

Before we tread any further, we need some definitions. Let's begin with *mission*. Many Christians think of *mission* in a fairly narrow sense, which focuses on the church's activities of evangelizing people and planting churches, particularly in crosscultural settings. It is largely something that God-called missionaries *do* and other Christians *support*. That definition isn't wrong; it's simply too limited. A truly biblical understanding of mission is far more sweeping than that. We need to start not with the activities of the church or a group of missionaries but with the mission of the triune God (in Latin the *missio Dei*). Mission begins with God. It is about God's massive purpose to bring wholeness and redemption to the entire creation, especially people from every nation, as well as what we as God's people are called to be, do, and say as we participate in God's great purpose.[10]

---

[8]Christopher J. H. Wright, *The Mission of God: Unlocking the Bible's Grand Narrative* (Downers Grove, IL: IVP Academic, 2006), 51 (italics deleted).

[9]See Michael J. Gorman, *Abide and Go: Missional Theosis in the Gospel of John* (Eugene, OR: Cascade, 2018), 2-3.

[10]Christians, especially in North America, often use the plural term *missions* as well as *mission*. Although these terms are sometimes treated interchangeably, *missions* is best understood to refer to "the multitude of activities that God's people can engage in, by means of which they

I use the term *missional* not in any technical way (e.g., the "missional church") but simply as an adjective referring to something that has to do with or participates in the mission of God.[11] It's also important to make clear what mission is *not*. I recognize that for some Christians the term *mission* itself can be problematic. It conjures up painful past entanglements between missionaries and colonial powers in which dominant groups coerced less powerful people to adopt their cultures or beliefs. But I am not convinced that the answer is to throw out the term altogether, and my students and colleagues in various global cultures have helped me to see that. *Mission* in a biblical understanding represents the very opposite of cultural imperialism. It is about getting caught up in God's healing, reconciling, and liberating purposes for all peoples of the world.

A comprehensive understanding of the *missio Dei* means that we need to rethink the relationship between the Bible and mission. In the past Christians looking for what the Bible had to say about mission often operated similar to a prospector panning for gold. Like a prospector, they sifted through the Bible until they uncovered a few golden mission nuggets that supported the church's task of world evangelization.[12] Nuggets like Jesus' Great Commission to "Go . . . and make disciples of all nations" in Matthew 28:19, or the Messiah's promise, "You will be my witnesses . . . to the ends of the earth" (Acts 1:8), or Paul's question in Romans, "How are they to hear without someone to proclaim him?" (Rom 10:14). It's thrilling to find nuggets. But making that our primary approach to "the Bible and mission" is at best incomplete and at worst misleading. Instead of surfing the Bible for isolated mission texts, we need to see *the whole of Scripture as a mission text*. This assumes that *mission* is bigger than the church's crosscultural evangelistic witness alone. Mission embraces God's comprehensive and loving purpose to bring about salvation and healing at every level.

---

participate in God's mission." Christopher J. H. Wright, *The Mission of God's People: A Biblical Theology of the Church's Mission* (Grand Rapids, MI: Zondervan, 2010), 25.

[11]Flemming, *Why Mission?*, xvii-xviii. Wright makes a convincing argument that *missional* is a better term for reading the whole message of Scripture than either *missionary* or *missiological*, both of which have a narrower focus. Wright, *Mission of God*, 23-25.

[12]See David J. Bosch, "Reflections on Biblical Models of Mission," in *Toward the 21st Century in Christian Mission*, ed. James M. Phillips and Robert T. Coote (Grand Rapids, MI: Eerdmans, 1993), 175-76.

What is true of the Bible at large applies no less to Revelation specifically. Instead of simply searching for passages in Revelation that might
underpin the church's crosscultural missionary activity (Rev 5:9 comes to
mind: "You [the Lamb] ransomed for God saints from every tribe and
language and people and nation"), we need to see *all* of Revelation as a
witness to the sweeping purpose of God to redeem all people and to renew
the whole creation. The Apocalypse invites, even *demands*, such a missional reading. It envisions the goal and triumph of God's mission in the
world, a mission that is about "the healing of the nations" (Rev 22:2), and
ultimately "making everything new" (Rev 21:5 NIV). *In the first place*, a
missional reading of Revelation assumes that not just certain verses
or passages but the entire book bears witness to the comprehensive
mission of God on behalf of all of creation and the role of God's people in
that mission.

But there's a *second* dimension to a missional reading of Revelation. That
has to do with how this book equips and energizes the people of God to get
caught up in the mission of God where they live. A missional reading of
Scripture concerns not only what the Bible *says* but also what it *does*. John's
visions in Revelation do much more than foretell the future. They are
intended to shape who God's people are and how they live out God's mission
now. Revelation itself serves as an instrument of the mission of God. It
addresses communities of Christ-followers who are already engaged in
God's saving mission, both in the first century and the twenty-first century.
And it seeks to enable those communities to embody the loving purposes of
God in the world.

Third, a missional reading of Scripture also concerns how the Bible speaks
into specific life circumstances. Missiologists call this task *contextualization*.
Every Christian community must ask, How might Revelation's witness to
God's mission and the church's participation in that purpose be *contextualized* both in our own setting and in that of people who are different from us?
Fortunately, Scripture itself offers models of contextualization that we can
learn from. New Testament writers such as John enabled the gospel to speak
in ways that were tailored to specific settings—for example, confronting a

culturally "normal" practice like eating food offered to idols in ancient Pergamum (Rev 2:14).[13]

Similarly, we need to continue to sing the gospel story in new keys for a host of diverse global settings today. Depending on our life situation, we will bring different questions to the text. Take, for example, Christ's words to the church in Laodicea in Revelation 3: "For you say, 'I am rich, I have prospered, and I need nothing.' You do not realize that you are wretched, pitiable, poor, blind, and naked. . . . To the one who conquers I will give a place with me on my throne, just as I myself conquered and sat down with my Father on his throne" (Rev 3:17, 21).

Christians who experience poverty and marginalization might ask how those words turn the tables on the rich and the powerful and how they bring hope of deliverance from economic injustice. But what about Christians who read from a place of relative power and affluence? They might probe how Christ's message challenges them to resist mindless materialism and its harmful effects on less privileged people so that they might share in Christ's ultimate victory. At the same time, the gospel will in some ways challenge *every* culture and setting, including our own.

The funny thing about contextualization is that it doesn't work as well second hand. As a result, you and your Christian community will need to do the bulk of this difficult contextualizing work within your setting. Throughout this book, however, I will offer examples of how Christian readers in my own North American context as well as those in other global venues *hear* the message of Revelation and how it addresses them where they are. Some of these appear in the form of sidebars that accompany the main text.

In summary, reading Revelation missionally invites us to approach this book with at least three vital questions in mind. First, what is God doing in the world, and how does Revelation bear witness to that sweeping mission? Second, how does Revelation invite and equip God's people to get caught up in what God is doing? And third, how might that understanding of God's mission and our participation in it speak to the church's diverse, global

---

[13]See Dean Flemming, *Contextualization in the New Testament: Patterns for Theology and Mission* (Downers Grove, IL: IVP Academic, 2005).

settings today?[14] These three questions lay out the primary concerns of this book. Making it more personal, what is God up to in the world? How are we a part of that? And what difference does all of this make for Christians who are like us and for those who are *not* like us?

WHERE ARE WE HEADED?

I confess that I am directionally challenged! My inner compass generally operates about 180 degrees off course. Consequently, when I begin a trip, I really need a GPS app or a map. As we embark on this journey together, let me map out where we're headed. In the first place, we are not going to take the usual route, which starts with Revelation 1 and traverses the book chapter by chapter. Instead, we will approach Revelation *thematically*, exploring various dimensions of a missional reading of this book. That trek begins with a framework for reading Revelation in chapter one, which answers questions like, What kind of book is this? and What is the first-century context that John addresses? This chapter sets the stage for a missional reading of Revelation by showing how John's visions invite his readers to see their world from an entirely different perspective than that of the social, political, and religious powers that claim to be in control.

From there, the heart of our journey leads us through different ways of approaching Revelation's portrait of the mission of God. In chapters two through four, we encounter the major characters in the story of God's mission that Revelation tells: *the God of mission*, whose loving purpose for the world spans from creation to new creation; *the slaughtered Lamb*, whose costly, redeeming death not only makes God's mission possible but also reveals *how* God carries out his renewing purposes in the world; and *the people of God*, whom God has chosen as an instrument for accomplishing his saving work on behalf of all people and all of creation. We will discover that Revelation pictures God's people as *both* the suffering, sometimes compromising congregations in first-century Asia Minor (Rev 2 and 3), who in

---

[14]These concerns reflect different dimensions of a missional interpretation of Scripture as laid out in George R. Hunsberger's seminal essay, "Proposals for a Missional Hermeneutic: Mapping the Conversation," *Missiology* 39 (2011): 309-21. Hunsberger discusses four "streams" or different understandings of a missional hermeneutic, which emerged out of a series of meetings held by the Gospel and Our Culture Network.

many ways resemble churches today, *and* as the multinational company of the redeemed (Rev 7:9) that is called to embody God's new creation now.

Chapters five through eight continue the journey by exploring some key elements in John's vision of what God is up to in the world. First, we will look at the *witness* of word and life that is the church's fundamental calling in Revelation (chapter five). Then we'll take up the sticky issue of how to square Revelation's violent visions of *judgment* with the loving mission of God (chapter six). We will discover that mission and judgment act as *partners*, not enemies. Chapter seven spotlights the *worship* of God's people and how that worship plays a crucial role in God's mission. And chapter eight tackles head-on the question of missional *politics*. What did loyalty to God's kingdom mean for John in light of the idolatry and exploitation of the Roman Empire? And how might God's mission call us to resist the politics of "Babylon and the beast" today? This might be the most challenging chapter for some readers, especially when I make applications to the present North American context. I invite you to read it with a prayerful and open spirit.

In chapter nine, our trek through Revelation reaches its goal with John's vision of a new heaven and a new earth and how that vision invites us to live as a foretaste of the new creation now. Finally, a concluding chapter reflects on the whole journey, especially what it means to read Revelation missionally and how that might work out in practice for the church in mission today.

To the Readers

I've already told you some of my story. Our life stories and the communities we are part of inevitably influence how we read Scripture. I'm no exception. I stand in the theological "tribe" of the Wesleyan holiness confession within the broader, historical evangelical tradition. I grew up in North America and live and work there now, but as I hinted earlier, I have spent most of my adult life ministering in Asia and Europe. Hopefully, you will see that intercultural part of my story coming through. I'm also aware that as a White male from the West, I have experienced privileges that many other readers of Revelation have not. This surely affects how I read these texts. But I've embarked on a journey of listening and learning from sisters and brothers in Christ whose life experience is different from my own.

This book is intended for several types of readers, including preachers and teachers, students, and laypeople who desire to read the Bible more faithfully. My aim is that it will appeal both to those who are interested in a more responsible approach to Revelation and to those who desire to learn how to read Scripture missionally. To make the book as accessible as possible, I've tried to cut out most of the technical jargon. I also include many Scripture references in parentheses, which are not cited in full. It will take extra effort and time to look them up, but I believe it will pay you rich dividends. Finally, I have included reflection questions relating to each chapter at the end of the book to facilitate further personal reflection and group conversations about how Revelation's message might apply practically.

Without apology, this book builds on the work of others. I have learned much from missiologists and biblical scholars such as David Bosch, Christopher Wright, Michael Goheen, and many others who have reflected seriously on reading the Bible missionally.[15] In addition, the Gospel and Our Culture Network in North America has sponsored an annual forum on missional hermeneutics (how we interpret the Bible) since 2002, which has helped to shape my thinking significantly.[16] I hope that this book can help advance this conversation. As far as I am aware, it is the first book dedicated to a missional reading of Revelation as a whole.[17]

---

[15]See David J. Bosch, *Transforming Mission: Paradigm Shifts in Theology of Mission* (Maryknoll, NY: Orbis, 1991), esp. 15-178; Wright, *Mission of God*; idem, *Mission of God's People*; Michael W. Goheen, *A Light to the Nations: The Missional Church and the Biblical Story* (Grand Rapids, MI: Baker, 2011); see especially Michael W. Goheen, ed., *Reading the Bible Missionally* (Grand Rapids, MI: Eerdmans, 2016), and its extensive bibliography.

[16]See the Gospel and Our Culture Network website for resources related to these meetings, www .gocn.org.

[17]I have reflected on a missional reading of Revelation in shorter book chapters and articles in the past, and this book stands on the foundations of those reflections. See Dean Flemming, "Revelation and the *Missio Dei*: Toward a Missional Reading of the Apocalypse," *Journal of Theological Interpretation* 6 (2012): 161-78; *Recovering the Full Mission of God* (Downers Grove, IL: IVP Academic, 2013), 231-52; *Why Mission?*, 109-27; "The Book of Revelation," in *Wesley One Volume Commentary*, ed. Kenneth J. Collins and Robert W. Wall (Nashville, TN: Abingdon, 2020), 908-34; "Locating and Leaving Babylon: A Missional Reading of Revelation 17 and 18 in Light of Ancient and Contemporary Political Contexts," *Missiology* 48.2 (2020): 112-26; "Divine Judgment and the *Missio Dei* in the Book of Revelation," in *Listening Again to the Text: New Testament Studies in Honor of George Lyons*, ed. Richard P. Thompson (Claremont, CA: Claremont Press, 2020), 171-91; "Following the Lamb Wherever He Goes: Missional Ecclesiology in Revelation 7 and 14:1-5," in *Cruciform Scripture: Cross, Participation, and Mission*, ed. Christopher W. Skinner et al. (Grand Rapids, MI: Eerdmans, 2021), 260-78. See also Michael J. Gorman's

I also hope that this effort can function as a case study of reading Scripture missionally, which might encourage you and your Christian community to read other parts of the Bible in similar ways. It is my prayer that this volume will kindle in readers a deeper desire to engage Scripture in light of the mission of God as well as a passion to discover how Revelation, a book so often misread or ignored, can shape the life and mission of God's people today. Now it's time to begin the journey.

Reading Revelation Responsibly: Uncivil Worship and Witness: Following the Lamb into the New Creation (Eugene, OR: Cascade, 2011). This excellent book engages Revelation theologically and, in part, missionally.

CHAPTER ONE

WHAT IS REVELATION TRYING TO DO?

Blessed is the one who reads aloud the words of the prophecy, and
blessed are those who hear and who keep what is written.

REVELATION 1:3

IMAGINE THAT YOU ARE PART of an early Christian gathering in the city of Ephesus in the late first century. You have joined other followers of Christ to hear the public reading of a long letter (see Rev 1:4, 9) addressed to seven Christian assemblies in your region, including your own. You listen intently as this "apocalypse" is read from start to finish. Your imagination surges into overdrive as you hear John, the author, describe a whole series of fantastical visions, which unfold like scenes in a cosmic drama. Here is one Revelation scholar's brief summary of the action:

> The risen Christ appears, eyes of fiery flame, with trumpet voice like mighty waves crashing against the shore, holding seven stars in his right hand. A throne in the heavenly sky appears, the Almighty seated on the throne, the heavenly court—zoological and humanoid—singing eternal praise. A slaughtered Lamb receives a sealed book, opens it, and great terrors strike not only the earth with its fish, animals, and humans, good and evil alike, but also the solar system, the planets, and the stars. Seven-headed beasts emerge, who demand the worship that is due only to the Lord God Almighty. Those who resist are beheaded; their death is called their "conquering." A beautifully

seductive whore rides one of the beasts, but she is destroyed, as are the beasts and Satan, who empowers them. The world is redeemed, the heavenly city New Jerusalem descends to earth, all God's people celebrate the ultimate happy ending.[1]

What effect would this imaginative drama have on you as a member of a first-century congregation? How would it speak to your world? What would be the effect of hearing it read publicly? How does John want your congregation to respond to what they have heard? And does Revelation ask Christian communities to think and act in similar ways today?

For most of us the answer to such questions is likely "I'm not sure." It's hard for us to put ourselves into the sandals of first-century Christians in Ephesus and grasp how utterly disruptive such a book would have seemed to them. But if we want to read Revelation missionally, we need to try to understand what this book is asking of its readers and how that fits into God's purpose for all people and the whole creation.

This chapter explores three fundamental issues: the *form* in which Revelation comes to us, how Revelation tries to *persuade* its audience, and the *missional context* it addresses. All three help to shape how believing communities then and now read Scripture's grand finale.

FORM MATTERS

Revelation is strange. It confronts us with a type of communication that seems closer to a fantasy video game than the accounts of Paul's travels in the book of Acts or the closely reasoned arguments of the letter to the Romans. It draws us into a world of angels and earthquakes, locusts and lampstands, beasts and bottomless pits. For many Western Christians, reading Revelation is not unlike the experience of traveling to a foreign country that has a mystifying culture. One reason many Christians react negatively to Revelation or want to avoid it is precisely that it is *so different.* Consequently, in order to grasp the missional *message* of Revelation, we need to understand the *form* in which that message is conveyed. Perhaps

---

[1]M. Eugene Boring, *Hearing John's Voice: Insights for Teaching and Preaching* (Grand Rapids, MI: Eerdmans, 2019), 9-10. Boring's description, of course, uses modern scientific language that would not have registered with first-century people.

more than any New Testament book, if we confuse the form, we'll misread the content.

Revelation, however, resists being pigeonholed into a single literary type or, to use a more technical term, *genre*. Rather, it represents "a *hybrid* document, a mixed breed."[2] Indeed, Revelation features at least three interrelated genres: apocalypse, prophecy, and letter.

Visions and symbols. Above all, Revelation belongs to a type of ancient writing called an *apocalypse*. Significantly, the first word in the Greek text of Revelation is *apokalypsis*, which means "revelation" or "unveiling." Although John doesn't use the term *apocalypse* in a technical sense, scholars came to employ the word for a kind of literature that flourished among Jews and Christians in the centuries right before and after Christ. As a result, apocalyptic literature seemed much more familiar and normal to John's readers than it does to most of us today. Like its name, apocalyptic literature is a revelatory form of writing. It runs thick with visions, images, and symbols. Douglas Moo and Jonathan Moo describe this well:

> John makes extensive use of symbolism, metaphor, and poetic language to convey the message of his Revelation. Readers are invited into a world of stories and images that are intended to communicate truth about God and his purposes but which are not intended—and in fact make no sense—if they are read as straightforward depictions of physical phenomena.[3]

The final point of this quotation deserves bold letters and an exclamation mark. Apocalyptic symbols and images *are not designed to be read literally.* Ancient people like John and his audience would certainly not have understood them that way. This is perhaps the strongest argument against popular dispensationalist ("Left Behind") interpretations of Revelation. They fail to let symbols be *symbols*. A "literal" reading of Revelation might, for example, assume that the description of John measuring "the temple of God" (Rev 11:1-3) refers to a literal rebuilt structure on Jerusalem's Temple Mount, that the infamous battle of Armageddon (which does not, in fact, take

---

[2]Michael J. Gorman, *Reading Revelation Responsibly: Uncivil Worship and Witness: Following the Lamb into the New Creation* (Eugene, OR: Cascade, 2011), 13 (italics Gorman's).

[3]Douglas J. Moo and Jonathan A. Moo, *Creation Care: A Biblical Theology of the Natural World* (Grand Rapids, MI: Zondervan, 2018), 162.

place—see Rev 16:16) corresponds to an actual clash of armies on a plain in northern Israel, or that the "mark of the beast" (Rev 13:16-18) denotes some kind of physical imprint or implant that allows someone to buy gas or groceries. Such readings force the square peg of an apocalyptic symbol into a round hole of describing historical events.

Nor can we fall into the snare of trying to *explain* John's apocalyptic symbols as a secret code (think of the Enigma Code from World War II) that might hide what he was *really* saying from the church's Roman persecutors. When John pictures Rome as the idolatrous harlot Babylon in chapter 17, for example, he makes no effort to give this figure a disguise. Descriptions like "the seven heads are seven mountains on which the woman is seated" (Rome as the city built on seven hills Rev 17:9) and "the woman you saw is the great city that rules over the kings of the earth" (Rev 17:18) would be as obvious to people living in the Roman world of John's day as a cowboy would be to an American football fan from Dallas today. What's more, *codes* simply tell us what something refers to. *Symbols* go deeper. The symbol of the harlot Babylon lets us *experience* the arrogance, injustice, and deception of human empires and anti-God powers in a way that straightforward language cannot.[4] Unlike codes, symbols operate at multiple levels. Although Babylon the prostitute represented Rome for John's first readers, Babylon isn't confined to Caesar's empire. As we will see in chapter 8, Babylon is present *anywhere* the powers of greed, injustice, and violence oppose the loving purposes of God.

John's language, then, functions more like poetry than prose. Eugene Peterson elegantly describes the book of Revelation as "theological poetry."[5] If we treat John as a news reporter, rather than as a visionary and a poet, we will misinterpret what he says. Reading an apocalyptic text like Revelation requires *imagination*.[6] For many Western Christians, myself included, this kind of reading doesn't come naturally. Speaking of Revelation's symbolic,

---

[4]See Boring, *Hearing John's Voice*, 62.
[5]Eugene H. Peterson, *Reversed Thunder: The Revelation of John and the Praying Imagination* (San Francisco: HarperSanFrancisco, 1988), xii.
[6]This is a large reason for including the illustrations you find in this book. Revelation has sparked the imaginations of visual artists over the centuries. Their creations offer us a way of *imagining* Revelation that goes beyond the written page.

Figure 1.1. Saint John the Evangelist on Patmos by Pietro Perugino (c. 1448–1523), Monastery of San Benedetto, Italy

pictorial language, Zimbabwean commentator Onesimus Ngundu observes, "This approach can sometimes be difficult to understand, especially for Western people, who tend to think in abstract terms. It is more familiar to Africans and people in Near Eastern cultures, who are used to expressing themselves in proverbial or concrete language."[7] Perhaps Majority World (non-Western) Christians can help those of us in the West learn to read Revelation more imaginatively—and more faithfully.

We can also talk about an apocalyptic *worldview* and *perspective*. Jewish apocalyptic works usually emerged from a time of crisis or perceived crisis. They addressed people who found their backs against the wall, people who felt threatened by oppressors and hostile powers. An apocalyptic perspective assumed a dramatic conflict between the forces of God and Satan, good and evil. This cosmic clash played out in the daily struggle between God's people and their oppressors who seemed to hold all the cards. Apocalyptic literature offered hope and assurance to politically powerless people, like the Jews of John's day who believed that God, against all appearances, holds the reins of history and will utterly triumph in the end. Ultimately God will intervene

---

[7]Onesimus Ngundu, "Revelation," in *Africa Bible Commentary*, ed. Tokunboh Adeyemo (Grand Rapids, MI: Zondervan, 2006), 1543.

to judge the wicked and reward the faithful with salvation. This big-picture perspective enabled people to see everyday realities through a different lens—God's sweeping purpose for all things. At the same time, apocalyptic writings functioned as *protest literature*. They encouraged God's people to resist the worldview of the dominant culture, which profoundly opposed God's end game for the world.[8]

In some ways, Revelation differs from Jewish apocalyptic writings, especially in its focus on Christ who has *already* conquered sin, evil, and death (Rev 1:5, 18; 5:5). Nevertheless, John shares much of this apocalyptic perspective. It is a worldview that still resonates with many Majority World Christians, who more easily recognize that unseen cosmic powers lie behind the earthly conflicts and injustices of their world than do many Christians from the West.[9]

How, then, does Revelation's *apocalyptic* character contribute to a missional reading of the book? *John's primary goal in Revelation is not to predict the future but to shape faithful, missional communities*—congregations of Jesus followers who worship the one true God and bear witness to what God is doing in the world. To that end, John challenges his readers to reimagine their world. He draws from the familiar apocalyptic symbols and images of their world in order to give them a new way of seeing what is happening around them. Revelation's theological poetry both uncovers what God is up to in the world (God's mission) and energizes God's people to get caught up in what God is doing (the mission of the church). New Testament scholar Richard Bauckham hits the nail on the head:

> John (and thereby his readers with him) is taken up into heaven in order to see the world from the heavenly perspective. . . . He is also transported in vision into the final future of the world, so that he can see the present from the perspective of what its final outcome must be, in God's ultimate purpose for human history.[10]

---

[8]Mitchell G. Reddish, *Revelation* (Macon, GA: Smyth and Helwys, 2001), 5.

[9]James Chukwuma Okoye, "Power and Worship: *Revelation* in African Perspective," in *From Every People and Nation: The Book of Revelation in Intercultural Perspective*, ed. David Rhoads (Minneapolis: Fortress, 2005), esp. 120-21; Gorman, *Reading Revelation*, 20.

[10]Richard Bauckham, *The Theology of the Book of Revelation* (Cambridge: Cambridge University Press, 1993), 7.

"The task of the apocalyptic imagination is to provide images that show us what is going on in our lives."[11]

EUGENE PETERSON

Revelation, then, is more about unmasking the present than unveiling the future.[12] Its apocalyptic images are disruptive and disorienting not because they are so confusing or scary but because they force us to see the world we live in through a wholly different lens; because they rock our confidence in the political and religious powers that claim to be in control of our world; because they shatter our trust in the American dream or any other illusion that promises meaning through money or salvation through success. John's apocalyptic visions seek to transform our imaginations, realigning them with God's great project of making everything new (Rev 21:5), both now and in the future.

Prophetic words. John is more than just an apocalyptic visionary. He is also a prophet. He makes that clear from the outset: "Blessed is the one who reads aloud the words of the *prophecy*" (Rev 1:3, italics added). Near the end of Revelation, John uses the word *prophecy* four times to describe what he has written (Rev 22:7, 10, 18, 19). Contrary to popular perceptions, prophecy in the Bible has less to do with *foretelling* the future than with *forthtelling* God's word for the present situation. Prophecy brings God's message to God's people in their concrete situation and calls people to act on that message.

It is difficult to make predictions, especially about the future.

DANISH PROVERB

John, then, sees himself marching in the long parade of Old and New Testament prophets. John's voice is the voice of a Christian preacher and

---

[11]Peterson, *Reversed Thunder*, 145.

[12]Harry O. Maier, "A First-World Reading of Revelation Among Immigrants," in Rhoads, *From Every People and Nation*, 78.

prophet who announces "a word from the Lord" for the church by the prophetic Spirit. Outside of the community of faith, Revelation makes little sense. Revelation's prophetic character comes to special prominence in the messages to the churches in Asia Minor in Revelation 2 and 3, but it is by no means limited to those chapters. Like the prophets before him, John at times speaks a word of comfort in dire circumstances ("Do not fear what you are about to suffer," Rev 2:10) and encourages God's faithful to persevere ("Here is a call for the endurance of the saints," Rev 14:12). At other times, John the prophet flashes a warning signal before people who are in danger of getting sucked into the very idolatrous and sinful activities that characterize their oppressors ("Come out of her [wicked Babylon], my people, so that you do not take part in her sins," Rev 18:4). John's visions of what God and the Lamb will do in the future are designed to transform the present lives of his readers.

Why is Revelation's claim to be prophecy important for a missional reading of this book? Like the churches in first-century Asia, we must read Revelation as God's word to *us* in *our* religious, social, and political circumstances. As prophecy, John's words challenge us to *act* on the message that we hear; to repent, to persevere, to be changed. On the one hand, they call us to turn our backs on the idols of our age and to prophetically resist those idols. On the other hand, Revelation beckons God's people to embrace God's great purposes for God's creation (God's mission) and to bear prophetic witness to that redeeming mission, with our lips and with our lives.

"People of the third [Majority] world, especially the people of our indigenous cultures, have shown much more sensitivity [than modern theologians] to the historical, this-worldly dimensions of the myths, symbols, and visions of the Apocalypse."[13]

PABLO RICHARD

---

[13]Pablo Richard, "Reading the Apocalypse: Resistance, Hope, and Liberation in Central America," trans. C. M. Rodriguez and J. Rodriguez, in Rhoads, *From Every People and Nation*, 149.

Words on target. "John to the seven churches that are in Asia: Grace to you and peace from him who is and who was and who is to come" (Rev 1:4; see also Rev 1:9).

What do those words recall? If you are reasonably familiar with the New Testament, they probably remind you of the way that New Testament letters, like the writings of Paul, begin (e.g., 1 Thess 1:1). Revelation may be an apocalyptic prophecy, but it is framed like a *letter*. More specifically, it comprises a *circular* letter, written to seven real churches in Asia Minor. The order of those churches, listed in Revelation 1:11 and duplicated in chapters 2 and 3, follows a clockwise circuit from Ephesus to Laodicea.

This is vital information for the way that we read Revelation. It means that the Apocalypse is not simply a collection of fantastical dreams or coded symbols but a pastoral letter written by John to local congregations he knows well.[14] Revelation represents God's word on target. John contextualizes his pastoral and prophetic message for real people living in specific circumstances. Once again, this becomes most apparent in Christ's messages to these churches in chapters 2 and 3 but remains true throughout the book.

A missional reading of Revelation must take seriously John's choice to

Figure 1.2. The seven churches in Asia

place his revelation in the framework of a letter. Addressing threatened churches with concrete needs, John seeks to shape faithful missional communities, churches that must get caught up in God's great project of making all things new, where they are. What's more, those churches hear God's targeted word out of their real-life circumstances. If they hear it well, that message will alter the way they engage the culture in which they live, whether

---

[14]Boring, *Hearing John's Voice*, 18.

distancing themselves from ordinary cultural practices like eating food offered to idols (Rev 2:14-16, 20-21) or launching into a costly witness of word and life that will ultimately lead others to worship God (Rev 11:13).

What about churches today? Revelation may not be written *to* us in the same sense that it was the churches in western Asia Minor in the first century, but it is surely written *for* us. Like all Scripture, this text holds the Spirit-energized capacity to transcend its historical circumstances and to address communities of faith of every generation and culture *within their concrete settings.* The good news must have a GPS location. No less than John's hearers in Sardis and Smyrna, this hybrid apocalyptic, prophetic, liturgical letter continues to address *us* in the high-rises of Manhattan and the barrios of Manila. Revelation still calls local Christian communities to hear and live by its transforming message.

THE POWER OF PERSUASION

Everything we have seen about Revelation's character as apocalyptic, prophecy, and letter affirms that Revelation was intended not simply to inform but to *persuade* those who encountered it. Like all New Testament texts, Revelation was intended to be delivered or "performed" out loud in a house church setting.[15] John was an accomplished oral communicator living in a primarily oral culture. He composed a work designed above all to be heard with the ears rather than read with the eyes. John fashioned Revelation to carry maximum effect on his listening audience and to bring about transformation in their lives.

For John, hearing rightly entails responding faithfully. At the outset he announces: "Blessed is the one who *reads aloud* the words of the prophecy, and blessed are those who *hear* and who *keep* what is written in it" (Rev 1:3 italics added; cf. Rev 22:17, 18). Seven times, John calls Christians in Asia "to hear, listen to *and follow* what the Spirit proclaims to all the churches" (Rev 2:7; cf. Rev 2:11, 17, The Voice). Throughout Revelation, John draws on strategies that would make his Apocalypse memorable and persuasive for a listening congregation. This begins, of course, with striking visual images,

---

[15]See Boring, *Hearing John's Voice,* 17-18.

like a heavenly throne encircled with multiple rings of worshipers (chapters 4–5) or a pregnant woman clothed with the sun and standing on the moon (Rev 12:1). But it involves other strategies as well, like repeating key words or phrases. For example, the phrase "every tribe and language and people and nation" (in different orders) surfaces on multiple occasions. It signifies *both* the multinational character of God's people (Rev 5:9; 7:9) *and* the universal sweep of those who oppose God (Rev 10:11; 11:9; 13:7; 14:6; 17:15).

We discover persuasive strategies as well in the way the drama of Revelation unfolds. Chapters 6–20 narrate a long sequence of judgment scenes, which grow in intensity until God says a final, "Enough!" to evil and ushers in the new creation (Rev 21–22). But these disasters don't pile up without any relief. Eugene Boring explains that John, as a skilled oral communicator, doesn't ask his hearers to wait until he describes every last woe before offering them any hope. Instead, he sprinkles visions of salvation and victory throughout the cycle of judgments, like sneak previews of the triumph to come (e.g., Rev 7:1-17; 11:15-19; 15:2-4; 19:1-10).[16] These alternating visions of judgment and salvation remind the listeners that they will not only experience God's victory in the future; they can already share in that salvation, in the midst of their present trials, anticipating the fullness of God's saving work that is to come.[17]

In addition, John makes use of the various forms of *rhetoric* (the art of persuasion) that would help convince an audience in his world of the truth of what he said and the need to act on it.[18] For example, Revelation especially seeks to persuade Christian listeners by stirring their emotions (what the ancients called *pathos*). So in chapter 17, John taps into the revulsion associated with the wicked Old Testament city of Babylon and cranks up the volume when he links Babylon with the bloodthirsty character of "the great whore" (Rev 17:1). By connecting both of these nauseating images with Rome, John asks Christians to *feel* the evil associated with the empire and break from its ways (Rev 18:4). In a different way, when the martyrs under

---

[16]M. Eugene Boring, *Revelation* (Louisville, KY: John Knox, 1989), 33.

[17]Boring, *Revelation*, 33.

[18]For John's use of Greco-Roman rhetoric, see David deSilva, *An Introduction to the New Testament: Contexts, Methods and Ministry Formation*, 2nd ed. (Downers Grove, IL: IVP Academic, 2018), 806-11.

the altar desperately cry out to God, in effect, "How long will you wait to vindicate us?" (see Rev 6:9-10), John arouses his readers' emotions, assuring them that their suffering is not in vain. God won't forget them.

John's effort to persuade and convict his audience aligns closely with a missional interpretation of this book. Revelation challenges missional communities, then and now, to see the world around them with new eyes and to allow that alternative vision to shape their mission in the world.

EXPERIENCING REVELATION

Revelation's character as an event that is spoken and heard reminds us that it is designed to be *experienced* as a whole, not simply read in bite-sized chunks.[19] John's Apocalypse unfolds like a magnificent cosmic drama or story. We meet a parade of characters, some good—God, the Lamb, the prophetic Spirit, and those who worship God, like angels, the twenty-four elders, and God's people—others evil, including Satan, the beasts, and the prostitute, along with their minions, like the kings and dwellers of the earth. As the drama progresses, settings change between the churches on earth and the throne room in heaven. Scenes shift, for example, from the utter devastation of Babylon to the victory of Christ, the heavenly warrior (Rev 18–19). Conflict ratchets up and resolves.[20] We cannot begin to do justice to Revelation if we approach it as a passive observer. John invites us to *enter* Revelation's story of God's now and coming triumph. He asks us to let that story disrupt and transform our vision of the world.

Perhaps it's not surprising that the most powerful rendering of Revelation I can remember involved an aged preacher who dramatically performed the Apocalypse from memory on stage, complete with costumes and musical accompaniment. I've never gotten over it. My own experience of quoting Scripture portions like Jesus' Sermon on the Mount publicly has convinced me that *hearing* the voice of God through the dramatically spoken word has the potential to change the hearers. Just as Revelation's stunning symbols and persuasive voice enabled Christians in Asia to experience

---

[19]Mark B. Stephens, *Annihilation or Renewal? The Meaning and Function of New Creation in the Book of Revelation*, WUNT 2.307 (Tübingen: Mohr Siebeck, 2011), 239.18.

[20]On Revelation's character as a drama, see Gorman, *Reading Revelation*, 37-38, 116-37.

the power of this text in their setting, so churches today must open themselves to the bottled energy in this book. To grasp Revelation, we must let it grasp us.

> *"Like a good movie, and about the same length (1 hour and 20 minutes of reading/hearing time), Revelation's effect is the way it works as a unit. The power of any individual text depends on its mediating the whole."*[21]
>
> EUGENE BORING

WHAT'S THE BACKSTORY?

A missional reading of Scripture can't avoid the issue of *context*. Specifically, how did Revelation speak into the circumstances of communities of worship and witness in John's world and how might it continue to address a variety of global contexts today?

Revelation's call to get caught up in God's missional purpose addressed local churches in the Roman province of Asia (western Turkey today), likely during the late first century when emperor Domitian dominated the Roman world. It wasn't an easy time to serve Christ in Asia Minor. The empire's propaganda boasted that Rome's destiny was to "bring the whole world under law's dominion."[22] Caesar was acclaimed as "lord of all the world."[23] A second-century Christian named Minucius Felix wrote of Rome that "it has propagated its empire beyond the paths of the sun, and the bounds of the ocean itself."[24] Inhabitants of the empire indeed perceived Rome as "the great city that rules over the kings of the earth" (Rev 17:18). When John and the Christians in Asia claimed that God, not Caesar, sits on the universal throne, they launched a frontal assault on the prevailing ideology in the Roman world.

---

[21]Boring, *Hearing John's Voice*, 71.
[22]Virgil, *Aeneid* 4.232.
[23]Peter Oakes, *Philippians: From People to Letter*, SNTSMS 110 (Cambridge: Cambridge University Press, 2001), esp. 149-50, 171-72.
[24]*Octavius* 6. Cited in deSilva, *Introduction to the New Testament*, 799.

Figure 1.3. Bust of emperor Domitian (81–96) from the Ephesus Museum, Selçuk, Turkey

Specifically, Rome's power and control over the empire was embodied in the emperor cult, which involved the worship of Caesar and of Rome itself. For the cities of Roman Asia, the imperial cult wasn't imposed from the top down but represented a grassroots movement. Cities in Asia Minor competed with one another for the status of "first of the province," normally by excelling in imperial worship and loyalty to Rome.[25]

The emperor cult touched all arenas of life. For many Westerners (like me), it's hard to grasp the seamless connection that existed between religion, politics, economics, and kinship ties in John's world. Citywide festivals, trade guild meetings (the labor unions of the day), private meals, and social gatherings like birthday parties all signaled occasions to honor the emperor and the local gods that sustained his reign. When Christians refused to participate in such occasions, as well as the meals that almost inevitably accompanied them, they came under suspicion for being dangerously disloyal and unpatriotic.

How did Rome push back against Christian dissenters? Christian communities in Asia almost certainly did not face a program of organized, state-sponsored persecution as often has been assumed. Nevertheless, sporadic, local oppression of Christians remained a constant possibility.[26] Antipas of Pergamum had already been martyred (Rev 2:13), John himself languished

---

[25]Laszlo Gallusz, *The Throne Motif in the Book of Revelation*, LNTS 487 (London: Bloomsbury T&T Clark, 2014), 278-79.

[26]David deSilva, "The Social Setting of the Revelation to John: Conflicts Within, Fears Without," *Westminster Theological Journal* 54 (1992): 274.

in exile (Rev 1:9), and Christians contended with the pressure to deny Christ's name (Rev 2:3, 13; 3:8). At the very least, refusing to join in practices like sacrificial meals carried a steep *social* and *economic* price. As a Christian, you might find yourself alienated from your friends and family members. If you were a shopkeeper, you might lose your customers, your business associates, even your livelihood itself. Your community might brand you as being subversive, antisocial, and "atheistic." The pressure to relieve these stresses by accommodating to Rome's ways would have been monumental.

> *"Like the Christians in John's day, Christians in South Asia are a minority. Adherents of other faiths surround them. Governments actively support some of these other faiths, which often results in Christians being persecuted as John's readers were. So we need to hear Revelation's answer to the questions, 'Who really rules the world—the political authorities or God?'"*[27]
>
> RAMESH KHATRY

CONTEXTUALIZING THE MESSAGE

How did the congregations in Asia respond to such pressures? It depends. For most of those churches the greatest threat was not persecution as such but rather the temptation to cozy up to the ways of the dominant Roman culture, perhaps to avoid persecution. This challenges a popular way of reading Revelation essentially as a book designed to offer hope to oppressed Christians by assuring them that God would defeat their persecutors in the end. That's too simplistic. To be sure, some of John's audience needed a word of encouragement to persevere in the midst of trial (see Rev 2:9-10; 3:8-11). But for other churches, John's messages sounded more like, "Wake up! Stop compromising! Turn around, or you risk facing God's judgment!"

---

[27]Ramesh Khatry, "Revelation," in *South Asia Bible Commentary*, ed. Brian Wintle (Grand Rapids, MI: Zondervan, 2015), 1770.

As we will see in chapter four, John tailors each of his messages in Revelation 2 and 3 to that church's concrete needs and failures. For example, Christ's word confronts Thyatira about dabbling in idolatry by eating food sacrificed to the gods (Rev 2:20), and it calls out Laodicea for blending in with the materialism of the surrounding culture (Rev 3:17-18). Today we might call this *contextualization*.[28] John not only speaks in ways that are *relevant* to each church's life situation but he also *challenges* that context in light of the gospel. Each missional community, then, must read the whole of Revelation out of their dust-on-the-sandals circumstances, even as they allow its visions to "shake up the dust" and transform how they live in the world.

For now, I will focus more broadly on how John used the cultural materials of his world, enabling Christians in Asia to see that world through a different lens. Sometimes John taps into popular cultural myths that would have resonated with his audience and reimagines them in light of what God is doing in Christ. The story of the pregnant woman and the dragon in chapter 12 provides a fascinating example.[29] Various ancient cultures told similar stories, including the Greco-Roman tradition. In that version of the tale, the great dragon Python pursues the pregnant goddess Leto, plotting to murder both Leto and her child. But the god Poseidon foils the scheme, rescuing Leto and hiding her below water on a remote island. There she gives birth to Apollo, who quickly avenges his mother by killing the dragon. Roman propaganda exploited the myth, picturing Leto as the goddess Roma, the deified representation of Rome, and Apollo as the divine emperor (particularly Domitian), the savior of the world.

John reworks the myth, drawing on elements from the Old Testament and Jewish tradition.[30] But he gives the story a distinctively Christian meaning. One writer explains the transformation this way:

---

[28]For a fuller treatment of contextualization in Revelation, see Dean Flemming, *Contextualization in the New Testament: Patterns for Theology and Mission* (Downers Grove, IL: IVP Academic, 2005), esp. 266-95.

[29]The following paragraph draws extensively from Flemming, *Contextualization*, 275.

[30]See G. K. Beale, *The Book of Revelation: A Commentary on the Greek Text* (Grand Rapids, MI: Eerdmans, 1999), 624-25.

> In [John's] version the woman in labor is not a Greek goddess, but the people of God; the child is not the emperor but Christ; and the dragon represents the forces that oppose Christ and threaten his church. In the end, a story that was used to celebrate the popular culture is now transformed in a way that helps readers resist being assimilated to that culture.[31]

For John, the cultural myth finds its historic fulfillment in Jesus, who rules "all the nations with a rod of iron" (Rev 12:5; cf. Ps 2:9). Christ, not Caesar, stands as the true victor over evil, the one and only Savior of the world. John knows his culture well, and he uses that knowledge both to connect with his Asian audience and to turn the worldview of the empire on its head.

Above all, John dips deeply into the well of Old Testament images to speak a fresh word to his audience where they are. It's striking that John *never cites Scripture explicitly*. Rather, he wallpapers Revelation with biblical echoes and allusions, some five hundred in all.[32] John's use of Scripture seems closer to the many uncited allusions to the Bible in the sermons of John Wesley than to the explicit quotations of Matthew's Gospel or the book of Hebrews.[33] John weaves these images so tightly into the fabric of Revelation that without them, the book would unravel.

In general, Revelation does not present Old Testament images or language simply as the fulfillment of prophecy. Instead, he recontextualizes them and adapts them for the new situation of his audience. Old Testament figures who opposed God like Balaam and Jezebel come to symbolize false teachers who threaten the churches in Asia (Rev 2:14, 20). The plagues on Egypt in Exodus are re-presented as God's end-time plagues of judgment on the whole earth (Rev 8:6–9:21; 16:1-21). The biblical ministries of Moses and Elijah foreshadow the church's faithful and prophetic witness in the world (Rev 11:3-13). What is more, major symbols in Revelation—the throne, Lamb,

---

[31]Craig R. Koester, *Revelation and the End of All Things*, 2nd ed. (Grand Rapids, MI: Eerdmans, 2018), 118.

[32]Boring, *Hearing John's Voice*, 69. Would John's audience in Asia "get" all these scriptural allusions? Probably not. But John continually invites his readers to enter the biblical story and in the process to learn to recognize the cadences of that story. For a full treatment of John's use of Scripture, see G. K. Beale, *John's Use of the Old Testament in Revelation*, JSNTSS 166 (London: Bloomsbury T & T Clark, 2015).

[33]See *The Sermons of John Wesley: A Collection for the Christian Journey*, ed. Kenneth J. Collins and Jason E. Vickers (Nashville, TN: Abingdon, 2013).

trumpets, and temple, to name just a few—all sprout from Old Testament roots. As I wrote in another setting, "John repeatedly, under the influence of the Spirit, recycles familiar events and images in ways that transcend the old meaning and frame of reference."[34] Scripture speaks once again in new circumstances. John subtly invites his readers to enter the biblical story of God's saving purposes in a way that reshapes their vision of what God is doing now and how he will fulfill his mission in the end.

CONTEXTUALIZING THE GOOD NEWS TODAY

Can we learn from John? Revelation's Spirit-energized prophecy uses the language, literary forms, symbols, and persuasive methods of its world even as it summons that world to change. Throughout Revelation John reworks Old Testament images and events, co-opts familiar symbols, and transforms pagan myths from his cultural world. John seizes the language of Rome, not so much to find common ground as to unmask the empire's lies and idolatry.[35] He speaks in ways that make sense in his culture precisely to give people a new lens through which to see their world. In similar ways, Christians today can draw from all the resources available to them in order to challenge people in their own settings to be transformed. That includes the treasures of Scripture and tradition as well as the images, values, stories, and songs from our various cultures.

For example, New Testament scholar Brian Blount shows how Black slaves used the form of the spiritual to portray a hope-filled vision of the future. That vision enabled them to endure hardship and resist the false narratives of the enslaving powers, not unlike what John was asking of his readers in the first century. Blount believes that the language of resistance through costly witness expressed in the spirituals still resonates:

> Because most African Americans in this country still count themselves among the most impoverished and oppressed, John's message to resist, to refuse to accommodate to the present social, economic, and political way of life, is still a necessary message. His language of resistance, as the slaves rightly understood in their time, must remain a vital part of the African American

---

[34]Flemming, *Contextualization*, 276-77.
[35]Flemming, *Contextualization*, 292.

language—if African American Christian language is to remain the language of hope for the future in the midst of an unbearable present.[36]

In a different setting, Jackson Wu reflects on how Christians in Chinese communities might draw on the cultural notion of *filial piety* (loyalty to one's parents) in service of the gospel.[37] Within the framework of Chinese culture, Wu explains, children live in debt to their parents, owing them honor and allegiance. Failing to properly respect and obey a parent brings public shame and utter loss of face. Further, since the nation functions like a large family, Chinese people often face the dilemma: Where does my ultimate allegiance lie, with my parents or with the nation or its ruler?

Wu shows how the good news of Christ can both connect with a cultural value like filial piety and transform it. "When we trust Christ," he writes, "we belong to a new family and enter a new kingdom. Becoming a Christian does not mean rejecting our family and country; rather we enlarge our sense of family and nation."[38] In this redefined understanding of family, we offer the fundamental debt of filial piety to our true Father. We don't have to choose between loyalty to family or nation because God is both King and Father. Family no longer ends with bloodlines but expands to embrace people from all nations.[39] Even as John urged Christians in first-century Asia to cast their ultimate lot of loyalty with God and the Lamb, and not with Caesar and Rome, Christians in twenty-first-century Asia and elsewhere must decide whether their ultimate allegiance lies with their parents and nation or with the true Lord and Father of all.

Conclusion

What is God doing in the world? And how are we a part of what God is doing where we live? These are the fundamental questions a missional reading asks of any biblical text. Let's summarize how Revelation's *form, rhetoric,* and *context* contribute to answering these questions.

---

[36]Brian K. Blount, "The Witness of Active Resistance: The Ethics of Revelation in African American Perspective" in Rhoads, *From Every People and Nation,* 43.

[37]Jackson Wu, *One Gospel for All Nations: A Practical Approach to Biblical Contextualization* (Pasadena, CA: William Carey, 2015), 127-71.

[38]Wu, *One Gospel,* 169.

[39]Wu, *One Gospel,* 163, 169.

As an *apocalypse*, Revelation reveals "what must soon take place" (Rev 1:1): God's sweeping purpose to defeat all adversaries and to restore all things. Drawing on symbols and images from the world of his readers, John seeks to perform spiritual eye surgery on his audience, to give them an entirely new vision of the world in which they live. Such a vision calls them to live as a foretaste of God's future *now* through their words and their lives.

As *prophecy*, Revelation unleashes the word of God and Christ by the Spirit and directs it to God's people where they live. They must not only *hear* that word but *act* on it. Revelation's prophetic word urges them to remain on mission in the face of opposition and to bear prophetic witness to what God is doing in the world.

As a *letter*, Revelation addresses real churches in their concrete life circumstances, seeking to shape them into faithful missional communities.

As *rhetoric*, Revelation seeks to *persuade* those who hear its words. This moves beyond merely understanding what it says. John's visions are designed to *convince* them that God, not Satan, Caesar, or any other power, is in control of history as well as to *convict* them to repent and align themselves with God's reconciling purpose.

As a *contextual document*, Revelation speaks into the lives of Christian communities living in a specific setting in first-century Asia, one that was dominated by the engines of Rome's power and idolatry. John contextualizes his message for that world. He recasts both the language of Scripture and the images and myths of Roman culture, enabling Christians to reimagine their world. Revelation doesn't ask Christians to *leave* their concrete circumstances but rather to bear witness to a different truth *within* those circumstances.

Revelation continues to address us today in similar ways, whatever our culture or life setting. John the visioner, prophet, letter writer, persuader, and contextual theologian continues to call God's people to embody God's mission where they live. But what does that mission look like? Let's find out.

CHAPTER TWO

THE GOD OF MISSION

Salvation belongs to our God who is seated on the throne,
and to the Lamb!

REVELATION 7:10

GOD IS THE LEAD ACTOR in the drama of justice and hope that Revelation tells. In his opening greeting to the seven churches, John shines an intense spotlight on the triune God—God the Father (Rev 1:6), "who is and who was and who is to come" (Rev 1:4), "Jesus Christ, the faithful witness" (Rev 1:5), and "the seven Spirits who are before his throne" (Rev 1:4), representing the fullness of the one Spirit of God sent into the world (Rev 5:6). It's crucial that we begin with God. If our reading of Revelation focuses on *events*—how the script of the end times unfolds—we will miss Revelation's God-centered focus. Revelation, above all, tells the story of a sovereign and loving God who is on a mission to save people of all nations and to bring the whole creation to its intended goal. And God accomplishes this magnificent purpose in and through Jesus Christ, the slaughtered Lamb, who by his death triumphs over sin and death, and by the Spirit, who empowers God's people to bear witness to what God is doing in the world (Rev 19:10).

It's appropriate, then, that our missional reading of Revelation begins where John begins—with the triune God. We sometimes talk about "the church's mission," and there's a sense in which that is true. First and foremost, however, the Bible tells the story of *God's* mission, the *missio Dei*. We, as

God's people, are given the calling and the privilege of participating in the
mission of God. Nowhere in Scripture is that emphasis on the divine mission
clearer than in the Apocalypse. This chapter focuses on the mission of God
the Father of Jesus Christ (Rev 1:6; 2:28; 3:5, 21; 14:1). We'll see that Revelation
pictures God as the Alpha and Omega, the Creator and renewer of everything, a Savior who is sovereign over the universe and utterly holy, a God
whose mission is driven by wounded love. Let's unpack this mind-bending
vision of God.

THE ALPHA AND THE OMEGA

Immediately before John begins to narrate his vision, which makes up the
bulk of Revelation, we hear the voice of God: "'I am the Alpha and the Omega,'
says the Lord God, who is and who was and who is to come, the Almighty"
(Rev 1:8).

This is the first of only two occasions that God speaks directly in
Revelation. The second occurs near the end of the book and holds similar
language: "I am the Alpha and the Omega, the beginning and the end"
(Rev 21:6; cf. Rev 21:5-8). I once heard a preacher say, "When people talk
about God, that is often a good thing. But when *God* talks about God, we
had better listen!" When God's words about God stand like brackets at the
beginning and end of Revelation, we *surely* must listen.

Alpha and *Omega* represent the first and last letters in the Greek alphabet.
As the Alpha and Omega, God reveals himself as the Lord of history. God is
before all things, and in him all things will reach their fulfillment when God
makes everything new (Rev 21:5). What's more, God is the one "who is who
was and who is to come" (Rev 1:4, 8; cf. Rev 4:8). This title recalls and interprets the divine name that God revealed to Moses in the burning bush.[1]
When Moses asked God what his name was, God responded, "I AM WHO I
AM," which in Hebrew can also mean, "I will be who I will be" (Ex 3:13-14).
In Revelation, this eternal character of God focuses particularly on God's
relationship to the world he created. As the God who was and is, he remains
faithful throughout the whole human history with all its risks and

---

[1]See Richard Bauckham, *The Theology of the Book of Revelation* (Cambridge: Cambridge University
Press, 1993), 28-29.

uncertainties. As the one who is to come, God is in control of the future. God is *coming* to make all that is wrong right, to bring his loving mission in the world to its intended goal through his acts of salvation and judgment.

CREATOR AND RESTORER OF CREATION

God's mission is massive. It encompasses far more than simply saving individuals from their sins so that they can punch their ticket to heaven. In Revelation, as in all of Scripture, God's mission embraces the whole creation. Revelation portrays God not only as Savior and judge of humanity but also as creator and renewer of all things. God's sovereignty over the world is anchored in the biblical confession that God is the Creator and sustainer of everything that exists (Rev 10:6; 14:7). In the incomparable heavenly throne room scene in chapter 4, John sees the twenty-four elders who symbolize the people of God cast their crowns before the Almighty and sing:

> You are worthy, our Lord and God,
> > to receive glory and honor and power,
> for you created all things,
> > and by your will they existed and were created. (Rev 4:11)

In the same scene, the four living creatures, which represent all of creation, encircle the throne, singing unending praise to God (Rev 4:7-8). The worship circle widens until finally "every creature in heaven and on earth and under the earth and in the sea, and all that is in them" is caught up in the song of adoration to God and the Lamb (Rev 5:13). Because God is Creator, he is worthy of worship. Later, in Revelation 14, an angel proclaims an "eternal gospel" to people from every tribe and nation. The content of that good news includes the call to turn to their Creator and worship the One "who made heaven and earth, the sea and the springs of water" (Rev 14:6-7).[2]

It's important to see God's work as creator as a *missional* role, one that spans the entire biblical story. It matters where we start. Here is a *profound* statement. The Bible's story begins in Genesis 1, not Genesis 3.[3] Obvious, right? Unfortunately, some Christians operate as if the story of God's

---

[2]Bauckham, *Theology*, 48.

[3]On this, see Andy Johnson, *Holiness and the* Missio Dei (Eugene, OR: Cascade, 2016), 3-5.

mission in the world activates in Genesis 3 *after* Adam and Eve thumb their noses at the commandment of God and ends in Revelation 20 when God pronounces a final judgment on sinful humanity. From that perspective, our reading of the biblical narrative can easily focus on dealing with peoples' individual sin and guilt so that they can avoid God's punishment and go to heaven when they die. But the story begins, as Genesis has it, "In the beginning" (Gen 1:1), with God's role as creator of the heavens and the earth. God's creation is "very good" (Gen 1:31); it flourishes with abundant life and harmonious relationships, involving God, humans, and creation itself. At the climax of his creative work, God breathes life into humans and gives them a creation task, a *mission*. Humans are called to "rule" (Gen 1:26, 28) and to serve (Gen 2:15) God's creation under his lordship so that creation flourishes in the way God intended.

But John knows well that God's good creation has come under captivity to sin and the evil powers that oppose God's life-giving purpose for the world. Revelation portrays a God who is irrepressibly faithful to his creation. God seeks to liberate creation from the powers that "destroy the earth" (Rev 11:18). That earth, which includes the people who live on it, suffers acutely under the devil's wrath (Rev 12:12) and wicked Babylon's corruption (Rev 19:2). In Revelation 11:18, God's judgment falls not on the earth itself but on its "destroyers"—all those who kill God's people and ruin God's creation.

This wasn't simply theoretical language for John's audience. In their world, the Roman Empire represented the poster child for "those who destroy the earth" (Rev 11:18). Micah Kiel details how Rome's thirst for luxury goods and power came at the price of exploiting the natural resources of its ever-expanding territory. That includes mining on a previously unknown scale, deforestation, and harvesting masses of exotic animals for public spectacles, which pitted beasts against one another or gladiators.[4] For example, at the festival opening the Coliseum in Rome in AD 80, nine thousand wild animals were slaughtered.[5] This all propped up Rome's propaganda that claimed eternal dominance over the earth. But John sees things as they *really*

---

[4]Micah D. Kiel, *Apocalyptic Ecology: The Book of Revelation, the Earth, and the Future* (Collegeville, MN: Liturgical, 2017), 47-64.

[5]Kiel, *Apocalyptic Ecology*, 53.

are. Those who exploit the earth and its people—the empire and the demonic powers that lie behind it—*will* be judged. God seeks to rescue the earth from its current destruction.

The Creator of heaven and earth still has a future for creation. In Revelation 21, God says something else of utmost importance about God: "See, I am making all things new" (Rev 21:5). God is not only the Creator but also the "everything-new-maker." Revelation 21 and 22 picture the goal of God's mission foretold by the prophet Isaiah (Is 65:17-19; 66:22-23), and that goal is *new creation*.

Without the new creation, God's activity as creator would remain a failed project; without God's original, good creation, a *new* creation would make no sense. In fact, Genesis 1–2 and Revelation 21–22 form bookends to the entire biblical story of God's mission.[6] That story launches with God creating the heavens and the earth and climaxes with God creating a *new* heaven and a *new* earth. It starts in a garden with two people sharing communion with God. It ends in a bustling city, an urban garden, in which people from every nation live in intimate fellowship with God and with one another. In the first Eden, humans are cut off from the tree of life because of their sin, but in the new Paradise, the leaves of the tree of life offer healing to the nations (Rev 22:1-2). The original garden became an instrument of death, pain, and a curse on the earth; the new city teems with life and fruitfulness, and the curse is reversed (Rev 22:3).

When God brings about the new heaven and the new earth, he does not reinstate the original pre-fall model. Nor does he simply give the first creation an upgrade like an improved version of software. Rather, God makes something *new*, which is qualitatively different from the original creation. Andy Johnson reminds us that the Bible's own framing in Genesis and Revelation helps us to read the biblical narrative "as the story of God's mission to bring his creation to its full potential and to do so through the agency of humanity."[7]

---

[6]See Michael J. Gorman, *Reading Revelation Responsibly: Uncivil Worship and Witness: Following the Lamb into the New Creation* (Eugene, OR: Cascade, 2011), 161. The rest of the paragraph is largely adapted from Dean Flemming, *Why Mission?* (Nashville, TN: Abingdon, 2015), 111.

[7]Johnson, *Holiness and the* Missio Dei, 6.

Figure 2.1. Manuscript illumination of the river of life in the new Jerusalem (Rev 22:1-2) from *The Apocalypse with Commentaries from Andrew of Caesarea,* c. 1800

God's work of *re*-creation carries two crucial implications for our understanding of mission. First, God's mission is inherently *creation focused*. The new Jerusalem comes *down* from heaven and merges with a renewed earth (Rev 3:12; 21:2, 10). Revelation is anything but otherworldly. God desires to *transform* the earth, not obliterate it. As Richard Middleton puts it, "The creator has not given up on creation and is working to salvage and restore the world (human and nonhuman) to the fullness of shalom and flourishing intended from the beginning."[8] God has a future for *the earth*.

---

[8]J. Richard Middleton, *A New Heaven and a New Earth: Reclaiming Biblical Eschatology* (Grand Rapids, MI: Baker, 2014), 27.

Revelation's creation focus cuts cross-grain to much popular eschatology (what we believe about the end), especially the expectation that the true church secretly will be "raptured" to heaven *out of* a world that is riding a bullet train to destruction. The original last verse of "Amazing Grace," recently rehabilitated in Chris Tomlin's revision of the iconic hymn, illustrates precisely this pessimistic view of the future of God's creation:

The earth shall soon dissolve like snow,
The sun forbear to shine;
But God, who called me here below,
Will be forever mine.[9]

This poem may have been penned by John Newton, but it couldn't have come from John the Revelator. Practically, if our hope lies in escaping a doomed world, then we might be tempted to think of *mission* simply in terms of getting people ready to leave this world for heaven. This mentality often has underpinned well-meaning revivalist preaching and its appeal to conversion. The influential nineteenth-century evangelist D. L. Moody famously said, "I look on this world as a wrecked vessel. God has given me a life-boat, and said to me, 'Moody, save all you can.'"[10] At its worst, an "otherworldly" view of the end leads to washing our hands of any responsibility to protect God's creation for future generations or to work for justice in the systems that oppress and degrade people. In contrast, Revelation's picture of God as the Creator who is intensely committed to *this* world and its ultimate liberation calls God's people to become channels of compassion, healing, and *shalom* at every level of human need.

Second, we need to begin to think of creation care missionally. If God's restoring mission includes creation itself, and if God has given humans the task of ruling and serving that creation, then caring for God's creation becomes integral to participating in the mission of God. Followers of Jesus should be the *last* people to deny the dangers of climate change or to support economic or political policies that are harmful to the environment, not, as

---

[9]John Newton, "Amazing Grace," 1779, www.hymnlyrics.org.
[10]Dwight L. Moody, "That Gospel Sermon on the Blessed Hope," sermon 16, in *New Sermons, Addresses and Prayers* (St. Louis: N. D. Thompson, 1887), cited in Middleton, *A New Heaven and a New Earth*, 301.

is too often the case, the *first*. Revelation calls us to engage in God's transforming purpose of "making everything new" (Rev 21:5 NIV). As Christopher Wright summarizes, "Our mission involves participating in [God's] redemptive work as agents of good news to creation, as well as to people."[11]

> *"Truly Christian environmental action is in fact also evangelistically fruitful, not because it is any kind of cover for 'real mission' but simply because it declares in word and deed the Creator's limitless love for the whole of his creation (which, of course, includes his love for human creatures) and makes no secret of the biblical story and the cost that the Creator paid to redeem both."*[12]
>
> CHRISTOPHER WRIGHT

If God's loving mission means good news for people, for societies, *and* for the earth, then the church's participation in that mission cannot ignore the task of caring for God's creation. We demonstrate love for God by loving and caring for what God delights in, what God owns, what God has redeemed in Christ, and what God desires to fully restore. Wright puts it well:

> To take good care of the earth, for Christ's sake, is surely a fundamental dimension of the calling on all God's people to love him. It seems inexplicable to me that there are some Christians who claim to love and worship God . . . and yet have no concern for the earth that bears his stamp of ownership. They do not care about the abuse of the earth and indeed, by their wasteful and overconsumptive lifestyles, they contribute to it.[13]

Revelation's perspective on God's loving purpose for *the earth* has never been more urgent for the church. In the face of overwhelming evidence of

---

[11]Christopher J. H. Wright, *The Mission of God's People: A Biblical Theology of the Church's Mission* (Grand Rapids, MI: Zondervan, 2010), 61.

[12]Christopher J. H. Wright, *The Mission of God: Unlocking the Bible's Grand Narrative* (Downers Grove, IL: IVP Academic, 2006), 419.

[13]Wright, *Mission of God*, 269.

accelerating environmental destruction and the abuse of God's creation, not least resulting in the loss of countless species and a menacingly changing climate, Christians cannot continue to treat this as a "secular" issue. The stakes are too high, the biblical mandate too clear.

"We need to listen to the cry of the earth and the cry of the poor in this apocalyptic biblical book. We need to see the connection between, on the one hand, Revelation's anti-imperial critique of the effects of militarism and violence against the earth in Roman imperial times and, on the other hand, the global exploitation of the earth and its peoples today. The earth and its peoples are crying out to God—and to those of us humans who have the resources to do something about it. God laments the devastation of creation. And we ought to lament it also!"[14]

BARBARA ROSSING

I will talk more about how Christians can practically respond in the book's final chapter. Nevertheless, Revelation's new creation vision invites the church to join the vanguard in the challenge of creation care. One dimension of that response involves encouraging, praying for, and supporting Christians who are called specifically to creation-care mission. A Rocha International, a Christian research, conservation, and advocacy group, demonstrates such a vocation.[15] One example involves its work to preserve the Atewa Forest in eastern Ghana in West Africa, an area of high biodiversity, including critically endangered birds, butterflies, frogs, and mammals. The region, which is threatened by commercial mining, illegal logging, and farm encroachment, also provides clean drinking water for five million Ghanaians. A Rocha has participated in a multipronged awareness and advocacy

---

[14]Barbara R. Rossing, "For the Healing of the World: Reading Revelation Ecologically," in *From Every People and Nation: The Book of Revelation in Intercultural Perspective*, ed. David Rhoads (Minneapolis: Fortress, 2005), 180.

[15]A Rocha International, accessed January 17, 2021, www.arocha.org.

campaign at both the international and local levels, including helping local communities develop alternative, nature-based sources of livelihood.[16] Such care for the planet enables God's people to bear witness to God's commitment to make everything new, as a foretaste of the new creation to come.

SEATED ON THE THRONE

Who's in control of the world? Revelation answers emphatically: *God* is. As creator of the cosmos, God is also sovereign over the universe. At the book's outset, God declares, "I am . . . the Almighty" (Rev 1:8).[17] The title "Almighty" (*pantokratōr* in Greek) is found almost exclusively in Revelation within the New Testament (Rev 4:8; 11:17; 15:3; 16:7, 14; 19:6, 15, 21:22). It signals that God is supreme and has control over all things.

Above all, Revelation demonstrates God's sovereignty by his place on the throne of the universe. This leads us to Revelation 4 and 5, the theological heart of the book. When John is taken up to heaven at the beginning of chapter 4, he immediately sees a throne with the divine ruler sitting on it (Rev 4:2). The throne room represents "Mission Control of the universe."[18] God's throne is at the center of everything. As the scene plays out in these chapters, ever-expanding circles of worshipers surround the throne, like ripples in a cosmic pond, until "every creature in heaven and on earth and under the earth and in the sea, and all that is in them" thunder their praise to God and the Lamb (Rev 5:13).

The throne constitutes one of Revelation's two signature symbols, along with the slaughtered Lamb (see chapter three). References to the throne of God or Christ appear no fewer than forty times in Revelation. The throne symbolizes God's power and rule. To say that the triune God is "the one seated on the throne" (e.g., Rev 4:9; 5:1, 7, 13; 6:16; 7:15; 21:5) means that God is sovereign over everything. The Creator of all things owns and sustains his

---

[16]"Protecting Atewa Forest," A Rocha Ghana, accessed November 24, 2020, https://ghana.arocha .org/projects/protecting-atewa-forest/.

[17]The designation "the Lord God the Almighty" appears seven times in Revelation (Rev 1:8; 4:8; 11:17; 15:3; 16:7; 19:6; 21:22), while the phrase "God the Almighty" occurs an additional two times (Rev 16:14; 19:15).

[18]M. Eugene Boring, *Hearing John's Voice: Insights for Teaching and Preaching* (Grand Rapids, MI: Eerdmans, 2019), 97.

creation. Revelation robustly reaffirms the Old Testament confession about the God of Israel: "To the Lord your God belong the heavens, even the highest heavens, the earth and everything in it" (Deut 10:14 NIV).

Figure 2.2. Woodcut of *Saint John Before God in the Heavenly Throne Room* by Albrecht Dürer from *The Apocalypse of Saint John*, 1496–1498

God's place on the cosmic throne bears profound missional implications. First, if God is sovereign over the whole universe, then *no other
rulers or powers, human or spiritual, can finally frustrate God's redeeming
purpose for the world.* Every earthly and cosmic power that opposes
God's mission is doomed, and the enthroned one will overcome all resistance to his rule in the end. John's vision of God seated on the throne
would surely communicate enormous hope and encouragement to John's
readers in Asia, assuring them that "he will reign forever and ever"
(Rev 11:15).

Second, if God rules over the whole world, then *God's mission is universal
in its scope.* If the one seated on the throne is truly "Lord and God," then
God's redeeming purpose extends to all people without exception. He is
"king of the nations" before whom "all nations will come and worship"
(Rev 15:3-4). Moreover, Scripture affirms that Christ shares the same sover-
eign lordship and the same universal mission. Revelation acclaims Jesus
"Lord of lords and King of kings" (Rev 17:14). In Matthew's well-known Great
Commission passage, Jesus claims, "All authority in heaven and on earth has
been given to me" (Mt 28:18). The phrase "heaven and earth" points back to
Genesis 1 and anticipates God's "new heaven and new earth" in Revelation 21.
It refers to Jesus' universal authority over every corner of creation. Jesus'
commission that follows, "Go therefore and make disciples of all nations"
(Mt 28:19), proceeds directly out of Christ's sovereign authority over the
whole world.

The basis for the church's mission, then, is not simply obedience to an
external command. Rather, that mission becomes an inescapable response
to the universal lordship of God in Christ. Because God is seated on the
throne of the universe and because God has given "all authority" to Jesus,
the church is defined by a mission that reaches out to all people everywhere.
"The missional task of God's people," notes Christopher Wright, "flows
directly from the universal offer of salvation. And that in turn flows from
the universal sovereignty of God—that is, from the very throne of God to
the world."[19]

---

[19]Christopher J. H. Wright, *Salvation Belongs to Our God: Celebrating the Bible's Central Story*
(Downers Grove, IL: IVP Academic, 2007), 145.

"We promote God's glory to the ends of the earth not principally because of any human need but fundamentally because of God's/Christ's unique worthiness as the Lord of heaven and earth. Promoting the gospel to the world is more than a rescue mission (though it is certainly that as well); it is reality mission. It is our plea to all to acknowledge that they belong to one Lord."[20]

JOHN DICKSON

Third, if God alone *reigns* over the world, then *only God can redeem the world*. In Revelation 7, a vast, multinational multitude stands before the throne and trumpets, "Salvation belongs to our God who is seated on the throne, and to the Lamb!" (Rev 7:10).

The God who rules over all is uniquely able to save. Here "salvation" likely means not only victory over God's enemies, but God's redeeming, healing, and restoring work in its most comprehensive sense. This far-reaching salvation belongs to *our* God, no other lord or savior. And *our* God is none other than the God we know from the biblical story, the God Yahweh who liberated a particular people, Israel, and who continues that redeeming activity on behalf of a particular people, those who are in Christ.[21] It is to this God and only this God that the nations must turn in order to be saved. As Isaiah the prophet announced centuries earlier:

> There is no other god besides me,
> a righteous God and a Savior;
>   there is no one besides me. (Is 45:21)

Likewise, Revelation reveals a God who is both universal and unique, both sovereign and Savior.

This is a highly relevant message for John's audience. In John's world, the notion of Israel's God as unique Savior posed a serious challenge to the

---

[20]John Dickson, *The Best Kept Secret of Christian Mission: Promoting the Gospel with More Than Our Lips* (Grand Rapids, MI: Zondervan, 2010), 35.
[21]Wright, *Salvation Belongs to Our God*, 140.

powers that be. We saw earlier that in the Roman Empire religion and politics made a cozy couple. Caesar sat on the throne, and that rule was propped up by a full menu of traditional gods for good measure. What's more, Roman emperors were acclaimed "savior" because of their power to offer people security, prosperity, and protection from danger. Emperor Claudius, for example, was hailed as "god who is *savior* and benefactor" and as "*savior* of the universe."[22] In return for this salvation, Rome demanded ultimate loyalty and total devotion. But John's vision shouts: there's only one throne, and if God occupies it, there's no room for Caesar. And while Rome may claim to provide salvation for its subjects, in doing so it is hijacking a role that belongs to God alone.

Figure 2.3. Coin of Emperor Nero (54–68) and *Salus* (Salvation) with a libation dish

The question of God's unique ability to save remains a vital one today. It may be increasingly popular to claim that just as many trails can lead to a mountain summit, there are many paths to salvation. To think otherwise might appear intolerant and judgmental toward the beliefs or religious traditions of others. But just as John confronted a religiously plural world with the scandalous truth that salvation is found uniquely in "our God" and in the slaughtered Lamb, we cannot water down the scandal of the gospel today. If God sits on the throne, he can have no rivals. At the same time, if this God remains the only source of salvation, then participating in God's mission involves seeking to draw people from every culture, nation, and religious background into the sphere of his sovereignty, so that they too can know him as "our God." As missional communities, we are called to mediate God's saving, reconciling, life-giving purposes at every level of human need.

Fourth, if God sits on the heavenly throne, then what *is* true in heaven must *become* true on earth. As one Revelation scholar says it, "The

---

[22]Cited in Peter Oakes, *Philippians: From People to Letter*, SNTSMS 110 (Cambridge: Cambridge University Press, 2001), 140.

heavenly throne is the vantage point from which John wants readers to look out upon the world of human affairs."[23] Faced with a battle of sovereignties, John's Christian readers in Asia must make a choice: either buy into Rome's bogus claim to control the universe or embrace the perspective of heaven where the true God and Savior reigns. Such a heavenly perspective means more than just a state of mind. It must translate into a daily lifestyle that affirms God's rule over his people through obedient living, as Christ's messages to the seven churches in chapters 2 and 3 make abundantly clear.

What does this conflict over who runs the world mean for Christian communities today? Surely opting for a heavenly perspective where God reigns supreme compels us to resist competing powers that make claims over us, whether traditional gods, nation-states, or material successes. At the same time, Revelation's *heavenly* perspective is by no means an *otherworldly* perspective. On the contrary, it invites Christian communities to live within their specific settings as a present embodiment of the sovereign reign of God in Christ. This concrete way of living serves as a signpost of the future when God's rule will saturate every nook and cranny of the earth.

HOLY TO THE MAX

In Revelation 4, a song reverberates in the throne room of heaven on permanent repeat mode, lifted by the four living creatures that surround the throne:

> Holy, holy, holy,
> the Lord God the Almighty
> who was and is and is to come. (Rev 4:8)

The Bible underlines by repetition, and here repeating the word three times announces that God is "holy to the max," distinct from his creation.[24] The heavenly pyrotechnics that explode from the throne—"flashes of lightning, and rumblings and peals of thunder" (Rev 4:5)—only drive home

---

[23]Craig R. Koester, *Revelation and the End of All Things*, 2nd ed. (Grand Rapids, MI: Eerdmans, 2018), 79.

[24]I borrow the phrase from Andy Johnson, *Holiness and the* Missio Dei, 157.

the point. In Revelation, holiness is not in the first place a lifestyle ideal for people, but the character and identity of God.[25]

The lyrics of the song extolling God's holiness in Revelation 4 recall an earlier song, lifted in another throne room. Instead of living creatures, the singers are seraphim who call out, "Holy, holy, holy is the LORD of hosts; the whole earth is full of his glory" (Is 6:3). The two songs, Revelation's and Isaiah's, begin the same, but *they end differently*. As Andy Johnson observes, the living creatures' song in Revelation says nothing about the earth being filled with God's glory, his visible holiness. Instead, the song goes on to describe God as the one "who was and is and is to come" (Rev 4:8). Johnson comments, "Such language implies that the creator God in the heavenly throne room is not satisfied with the way things are on the earth. For this God 'is coming' to make things right so that the whole earth will be full of his glory."[26] God's holiness, already fully acknowledged in heaven, will fill the earth only when the new Jerusalem comes down from heaven and God makes everything new (Rev 21:2, 5).

Once again, from John's missional perspective, what is already true in heaven must come to earth. Richard Bauckham keenly perceives that in one sense John's prophetic vision in Revelation fulfills the first three petitions in Jesus' prayer: "Hallowed be your name. Your kingdom come. Your will be done, *on earth as it is in heaven*" (Mt 6:9-10, italics added).[27] The facts on the ground, however, told a different story. "John and his readers," notes Bauckham, "lived in a world in which God's name was not hallowed, his will was not done, and evil ruled through the oppression and exploitation of the Roman system of power."[28] Because God is ultimate holiness, he cannot allow the powers that seek to destroy the earth to win the day (Rev 16:5). For God's name to be hallowed on earth, for God's will to be done universally, for God's kingdom to come in its fullness, *evil must be destroyed*. Consequently, judgment and punishment become unfortunate but necessary aspects of

---

[25]Dean Flemming, "'On Earth as It Is in Heaven': Holiness and the People of God in Revelation," in *Holiness and Ecclesiology in the New Testament*, ed. Kent E. Brower and Andy Johnson (Grand Rapids, MI: Eerdmans, 2007), 345.

[26]Johnson, *Holiness and the Missio Dei*, 157.

[27]Bauckham, *Theology*, 40, italics added.

[28]Bauckham, *Theology*, 40.

God's life-giving mission. I'll say more about this in chapter six. For now, I simply note that in the chapters that follow the throne room scene (Rev 6–20), God's holiness expresses itself in righteous and merciful judgments on the evil powers and those who persist in worshiping them.

John not only pictures a holy, sovereign God but also an exalted Christ who shares the same holy character. He is "the holy one, the true one" (Rev 3:7) who appears in blazing glory as Daniel's "one like the Son of Man" (Rev 1:12-16; cf. Rev 14:14; Dan 7:13-14). However, we need to return to the heavenly throne room scene in Revelation 5 to grasp the full meaning of Christ's holiness. There Jesus, the bleeding Lamb, shares the heavenly throne and receives the same praise from all creation that is accorded to God (Rev 5:6-14; cf. Rev 3:21). Through his shameful, sacrificial death the Lamb "not only redefines the nature of true power, he reconfigures what it means to be the almighty, thrice holy God."[29] God's holiness, then, must be seen through the lens of the vulnerable, crucified, and risen Lamb.

Throughout the Apocalypse, God's holiness is inseparable from God's mission. In chapter 15, God's victorious people, standing beside the sea of glass, lift the song of Moses and of the Lamb (Rev 15:2-4). The song's lyrics ask, "Lord, who will not fear and glorify your name?" Immediately the answer resounds:

> For *you alone are holy.*
>   All nations will come
>   and worship before you,
> for your judgments have been revealed. (Rev 15:4, italics added)

From John's perspective, as people from the world's nations genuinely grasp God's unique holiness and his righteous ways and judgments (see Rev 15:3), they will be drawn to repent and worship such a God.[30] God's holiness comes to its ultimate expression in his purpose not to destroy the world's rebel nations but to reconcile and redeem them.

What is more, a holy God and a holy Christ desire a holy people, a people who are caught up in God's life-giving purposes for all creation. Repeatedly,

---

[29]Johnson, *Holiness and the Missio Dei*, 158.
[30]Craig R. Koester, *Revelation: A New Translation with Introduction and Commentary* (New Haven, CT: Yale University Press, 2014), 633, 636.

John calls God's people the "holy ones" (e.g., Rev 5:8; 8:3-4; 11:18 translation mine). They are holy not because of their own innate goodness but because of their relationship with a holy God. At the same time, they are called to *be* a holy people as God is holy. They "keep the commandments of God" (Rev 14:12) and are clothed in righteous deeds (Rev 19:8). As we'll see in chapter four, only as Christians reflect God's holy character can they participate in God's work of bringing wholeness to the whole creation.

That mission reaches its goal in the new Jerusalem, the "holy city" (Rev 21:2). New Jerusalem's perfectly cubed shape is patterned after the inner sanctuary of God's temple in the Old Testament, the holy of holies (Rev 21:16; cf. 1 Kgs 6:19-20). A temple would be utterly superfluous there; the entire city and its people are drenched with the presence of a holy God (Rev 21:3, 11, 22; 22:3-5). New Jerusalem is one giant holy of holies. But this vision isn't only about the future. John's readers, and readers today, are called to embody the life of holy New Jerusalem here and now. For that to happen, we must allow God's holy, indwelling presence to so transform our Christian communities that our attitudes and actions show a watching world a sneak preview of what's to come—a community that is wholly conformed to the character of its holy God.

WOUNDED LOVE

To this point, we have seen primarily Revelation's portrait of the almighty Creator God, the holy one, who sits on the universal throne and overcomes evil with righteous judgments. But what about love? Is the God of Revelation also a God of love? Oh, yes!

It's true that Revelation offers few explicit references to divine love, all of which relate to the risen Christ (Rev 1:5; 3:9, 19).[31] But that's far from the whole picture. The God of holiness and justice is also a loving God. He loves his good creation enough to fulfill his life-giving purposes for creation, despite all the powers of sin and evil that oppose him. God does not remain unmoved by the suffering and pain of the martyrs but responds to their cries for justice (Rev 6:10; 16:4-5). His loving mission reaches its goal only in the

---

[31]These references use two different Greek words for "love": *agapaō* in Rev 1:5 and Rev 3:9 and *phileō* in Rev 3:19.

new creation when God dwells with his people and, like a tender parent, wipes every tear from their eyes (Rev 7:17; 21:3-4). God does not turn his back on rebellious sinners but graciously seeks to reach them with the good news and bring them to repentance (Rev 9:20-21; 14:6-7; 16:9, 11).[32] In Revelation, as in the rest of the New Testament, "there is mission because God loves."[33]

Above all, however, God's love is embodied in the slaughtered Lamb, who "loves us" (Rev 1:5), whose blood is spilled to redeem people from every tribe, language, and nation (Rev 5:9). Consequently, "The Sovereign God of the universe is driven by self-giving love and is able to be wounded in reaching out to humanity."[34] As commentators Thomas and Macchia point out, we meet "a creative tension" in Revelation between divine sovereignty and divine love. "There is no contradiction," they insist, "between the God who sits on the throne and the God revealed in the crucified Lamb."[35] God's love is never squishy and sentimental, like a parent who indulges the destructive behavior of a spoiled child. Rather, God's love is a holy love, which judges and conquers those who are bent on sabotaging God's restoring work in the world. But God's love triumphs through the shed blood of the Lamb (Rev 5:6; 12:11). Victory comes not through violence but through a mission of suffering, wounded love.

CONCLUSION

Years ago, I heard a story about a young girl whose mother found her eagerly sketching on a piece of white paper. "What are you drawing?" the mother queried. "I'm drawing a picture of God," came the answer. "Dear, no one knows what God looks like," the mother gently corrected. Without raising her head, the child shot back, "They will when *I* get done!"[36]

One of the crucial questions asked by Christians (and non-Christians as well) is, What is God like? In this chapter, we've looked at how Revelation

---

[32]John Christopher Thomas and Frank D. Macchia, *Revelation* (Grand Rapids, MI: Eerdmans, 2016), 409.

[33]John R. Franke, *Missional Theology: An Introduction* (Grand Rapids, MI: Baker Academic, 2020), 8.

[34]Thomas and Macchia, *Revelation*, 409.

[35]Thomas and Macchia, *Revelation*, 410-11.

[36]Dean Flemming, *Self-Giving Love: The Book of Philippians* (Bellingham, WA: Lexham, 2021), 10.

answers that question. In the first place, the God of the Apocalypse is not a scary, spooky God, a violent God who behaves badly, or a different God than we see in the rest of the Bible. Unfortunately, I often encounter students whose perception of God in Revelation is precisely that. Rather, the God of Revelation is the same God we know throughout the entire biblical story, a God of love who is unswervingly committed to reconciling people of all nations to himself and to bringing *shalom* to the whole of creation. Within that sweeping story, Revelation spotlights several dimensions of the divine mission:

- God is the Creator of everything, whose mission seeks to bring a wounded and alienated world to its intended purpose of wholeness and abundance. To that end, God acts as creation's *restorer*, who can be trusted to make everything new (Rev 21:5).

- God is the sovereign Lord of history, who rules everything from the universal throne. Because God is Lord of the world, his redeeming, healing mission reaches out to every person *in* that world, regardless of their nation, ethnicity, gender, socioeconomic status, or religious tradition. God is unique in his power to save. No rival power can threaten God's restoring purpose for the world.

- God is "holy to the max." Because God is holy, he is unrelentingly committed to making things right in the world, so that the earth may be filled with his glory. The holy God cannot compromise with the sinful powers that try to frustrate his loving mission to the world but overcomes them with righteous judgments.

- Revelation reveals a creative tension between God's sovereignty over creation and God's love for what he has made. Ultimately, God's holiness, sovereignty, and love embrace in the mission of Jesus, the slaughtered Lamb, who defeats the evil powers through his spilled blood. At the end of the day, Revelation doesn't define what it means to be God by speculating on the divine attributes but by telling the saving story of the slain, victorious Lamb.

It's to the mission of the crucified Lamb that we now turn.

CHAPTER THREE

THE MISSION OF THE SLAUGHTERED LAMB

Then I saw a Lamb, looking as if it had been
slain, standing at the center of the throne.

REVELATION 5:6 NIV

MY HIGH SCHOOL HAD A MASCOT. We were the Leopards. The mighty, mighty Leopards! Nearly all schools, universities, and professional sports teams in the United States boast mascots, and the fiercer the better. Mascots like tigers or panthers or bears are designed to communicate power and dominance over adversaries on the athletic field. Granted, a few outliers buck the trend, such as the Banana Slugs, the Poets, or the Fighting Pickles.[1] But for the most part, mascots send a *We're gonna rip you to pieces!* message.

One mascot, however, that I have never come across (nor am I likely to do so) is the *Lambs*.[2] Lambs make *terrible* mascots. They are entirely too docile, too passive, too weak. A chant such as, "We are the mighty, mighty lambs!" would hardly strike fear in the hearts of opponents!

How strange, then, that John would choose a lamb as the master symbol of the Apocalypse, a book that narrates God's utter triumph over all his

---

[1] These university mascots belong to UC Santa Barbara, Whittier College, and the University of North Carolina School of the Arts respectively.
[2] I owe this thought to a sermon by Jon Middendorf.

enemies. Yet apart from the identity and mission of the slaughtered Lamb, what God is doing in Revelation makes little sense. It is precisely in the activity of Jesus, the slain Lamb, that God's redeeming, restoring purpose for all people and all of creation comes into clearest focus.

In this chapter, we will explore how Jesus, the crucified and risen Lamb, reveals both the content and the character of God's mission in the world. We'll also see that the church's mission, if it is truly Christian, must follow a Lamblike pattern.

THE LION AND THE LAMB

Imagine once again that you are sitting in a gathering of Christians in first-century Ephesus. A gifted reader unravels the scroll that contains John's Apocalypse and begins to read. You and those around you are struck by the first words you hear: "The revelation of *Jesus Christ*" (Rev 1:1, italics added). Then as the reader dramatically unfolds John's visions, your assembly encounters Christ in a flurry of names and images: the faithful witness, the firstborn of the dead, the ruler of the kings of the earth, the one like the Son of Man, the first and the last, the living one, the one who holds the keys of Death and Hades, the holy and true one, the Lion of the tribe of Judah, the root of David, the shepherd who guides people to springs of the water of life, the King of kings and Lord of lords, the conqueror who rides a white horse, the one who judges and makes war, the lamp and temple of New Jerusalem, the Alpha and Omega, the beginning and the end, the root and descendant of David, the bright and morning star. Finally, after the reading arrives at its stirring conclusion, Jesus' threefold promise, "See, I am coming soon" (Rev 22:7, 12, 20) still rings in your collective ears. Your congregation surely would harbor no doubt that what you just heard was a revelation of *Jesus Christ*.[3]

At the heart of God's mission in Revelation lies the story of Jesus, a narrative that gives meaning to all of history. That story encompasses both a past and a future. Regarding the past, John refers briefly to Jesus' preexistence. He is the "first and the last" (Rev 1:17), the "origin" or "source" of God's

---

[3]The phrase "revelation of Jesus Christ" (Rev 1:1) likely describes a revelation that is *about* Christ and *from* Christ.

creation (Rev 3:14; cf. Rev 13:8). In addition, the Apocalypse makes a symbolic allusion to Jesus' birth, as the child borne by the woman clothed with the sun (Rev 12:1-6). But Jesus' prehistory and earthly life are not John's main talking points. Above all, Revelation spotlights Jesus' death, resurrection, and exaltation as the epicenter of Christ's mission.

That takes us directly to Revelation 5. We've already seen that the heavenly throne room scene in chapters 4 and 5 forms the theological core of the book. Chapter 5 opens with God holding a scroll, which symbolizes God's sweeping plan to redeem and judge the world. Suddenly a powerful angel poses a question that echoes through the halls of heaven: "Who is worthy to open the scroll and break its seals?" (Rev 5:2). In response, John weeps because no qualified candidate can be found. But then one of the twenty-four elders consoles him, "See, the Lion of the tribe of Judah, the Root of David, has conquered." He alone is worthy to open the scroll (Rev 5:5). Such titles evoke Israel's nationalistic hopes of a mighty messiah from the line of David, a military figure who would crush Israel's enemies with overpowering force. As Eugene Boring notes, time and time again, "Israel found itself as lambs at the mercy of the lion-like empires that had often surrounded it." But at last the mighty Lion of God has come to turn the tables and deliver his powerless people.[4] We naturally expect a glorious figure to appear, such as the one John describes in Revelation 1:12-20, with eyes blazing with fire, a voice thundering like the waters of Victoria Falls, a sharp, two-edged sword issuing from his mouth, and a face glowing like the sun at high noon. But in a shocking reversal of expectations, we see something very unlionlike—"a Lamb standing as if it had been slaughtered" (Rev 5:6). It's as if the team mascot has suddenly morphed from a roaring lion to a *dead lamb*!

As Richard Bauckham reminds us, the difference between what John *hears* and what he *sees* matters a great deal in Revelation, and never more so than here.[5] John *hears* that the powerful Lion of Judah has triumphed over

---

[4]M. Eugene Boring, *Hearing John's Voice: Insights for Teaching and Preaching* (Grand Rapids, MI: Eerdmans, 2019), 100.
[5]Richard Bauckham, *The Theology of the Book of Revelation* (Cambridge: Cambridge University Press, 1993), 74.

God's enemies, but he *sees* a slaughtered Lamb. The Lion becomes the Lamb. This is the magnificent mystery of Revelation. The powerful Creator God who sits on the throne of sovereignty has chosen to enact his restoring purpose for humanity and all creation *through the spilled blood of the Lamb* (Rev 5:9). The symbol of the slaughtered Lamb bursts and reconfigures all human categories of what it means to be the Messiah. As Thomas and Macchia put it, "The vulnerable Lamb does not simply qualify our understanding of the ferocious Lion but is rather the lens through which the Lion's acts are to be understood."[6] Like Aslan, the Christ figure in C. S. Lewis's *The Lion, the Witch and the Wardrobe*, he is a lion who suffers and dies. God *conquers* the enemies of his saving purposes not by sheer force but by suffering love. By a dying Lamb!

The Lamb that was slain becomes the interpretive key to the nature of the divine mission in the Apocalypse. It is Revelation's centering and defining symbol. Michael Gorman observes, "As a narrative whole, Revelation first builds to this astonishing image, and then everything afterwards flows from it."[7] Revelation's slaughtered Lamb leans on powerful Old Testament

Figure 3.1. *Adoration of the Mystic Lamb* by Jan Van Eyck from the Ghent altarpiece, 1432

---

[6]John Christopher Thomas and Frank D. Macchia, *Revelation* (Grand Rapids, MI: Eerdmans, 2016), 442.

[7]Michael J. Gorman, *Reading Revelation Responsibly: Uncivil Worship and Witness: Following the Lamb into the New Creation* (Eugene, OR: Cascade, 2011), 108.

pictures such as the Passover lamb by which God liberated his people from their bondage in Egypt (Ex 12:1-27; 1 Cor 5:7) and Isaiah's suffering Servant, who is "like a lamb that is led to the slaughter" (Is 53:7). John's picture of the Lamb's mission, however, stretches us beyond even these. The four living creatures and the elders exclaim:

> You are worthy to take the scroll
> and to open its seals,
> for you were slaughtered and by your blood you ransomed for God
> saints from every tribe and language and people and nation;
> you have made them to be a kingdom and priests serving our God,
> and they will reign on earth. (Rev 5:9-10)

Revelation reveals that the Lamb holds the key to unlocking God's great plan to redeem the world precisely because he *suffers* and *dies*. Why is the Lamb's violent death worth celebrating? The heavenly song provides a comprehensive answer:

- It is *sacrificial*. As the Passover Lamb, Christ opens the way to redemption *by his blood*, shed for others.

- It is *liberating*. Christ's death enacts a *new exodus*. It ransoms, liberates, and redeems people who were enslaved by the beastly powers.

- It is *universal*. Whereas the first exodus delivered God's people Israel from bondage, in the new exodus, Christ's sacrificial death redeems a globally inclusive people from every tribe, language, and nation.

- It is *missional*. Drawing on language from Exodus 19:6, Christ's death forms a people who serve God and are caught up in his mission. As priests, they mediate God's presence in the world on behalf of others (Rev 5:10; cf. Rev 1:5-6; 20:6).

It's clear that John sees the Lamb's redeeming work in strong continuity with what God has done in the past to liberate his people from their slavery in Egypt. Later, God's redeemed people stand beside a sea of glass, which recalls the Red Sea of the exodus, and sing "the song of Moses . . . and the song of the Lamb" (Rev 15:2-3). It is the song of *both* Moses *and* the Lamb "because essentially it is one song celebrating one great redeemer and his one great redemptive work in history."[8] What is more, Christopher Wright points out that the mission of the slaughtered Lamb also fulfills God's promise to Abraham that in him and his descendants "all the families of the earth shall be blessed" (Gen 12:3).[9] Through his death, the Redeemer-Lamb, who embodies Israel's mission, brings salvation and blessing to "saints from every tribe and language and people and nation" (Rev 5:9).

THE LAMB IS THE LION (AND VICE VERSA)

The Lamb in Revelation may be vulnerable, but he is no weakling. Don't picture a cute, cuddly stuffed animal. *This* Lamb has seven horns, which symbolize perfect power, and seven eyes, which represent complete wisdom (Rev 5:6). He is the risen, exalted Lord, the "living one," who "was dead and came to life" (Rev 1:18; 2:8; cf. Rev 1:5). The Lamb has conquered sin, death, and evil and keeps the keys of Death and Hades (Rev 1:18; 5:5). In short, *the Lamb is still the Lion.* The Lamb does not *replace* the powerful messianic Lion of Judah; he *redefines* that role. The wounded Lamb is also the triumphant, victorious Lord, who receives the praise of myriads of angels in heaven and the whole of creation (Rev 5:11-13). Gorman astutely notes that the whole scene in Revelation 5 shows "a vivid enactment of the poetic text in Phil 2:6-11, where the one who was obedient to death is acknowledged as Lord, worthy of the acclamation due God alone, by all who are 'in heaven and on earth and under the earth' (Phil 2:10)."[10]

John underscores in chapter 5 that Christ, the Lion of Judah, conquers through *death*, his self-giving, vulnerable, yet victorious death on the cross. The exalted Jesus, whom Revelation acclaims as "King of kings and Lord of lords" (Rev 19:16), forever remains the suffering, wounded Lamb. As the theologian Karl Barth once observed, it is no coincidence that when ancient Christian artists portray the risen and exalted Christ enthroned in heaven, we still see the wounds of the cross.[11] Revelation 5 paints a powerful paradox, which we discover throughout the New Testament: the crucified is the

---

[8]Christopher J. H. Wright, *The Mission of God's People: A Biblical Theology of the Church's Mission* (Grand Rapids, MI: Zondervan, 2010), 109.

[9]Wright, *Mission of God's People*, 76-77.

[10]Gorman, *Reading Revelation*, 110.

[11]Karl Barth, *The Epistle to the Philippians*, trans. J. W. Leitch (London: SCM, 1962), 66.

conqueror, the victim is the victor, the dying Lamb is the reigning Lord. What does this reality tell us about the mission of God?

GOD'S LAMBLIKE MISSION

One of Revelation's most striking features concerns the way John identifies the slaughtered Lamb with God on the throne. In chapter 5, the Lamb stands at the center of God's throne (Rev 5:6).[12] At the climax of the scene, every creature under heaven offers the identical praise and worship "to the one seated on the throne" as they do to the Lamb (Rev 5:13). That shared identity between God and the crucified Jesus courses through the Apocalypse like a river through a deep canyon. God the Father and the Lamb share

- rule and sovereignty (e.g., Rev 1:5; 11:15; 22:5),

- the divine throne (Rev 3:21; 5:6; 7:17; 22:1, 3),

- a divine identity as "the Alpha and the Omega" (Rev 1:8; 21:6; 22:13) and "the beginning and the end" (Rev 21:6; 22:13),

- the promise that God and the Lamb will "come" (Rev 1:4; 7, 8; 3:11; 4:8; 22:7, 12, 20),

- hair white as wool, like the Ancient One in Daniel 7:9 (Rev 1:14),

- a name (Rev 14:1; 22:3-4),

- holiness (Rev 3:7; 4:8; 15:4),

- salvation (Rev 7:10),

- care for God's people, leading them to the fullness of life (Rev 7:17; 21:6),

- wrath and judgment (Rev 2:5, 16; 6:16-17; 14:14, 17-20; 19:15),

- receiving the prayers of God's people (Rev 5:8; 8:3-4),

- a role as the temple (Rev 21:22) and the light (Rev 21:23; 22:5) in New Jerusalem, and

- worship (Rev 5:9-14; 7:10; 22:3).

---

[12]"In the midst of the throne" is a more natural translation of the Greek phrase *en mesō tou thronou* (Rev 5:6) than the NRSV's "between the throne."

As we'll see throughout this book, nearly all these touchstones of common identity are *missional* concerns. In Revelation, the mission of the Lamb *is* the mission of God and vice versa; or, in Bauckham's staccato summary: "What Christ does, God does."[13] God's redeeming work in the world happens and can *only* happen through a vulnerable, crucified Lamb.

But the image of the slaughtered Lamb doesn't just tell us *that* God brings restoration to the world through the crucified Jesus. It also shows us *how* God fulfills his purposes of judgment and salvation. God's mission is *Lamblike*. Self-giving love lies at the very heart of the divine mission. In his opening greeting to the seven churches in Asia, John describes Christ as the one "who loves us and freed us from our sins by his blood" (Rev 1:5). The Lamb routs evil not by violence or coercion but through wounded love (Rev 12:11).

"The most surprising thing about this book is that at the center of the throne, holding together both the throne and the whole cosmos that is ruled by the throne, we find the sacrificed Lamb (cf. Rev 5:6; 7:17; 22:1). At the very heart of 'the One who sits on the throne' is the cross. The world to come is ruled by the one who on the cross took violence upon himself in order to conquer the enmity and embrace the enemy. The Lamb's rule is legitimized not by the 'sword' but by its 'wounds'; the goal of its rule is not to subject but to make people 'reign for ever and ever' (Rev 22:5). With the Lamb at the center of the throne, the distance between the 'throne' and the 'subjects' has collapsed in the embrace of the triune God."[14]

MIROSLAV VOLF

For John's first readers, a more countercultural truth can hardly be imagined. The Romans were experts at *conquering*. Rome milked the myth of the

---

[13]Bauckham, *Theology*, 63-65.

[14]Miroslav Volf, *Exclusion and Embrace: A Theological Exploration of Identity, Otherness, and Reconciliation* (Nashville, TN: Abingdon, 1996), 300-301.

Pax Romana (Roman peace), which promised peace, security, and order for the empire. But with more than a sprinkling of irony, Rome pacified its subjects through military conquest, public crucifixions, and other forms of violence (see Rev 13:7; 17:6; 18:24). John then asks Christians in Roman Asia to do nothing less than reimagine the way things work in the world. Rome rules by brute force. But God overcomes his enemies through weakness and self-giving love, in solidarity with the weak and the marginalized. Revelation turns the popular notion of power on its imperial head.

This is vital to remember as we read the later visions of judgment in Revelation. As Gorman reflects, "Human beings, even apparently faithful Christians, too often want an almighty deity who will rule the universe with power, preferably on their terms, and with force when necessary."[15] A wounded God seems far too weak to deal with our complicated moral and global realities. Our lens, however, for reading the whole of Revelation is not the fearsome Lion but the suffering Lamb. Richard Hays rightly insists, "A work that places the Lamb that was slaughtered at the center of its praise and worship can hardly be used to validate violence and coercion."[16]

"The church does not understand, nor does it seek to understand, the ways of worldly power. The church does not seek to master what is called the power game, nor employ what the world calls power. There is no question of becoming the world's equal in this regard, of finding an equal stand where we can be as strong, as threatening, as powerful as the world. . . . True power is not the ability to claim but to serve. It is not the ability to destroy life in order to survive or feel secure, it is the ability to give one's own life so that others may live."[17]

ALAN BOESAK

---

[15]Gorman, *Reading Revelation*, 111.

[16]Richard B. Hays, *The Moral Vision of the New Testament: Community, Cross, New Creation: A Contemporary Introduction to New Testament Ethics* (San Francisco: HarperCollins, 1996), 175.

[17]Alan Boesak, *Comfort and Protest: Reflections on the Apocalypse of John of Patmos* (Philadelphia: Westminster, 1987), 82-83.

It is true that divine love will ultimately conquer the idolatrous powers and destroy those who destroy the earth (Rev 11:18), but the ultimate goal of the Lamb's sacrifice remains the healing of the nations (Rev 22:2). As Thomas and Macchia elegantly frame it, "Divine love is wounded so that we may be healed."[18]

THE COMING LAMB

In this chapter, we have been exploring the story of Jesus, the slaughtered Lamb, the one who shares the Father's identity and embodies God's mission in the world. So far, we have focused on what Christ *has done* in the past. He is the crucified, risen, and victorious Lamb, whose sacrificial death has liberated God's people in a new exodus and formed an inclusive, international community of Lamb-followers.

As important as it is to know what the Lamb has done, Revelation, more than any other New Testament writing, spotlights what Christ *will do*. The story of Jesus is an unfinished story. In his opening prologue, John introduces Christ with the announcement, "Look! He is coming with the clouds" (Rev 1:7; cf. Dan 7:13), and as the book's curtain drops, Jesus leaves us with his personal assurance, "See, I am coming soon!" (Rev 22:7, 12, 20). He is the bridegroom, who will take God's people as his holy bride (Rev 19:7-9; 21:2, 9). The Lamb will be the temple and the lamp of the new Jerusalem to come (Rev 21:23-23). Along with God the Father, Christ will welcome and tenderly care for the redeemed in the new creation (Rev 7:15-17; cf. Rev 21:3-4). With delightful irony, John promises that the *Lamb* will be their *shepherd* (Rev 7:17). Like God's Servant in Isaiah, he will nourish and protect the flock, leading them to life-giving springs (Rev 7:16-17; Is 49:10). Such future visions not only assure the Lamb's community, then and now, that the God of Israel will fulfill everything he has promised his people through the slaughtered Lamb. They also remind us that we are called to live as a foretaste of God's future—to *become* the healing, restoring, life-giving mission of the slain Lamb in the broken places of our world.

---

[18]Thomas and Macchia, *Revelation*, 442.

As with God the Father, the Lamb's mission seeks salvation, wholeness, and healing not only for all people but also for creation itself. In Revelation 22, the river of the water of life flows from the throne of God and the Lamb. As a result, a lush urban garden erupts, so to speak, through the main street of the city, creating a "green belt" of abundance and fruitfulness (Rev 22:1-2).[19] If, as the New Testament repeatedly affirms, God created all things in heaven and earth through Christ (Col 1:16; cf. Jn 1:3; 1 Cor 8:6), then it shouldn't surprise us that the Lamb will play a central role in God's work of *new* creation. Given that the wounded Lamb will not only ransom his bride the church but also share in God's purpose to make *everything* new, it's little wonder that the hosts of heaven shout:

> Worthy is the Lamb that was slaughtered
> to receive power and wealth and wisdom and might
> and honor and glory and blessing! (Rev 5:12)

THE WARRIOR LAMB

The Lamb's unfinished story, however, has a shadow side. For Christ to reign, evil must fall. Bauckham's comment is on target: "The role of Christ in Revelation is to establish God's kingdom on earth; in the words of 11:15, to turn 'the kingdom of the world' (currently ruled by evil) into 'the kingdom of our Lord and his Messiah.' This is a work of both salvation and judgment."[20] Satan and the powers of evil, especially the idolatrous power of Rome, persist in opposing God and the Lamb. Unless Christ defeats and judges them, God's restoring mission cannot reach its goal. On the one hand, Revelation assures us that the decisive and defining victory is already won in Jesus' death and resurrection. God's people have *conquered* the accuser, Satan, "by the blood of the Lamb and by the word of their testimony" (Rev 12:10-11; cf. Rev 3:21). As with a fatally wounded animal, evil's end is assured.

On the other hand, John recognizes the tension between the triumphant Lamb and the ongoing struggle of God's people. Christ's victory isn't yet

---

[19]See Wes Howard-Brooke and Anthony Gwyther, *Unveiling Empire: Reading Revelation Then and Now* (Maryknoll, NY: Orbis, 2003), 190-91.

[20]Bauckham, *Theology*, 67.

complete. In Revelation's future vision, when the rebellious powers of this world, symbolized by the beast and the ten kings, join forces to make war on the Lamb, he "*will conquer* them, for he is Lord of lords and King of kings" (Rev 17:14, italics added). Christ's triumph is both now won and yet to come.

The final battle scene in Revelation vividly portrays Christ as a divine warrior, mounted on a white steed (Rev 19:11-21). John's description of his flaming eyes, his flowing robe, and the sword extending from his mouth reminds us of the vision of Christ as "one like the Son of Man" in chapter 1. In chapter 19, the rider comes to judge and make war in righteousness, with a heavenly cavalry riding in his wake (Rev 19:11, 14). He wears a robe dipped in blood, and his razor-sharp sword will strike down the nations. He will rule them with a rod of iron, even as he tramples them in the winepress of God's wrath (Rev 19:13-15; cf. Is 63:1-3; Rev 6:16). We see the name "King of kings and Lord of lords" emblazoned on his thigh (Rev 19:16). This triumphant, military figure recalls Jewish hopes for a messiah who would wage war on God's enemies and establish God's rule over the nations of the world.[21]

---

*Speaking of Aslan, the Christ figure in the
Chronicles of Narnia, Lucy asks,
"Then he isn't safe?" "Safe?" said Mr. Beaver.
"Who said anything about safe? 'Course he isn't safe.
But he's good. He's the King, I tell you."[22]*

But can we reconcile this picture of Jesus as a warrior-king, charging into battle, with the image of the slaughtered Lamb? To answer that, we need to take a closer look at John's vision of the victorious rider. Christ is called the "Word of God" (Rev 19:13) and the Faithful and True one (Rev 19:11). Revelation envisions the Lamb's sharp sword as the sword of

---

[21]Bauckham, *Theology*, 67-70.
[22]C. S. Lewis, *The Lion, the Witch and the Wardrobe*, Chronicles of Narnia, book 2 (New York: Harper Collins, 1994), 80.

the word (cf. Eph 6:17)! Further, blood stains the warrior's robe *before* he goes into battle, making it unlikely that the blood comes from his foes. John, as is his habit, turns our assumptions inside out. Commentator Joseph Mangina states it well: "The blood in which the rider's robe is dipped is not the blood of his enemies. It is *his own* blood. . . . We see no sword flashing in the hand of this warrior. The only weapon he wields is the word of truth, issuing from his mouth (Rev 19:15)."[23] The divine Warrior remains the slain Lamb.

Even the heavenly armies of God's people that follow him explode our expectations.[24] Instead of combat gear, they wear white festal robes that are washed in the Lamb's blood (Rev 7:14; 19:14). In John's vision, this nonviolent army doesn't *do* anything, except follow their leader. The battle is over before it can start. Christ has already triumphed by his death. Christ's judgment on those who refuse to repent is the judgment that occurs through God's proclaimed word (Rev 19:15, 21). As the writer to the Hebrews also knew, "The word of God is living and active, sharper than any two-edged sword" (Heb 4:12).

The final scene in Revelation 19:17-21 contains highly graphic images. If this vision were made into a video, it would post a warning for violent content! John envisions a weirdly macabre banquet, in which the main course consists of the flesh of humans, from the poor to the powerful, who continue to wage war against Christ. By the end of the passage, the false prophet and the beast, the devil's advocates, are unceremoniously tossed into a lake of fire. The divine warrior's sword mows down their human allies, who end up as a feast of carrion for gorging birds. These ghastly images shock and disturb us—precisely what they are meant to do. They are intended to flash a warning sign to John's Christian audience of the horrific consequences of

---

[23]Joseph L. Mangina, *Revelation* (Grand Rapids, MI: Brazos, 2010), 221-22. This interpretation goes back to the church fathers, e.g., Origen, *Commentary on the Gospel of John* 2.61, cited in William C. Weinrich, ed., *Revelation*, Ancient Christian Commentary on Scripture, New Testament (Downers Grove, IL: IVP Academic, 2005), 310. For the view that the blood stains on the rider's robe come from his enemies, see Grant R. Osborne, *Revelation* (Grand Rapids, MI: Baker Academic, 2002), 682-83.

[24]The next two paragraphs adapt material from Dean Flemming, "Revelation," in *The Wesley One-Volume Commentary*, ed. Kenneth J. Collins and Robert W. Wall (Nashville, TN: Abingdon, 2020), 930.

Figure 3.2. Manuscript illumination of the Lamb defeating the ten kings from *Commentary on the Apocalypse,* Beatus of Liébana, 1220–1235

compromising with the beast, as well as to urge them to repent and follow the way of the Lamb.

Unfortunately, some popular interpretations of Revelation treat the militant scenes in chapter 19 like an advance screening of literal history. Tim LaHaye, for one, expects a Warrior-Christ to lead a real army into a battle that will actually kill all unbelievers, an event he labels "the most horrible experience in the annals of human history."[25] But such a reading butts heads not only with Revelation's picture of the slaughtered Lamb but also with the rest of the New Testament, which affirms that Christ gains victory over the world through his self-giving death on the cross.[26] The gruesome visions of Revelation 19 use poetic language to graphically symbolize Christ's final defeat of evil; *they don't give us a literal description of it.* To read them as predictions of future events grossly misunderstands John's bigger purpose.

At the same time, Christ's role as the one who "judges and makes war" (Rev 19:11) does not deliver Revelation's final word. This scene shows vividly that the "King of kings" has not abandoned his world to the evil powers. God rids the world of evil in order to fulfill his mission of making everything new (Rev 21:5).

In its portrayal of both judgment and salvation, Revelation gives special emphasis to the conclusion of the Jesus story. John is a skilled contextual theologian, and this is something the Christians in Roman Asia need to hear. They lived under an imperial power that seemed to hold all the cards, a "kingdom of the world" (Rev 11:15) that proudly claimed to rule over everything. Revelation's gripping picture of Christ's final victory over God's enemies offers them the rock-solid assurance that they can endure triumphantly, whatever their present circumstances. What's more, Jesus' promise, "I am coming soon" speaks a two-pronged message to the church. It encourages faithful Christians to remain so, even as they await Christ's return. At the same time, it shakes up complacent churches like a splash of cold water, calling them to wake up and repent.

FOLLOWING THE LAMB

The story of Christ, the slain but conquering Lamb, not only has a past and a future but also a *present*. In the "present" time of John and the churches in Asia, the story of the blood-stained Lamb is inseparable from the story of his followers. They play a crucial role in the working out of the Lamb's

---

[25]Tim LaHaye, *Revelation Unveiled* (Grand Rapids, MI: Zondervan, 1999), 308-16; here 308.
[26]See Richard B. Hays, "Faithful Witness, Alpha and Omega: The Identity of Jesus in the Apocalypse of John," in *Revelation and the Politics of Apocalyptic Interpretation*, ed. Richard B. Hays and Stefan Alkier (Waco, TX: Baylor University Press, 2012), 81.

victorious mission.[27] Even as *Jesus* conquers, *they* must overcome the enemies of God (Rev 3:21; 12:11; 15:2). As *he* suffered and poured out his life on the cross, they, too, must be willing to endure suffering and martyrdom (Rev 1:9; 2:10; 6:9-11; 13:7-10). In this way, they already partner in Christ's triumph over Satan:

> But they have conquered him by the blood of the Lamb
>   and by the word of their testimony,
> for they did not cling to life even in the face of death. (Rev 12:11)

Then and now, the mission of the slain Lamb brings a costly call to discipleship to Christian communities. God's people "follow the Lamb wherever he goes" (Rev 14:4), even to the cross. This isn't simply about dying as a martyr, although for some in John's audience, that might be necessary. It is also about *living* daily in the likeness of the slaughtered Lamb. Jesus' sacrificial death on the cross is not only the source of our salvation; it is the pattern of our lives.

What does sacrificial, Lamblike mission look like in practice? It takes many forms in a multitude of contexts. But my friend Teena's story offers one example, as told by her pastor:

> Teena worked as a server at a local restaurant. A few years ago, her coworker's girlfriend suddenly died. This man was obviously devastated and needed to take some time off work. So in the spirit of sacrificial love, Teena offered to cover his shift. Along with the pain of losing his girlfriend, her friend was also in financial trouble, living paycheck to paycheck. He couldn't afford to take much time off. He knew he needed to pick up more shifts to make up for the lost hours. But when he returned to work, he was shocked to find out that even though Teena had worked all those hours on his behalf, every dime she made during those weeks was being paid to *him*.[28]

Teena had little discretionary income herself at the time. However, she loved sacrificially because she knew that was the way of the slaughtered Lamb.

The church's present isn't easy. But the Lamb has not left his followers alone in their weakness and suffering. The same risen Christ who will come

[27]Bauckham, *Theology*, 75.
[28]Michael W. Goheen and Jim Mullins, *The Symphony of Mission: Playing Your Part in God's Work in the World* (Grand Rapids, MI: Baker Academic, 2019), 106.

to finish his work of salvation and judgment is *already present* with his people. He stands in the midst of the seven lampstands, which represent the churches, and walks among them (Rev 1:13, 20; 2:1). Repeatedly, he calls them to repent, as discerned in the Spirit: "I am the one who searches minds and hearts, and I will give to each of you as your works deserve" (Rev 2:23; cf. Rev 2:5, 16; 3:3). The one who loves them enough to redeem them by his blood loves them enough to discipline and correct them (Rev 1:5; 3:19). Given their experience of suffering (Rev 1:9), the assurance that Christ is present among them comes as a word on target for Christians in crisis. Thomas and Macchia put it beautifully: "The Presence of the risen Christ . . . offers readers who suffer in the midst of a dark world a glimpse of the coming victory, as well as a foretaste of its future glory."[29] At the same time, for Christians who have struck up a friendship with the sinful powers or whose practices resemble the dominant culture more than the way of the Lamb, Jesus' presence among them shouts, "I love you; so come back to me, while there is still time!"

CONCLUSION

Near the end of the first book in the Harry Potter series, Harry learns from the headmaster, Dumbledore, that his mother foiled the evil designs of Lord Voldemort by sacrificing her life on his behalf. "Your mother died to save you," Dumbledore declares. "If there is one thing Voldemort cannot understand, it is love. He didn't realize that love as powerful as your mother's for you leaves its own mark."[30] Revelation reveals a love whose mark is etched across the horizons of the cosmos and along the corridors of human history. It is the mark of wounded love, cut into the side of the bleeding Lamb.

Revelation's vision of Christ is both paradoxical and stunning. He is the roaring Lion and the slaughtered Lamb; the conquering warrior and the tender shepherd; the reigning Lord and the wounded redeemer. Which side of the paradox that Christians emphasize depends a great deal on their context. I recently attended a theology conference on the person and mission of

---

[29]Thomas and Macchia, *Revelation*, 444.
[30]J. K. Rowling, *Harry Potter and the Sorcerer's Stone* (New York: Scholastic Press, 1998), 299.

Christ. It included presentations from Christians who lived in a potpourri of global settings. Presenters and participants who came from contexts where people feared unseen spiritual forces in their daily lives emphasized Christ's role as victor over Satan, the powers, and the grave—in Revelation's language, the powerful Lion and the Warrior-King. Others, however, situated in settings of widespread poverty and oppression, tended to stress Jesus' humble identification with the dispossessed and the implications of his shameful, sacrificial death for how the church lives out its faith. They appealed to the pattern of the slain Lamb.

> *"The image of the warring and victorious Lamb of Revelation has great value for the ordinary African Christian. When Jesus is called 'savior,' the experience of deliverance for many Africans is not primarily from sin; rather salvation is deliverance from the power of evil principalities and enclaves of human enemies, deliverance from ill-health and misfortunes of life as a means to bring wholeness and peace. . . . Hence, Christ is savior in the* present *situation of the believer more so than in the* past *event of the cross."*[31]
>
> JAMES CHUKWUMA OKOYE

Could it be, however, that each of us could benefit from looking at the saving mission of Christ through a different pair of glasses than the ones we wear? While living in the Philippines, I discovered that images of the suffering or entombed Jesus shaped the imagination of the popular culture. Each year, for example, the iconic statue of the "Black Nazarene" bearing his cross is led through the streets of Manila in solemn procession, surrounded by millions of devotees. Such representations of Jesus' suffering resonate deeply with people who endured centuries of colonial rule and who face daily

---

[31]James Chukwuma Okoye, "Power and Worship: *Revelation* in African Perspective," in *From Every People and Nation: The Book of Revelation in Intercultural Perspective*, ed. David Rhoads (Minneapolis: Fortress, 2005), 123. Italics original.

physical and economic hardship. But they only provide a half-portrait of Jesus, in isolation from a corresponding picture of Jesus as the Lion of Judah, the risen, coming, and victorious King. Filipina theologian Melba Maggay's plea makes just this point: "We need to make the emphatic transition from the cross to the empty tomb! Failure to do so consigns our people to the subtle demonic lie of seeing the work of Jesus, and life itself, as an endless passion, a picture of eternal defeat and unrelieved tragedy."[32]

In contrast, for many Christians in the West, as well as those influenced by a prosperity gospel in various global settings, the greater danger becomes a one-sided portrait of a powerful, triumphant Christ, who lacks the wounds of the cross. Too often this "superhero" Jesus spawns preaching and theology that "promise power without weakness, success without suffering, prosperity without sacrifice, salvation without discipleship, religion without righteousness."[33] Instead, a missional reading of Revelation invites us to embrace the paradox of a crucified conqueror, a strong Lion who redeems as a slaughtered Lamb.

At the end of the day, we can't forget that the master symbol of Revelation, which gives meaning to the whole, remains the Lamb who was slain. This is

Figure 3.3. Procession of the Black Nazarene in Quiapo, Manila, Philippines

---

[32]Melba Padilla Maggay, *The Gospel in Filipino Context* (Manila: OMF Literature, 1987), 8. This paragraph is adapted from Dean Flemming, *Contextualization in the New Testament: Patterns for Theology and Mission* (Downers Grove, IL: IVP Academic, 2005), 211.

[33]Dean Flemming, *Philippians: A Commentary in the Wesleyan Tradition* (Kansas City, MO: Beacon Hill, 2009), 180.

the *good news* of the Apocalypse: the God who sits on the universal throne fulfills his transforming mission in the world in no other way but through a wounded, dying Lamb. If we are serious about participating in *God's* mission, then *our* mission, too, must be Lamblike. The slaughtered Lamb becomes our mascot, our emblem, our song.

And all God's people sang: "We are the lambs! The suffering, conquering lambs!"[34]

---

[34]Our chant could just as well be, "We are the *Lamb's*! The suffering, conquering *Lamb's*!"

CHAPTER FOUR

THE MISSION OF GOD'S PEOPLE

There before me was a great multitude . . . from every nation, tribe,
people and language, standing before the throne and before the Lamb.

REVELATION 7:9 NIV

SOME YEARS AGO, a friend was traveling in the southern part of the
United States, along with several colleagues. They stopped at a local restau-
rant for breakfast, and my friend, who hailed from the North, ordered some
bacon and eggs. "Do you want grits with that?" the server questioned.
Unfamiliar with this Southern specialty (a kind of corn porridge), he paused
for a moment and then replied, "I'm not sure I like them, so I'll just start
with *one grit.*" With a broad smile on her face, the server shot back, "Honey,
they don't come by themselves!"

From Revelation's perspective, as well as that of the whole New Testament,
Christians "don't come by themselves." In fact, it might surprise you that
Revelation turns out to be one of the most important sources for *ecclesiology*—
what we believe about the church—in all of Scripture. And we can't talk
about the *nature* of the church apart from the *mission* of the church. As the
Swiss theologian Emil Brunner once observed, it would be like trying to
separate "fire" from "burning."[1] It simply can't be done.

---

[1]Brunner famously wrote, "The Church exists by mission just as fire exists by burning. Where
there is no mission, there is no Church." Emil Brunner, *The Word and the World* (London: SCM
Press, 1931), 108.

Before we begin, here's a disclosure. What I say in this chapter runs counter to much popular interpretation of Revelation. Teaching on this book often is so focused on figuring out the future that the church's life and mission in the present becomes, at best, a side issue. What's more, in many popular dispensationalist ("Left Behind") readings of Revelation, *the church is* "raptured" to heaven ("Come up here," Rev 4:1) before the Great Tribulation that will ravage those left behind on earth.[2] Such a view carries profound and, frankly, devastating implications for the mission of God's people. If the church is literally "out of this world," then it effectively *escapes* any responsibility for mission *in* the world. Such an escapist eschatology not only lacks support in the rest of Scripture; it also breaks contact with the mission of God.

In contrast, this chapter explores how the mission of God's people plays out throughout the Apocalypse. First, we'll look at the Spirit's messages to seven local congregations (Revelation 2 and 3) and how those messages intersect with the mission of God. Then we will focus on Revelation's rich reservoir of images for the church and what they tell us about the identity and mission of God's people.

THE CHURCHES IN ASIA: MESSAGES AND MISSION (REVELATION 2 AND 3)

For the most part, Revelation's *direct* instruction to the church is found in the messages in chapters 2 and 3, which come from both the risen Christ (e.g., Rev 2:1) and the Spirit (e.g., Rev 2:7); the rest of the Apocalypse largely *implies* what the church should do and be. The seven messages, then, make a good starting point.

Targeted messages. In Revelation 2 and 3, Christ addresses real Christian communities in specific missional contexts within the cities of Asia Minor. We should not rip these churches out of their concrete historical settings, say, by reading them as symbols for different periods spanning the history of the church, as some popular interpretations of Revelation hold.[3] Christ, by the

---

[2]The term *rapture* never appears in the Bible.
[3]This approach had advocates during the Reformation, but it was popularized by twentieth-century dispensationalist interpretation, including that of the Scofield Reference Bible. See Judith

Spirit, speaks a focused, contextualized word to each congregation. For example, the reference to "Satan's throne" in the message to Pergamum (Rev 2:13) probably alludes to the city's prominence as a center of the emperor cult. Likewise, the church in Laodicea's "lukewarm" condition recalls this city's tepid, putrid water supply. In contrast, nearby Colossae boasted cold, refreshing drinking water, and neighboring Hierapolis was renowned for its hot medicinal springs—both good things! (Rev 3:15-16).

What's more, the messages not only speak to the churches' specific historical circumstances, but they also address each congregation's spiritual condition and needs. As we saw in chapter one, the churches in Roman Asia Minor met pressures both from without and within. From the *outside*, they faced the possibility of persecution, ranging from economic exclusion to harassment by local authorities to potential violent death (Rev 2:10), as happened with Antipas of Pergamum (Rev 2:13). The greater danger, however, loomed in the form of accommodating to the values and practices of the "divinely sanctioned" empire of Rome, perhaps to avoid being hassled or harassed. The various negative examples we find in chapters 2 and 3 (Jezebel, the Nicolaitans, Balaam) demonstrate that some who were *a part of* these congregations lobbied for just such a compromise.

Varied responses. Did each of the seven churches respond to these internal and external pressures the same way? By no means. Revelation 2 and 3 reveal that "both churches and individual Christians live somewhere on a spectrum ranging from faithfulness to faithlessness."[4] Like a good pastor, John does not force a one-size-fits-all approach.

The churches in **Smyrna** and **Philadelphia** lie on the "faithful" end of the spectrum. Christians in Smyrna, materially poor and afflicted, apparently faced hostility from some Jews living in their city ("the synagogue of Satan," Rev 2:9) who likely denounced the Christian minority to the Roman authorities. Christ promises that, if they remain faithful unto death, they will receive the crown of life in the end (Rev 2:10). Likewise,

Kovacs and Christopher Rowland, *Revelation: The Apocalypse of Jesus Christ* (Malden, MA: Blackwell, 2004), 54-56. For a critique, see Michael J. Gorman, *Reading Revelation Responsibly: Uncivil Worship and Witness: Following the Lamb into the New Creation* (Eugene, OR: Cascade, 2011), 84-86.

[4]Gorman, *Reading Revelation*, 130.

Figure 4.1. Manuscript illumination of the seven churches of Asia from the Trier Apocalypse, 800–850

Christ urges the vulnerable congregation in Philadelphia to "hold fast" to what they have (Rev 3:11). With their faithfulness comes Christ's promise of protection in their coming trials (Rev 3:10) and the privilege of bearing his name in the new Jerusalem (Rev 3:12). John's targeted word to these threatened and faithful churches centers on endurance in the present and hope for the future.

The other five messages, however, tell a different story. For believers in **Pergamum** and **Thyatira**, the main temptation involves *compromising* with the practices of the dominant imperial culture. To their credit, the Christians in Pergamum have remained steadfast in the face of persecution, despite the martyrdom of Antipas, one of their number (Rev 2:13). But some in that city have listened to false teachers within the church, called Nicolaitans (Rev 2:15), who apparently recommended that the best way to get along in a pagan (not Jewish or Christian) society was to accommodate with its ways. Specifically, John targets the practice of eating food offered to idols, which could have taken place at venues like citywide festivals, honoring the emperor or various pagan gods.

The Christians at Thyatira likewise wrestled with the temptation to return to eating idol food, advocated by a deceptive prophet, nicknamed Jezebel (Rev 2:20). Given the pervasive presence of trade guilds in Thyatira, it's plausible that these Christians were seduced into attending guild banquets, where both idol meat and worship of local gods were featured on the menu. To opt out of the guilds could bring a severe economic price. But what might

Figure 4.2. Columned street in ancient Ephesus

seem normal within Roman culture John pictures as a dangerous compromise with idolatry. As a result, he offers these two churches, not words of comfort, but a stinging call to repent—or face Christ's judgment.

Unlike the previous two churches, the congregation in **Ephesus** refused to tolerate false teaching (Rev 2:2, 6). But John exposes a glaring gap in their loyalty to Christ: they have *forsaken their former love* for God, and especially for one another (Rev 2:4). So serious is this flaw in their faithfulness that Christ warns that he will "remove [their] lampstand from its place" unless they repent (Rev 2:5). A church that does not love is no longer the church.

The Spirit's message to **Sardis** and **Laodicea** homes in on a somewhat different problem. These churches apparently face neither persecution from without nor false teachers from within. Their pitfall is *complacency*, due to their own self-sufficiency and material success.[5] Both churches appear to

Figure 4.3. Ruins of the temple of Artemis in ancient Sardis

---

[5]See Craig R. Koester, *Revelation and the End of All Things*, 2nd ed. (Grand Rapids, MI: Eerdmans, 2018), 70-74.

be something they're not. The church in the prosperous city of Sardis carries a reputation for spiritual life, but in fact hovers on the brink of death (Rev 3:1). Likewise, the congregation in Laodicea—a city that boasted in its wealth and self-sufficiency—thought it was rich and needed nothing. But in Christ's eyes, it is spiritually poor and wretched (Rev 3:17). Of the seven churches, this one has accommodated most with the values and affluence of the surrounding culture. Like the city's undrinkable water supply, this prosperous congregation's smugness and self-indulgence make Christ vomit (Rev 3:16)! For both Sardis and Laodicea, the regimen is radical surgery if the patient's life is to be saved. They must wake up, see themselves as they truly are, and repent (Rev 3:3, 17-19)!

Missional implications. Seven churches. Seven targeted messages. What are the implications of these messages for how Christian communities participate in the mission of God?

First, Revelation shows a concern for both the local and the universal in addressing God's people. Each message takes seriously the concrete circumstances of a church embedded in a particular city in Asia Minor, as well as the spiritual condition and needs of that congregation. The message to Sardis wouldn't fit Smyrna, nor would the Spirit's word to Thyatira work for Laodicea. The prophetic messages both commend when needed and confront when demanded. At the same time, it becomes clear as Revelation unfolds that each of these churches plays a part in a greater cosmic struggle—the victory of the slaughtered Lamb over the beastly powers that oppose him. Richard Bauckham writes, "While the book as a whole explains what the war is about and how it must be won, the message to each church alerts that church to what is specific about its section of the battlefield."[6]

Similarly, we must allow Revelation to speak a context-specific word to churches within their life settings today. There is no fold-out theology or interpretation of Scripture that we can carry in a backpack from place to place. At the same time, each local body and national church must see itself as part of the greater unfolding drama of God's purpose to restore the whole of creation to what he intended it to be. We cannot allow our contextual

---

[6]See Richard Bauckham, *The Theology of the Book of Revelation* (Cambridge: Cambridge University Press, 1993), 14.

readings of Scripture to isolate us from the wider community of Lamb-followers who also are caught up in the mission of God.

Second, faithful participation in God's mission requires a willingness for churches to repent and change their attitudes and practices. I agree with Michael Gorman that the fundamental issue for these churches involves whether or not to compromise with the pagan culture around them, whatever specific form that might take.[7] How they answer that question carries a direct effect on their witness to the world. As Gorman poses the question, "Will they join the Nicolaitans, Balaamites, followers of Jezebel, and Laodiceans who are participating in various forms of compromise and accommodation, . . . or will they abstain—'come out' (Rev 18:4)—and be willing to suffer like John, like Antipas of Pergamum (Rev 2:13), and like Jesus himself?"[8] For compromising churches, repentance not only ensures their own spiritual survival but also enables them to maintain a faithful, Lamblike witness to the world.

Furthermore, repentance and transformation are musts for Christians to share in God's purpose to make everything new. This is the point of the new creation promise to those who "conquer" at the end of each of the Spirit's seven messages. Even the Christians in Laodicea who don't get a hint of praise from Christ hear this promise: "To the one who conquers I will give a place with me on my throne, just as I myself conquered and sat down with my Father on his throne" (Rev 3:21). Only if God's people turn from flirting with idolatry to following the Lamb will they be granted a share in Christ's eternal kingdom and reign.

Third, the targeted messages in Revelation 2 and 3 provide a lens through which each congregation can read the rest of the book.[9] For example, the persecution faced by Christians in Smyrna and Philadelphia foreshadows more intense pressure to come; it spotlights the need to persevere, even to the point of death (Rev 6:9-11; 13:10, 15; 18:24). Likewise, the self-satisfied prosperity of Laodicea prefigures Babylon's arrogance and thirst

---

[7]Gorman, *Reading Revelation*, 96.

[8]Gorman, *Reading Revelation*, 97.

[9]For this point, see Dean Flemming, *Contextualization in the New Testament: Patterns for Theology and Mission* (Downers Grove, IL: IVP Academic, 2005), 271-72.

to consume in chapter 18. For them, repentance "will be equivalent to coming out of Babylon, as God's people are urged to do, renouncing her sins lest they share her judgment."[10] Each congregation must hear and respond to Revelation's visions of salvation and judgment in the remainder of the book in a somewhat different way, depending on its spiritual condition and needs.

This speaks to how churches read Revelation today. Those under fire for their faithfulness might resonate with Christ's words of consolation to Smyrna and Philadelphia and take encouragement from God's victory over evil in the rest of the book. When I've been privileged to teach Revelation in places in Asia and the former Soviet Union where Christians faced persecution and suffering, I found strong interest in this book and its message of hope for the hard-pressed. Churches, however, in comfortable and affluent settings might need to read John's visions of the bowls and the beasts as people who show a strong family resemblance to the Laodiceans. For such Christians, Revelation does not speak a steadying word of assurance; rather, it blares a warning siren, calling them to return to obedience or face God's judgment.

Fourth, a missional reading will take to heart *all the messages* to the churches. This isn't private mail. Despite their targeted character, John intends that "all the churches" (Rev 2:23) listen to *all seven* messages. What's more, it is no coincidence that Revelation addresses *seven* churches—the number of completion in Revelation. These seven congregations represent *all* the churches, including those of our own time.[11] As one writer admits, "Reading the messages to the seven churches occasions much the same shock of recognition we have when reading Paul's letters. We know these people."[12] Although certain messages may speak to any given situation more directly, the variety of issues they address—compromising with cultural values, persevering in the face of pushback, Christians who are more concerned with defending the faith than loving others, to name a few—continue to challenge

---

[10]Bauckham, *Theology*, 123.

[11]Bauckham, *Theology*, 16.

[12]Joseph L. Mangina, "God, Israel, and Ecclesia in the Apocalypse," in *Revelation and the Politics of Apocalyptic Interpretation*, ed. Richard B. Hays and Stefan Alkier (Waco, TX: Baylor University Press, 2012), 89.

churches in mission today. "Let anyone who has an ear listen to what the Spirit is saying to the churches" (Rev 2:7).

Visions of the Church's Future (and Present)

Outside of the messages to the churches in Revelation 2 and 3, John pictures the people of God with a feast of images, including servants, saints, lampstands, a kingdom and priests, the two witnesses, the sealed 144,000, the woman clothed with the sun, the redeemed, a multinational multitude, brothers and sisters, "virgins," messianic warriors, the called and chosen, the temple, the bride of the Lamb, and the new Jerusalem. Most of these relate to the future destiny of God's faithful, the end-time people of God. It's noteworthy that the term *church* (*ekklēsia*), which occurs twenty times in Revelation, drops completely from sight between the end of the messages to the churches (Rev 3:22) and John's final epilogue in 22:16. For John, the churches are the vulnerable, imperfect, often-compromising communities in Asia, the people that pastor John seeks to shape (and *shape up*) into faithful missional communities.

What, then, is the relationship between the eschatological people of God pictured in Revelation 4–22 and John's audience, whether churches in Smyrna and Sardis or those in Seoul and Sydney? Joseph Mangina helpfully notes that the churches, embedded in their concrete circumstances, represent who God's people *are*. The later visions reveal who they must *become*.[13] Specifically, what the church *becomes* works in two ways. On one level, the visions of God's people, whether an international chorus of worshipers (Rev 7:9-17) or the 144,000 redeemed standing before God's throne (Rev 14:1-5), unveil the church's future, when God makes everything new. But on another level, these end-time visions show what the churches must *become* in their present life in the world. Negatively, Revelation's pictures of the church's future give local congregations a transformed perspective that enables them to resist compromise with the idolatrous culture around them. Positively, John's future visions energize communities of believers in Asia to follow the slaughtered Lamb and courageously bear witness to God's truth.

---

[13]Mangina, "God, Israel, and Ecclesia," 95.

Revelation's visions of the triumphant church pose a similar challenge to Christian communities today. They invite us to pray with utmost serious-ness, "Your kingdom come, your will be done *on earth as it is in heaven*."

Let's look, then, at some of the key images of the church's future in Revelation and how those visions shape the church in mission today.

Priests and rulers. Twice, Revelation pictures the church as a kingdom and as priests: "To him who loves us and freed us from our sins by his blood, and *made us to be a kingdom, priests serving his God and Father*, to him be glory and dominion forever and ever. Amen" (Rev 1:5-6, italics added).

> You were slaughtered and by your blood you ransomed for God
>   saints from every tribe and language and people and nation;
> *you have made them to be a kingdom and priests, serving our God,*
>   *and they will reign on earth.* (Rev 5:9-10; cf. Rev 20:6, italics added)

Echoes of Exodus. This is rich Exodus language. It recalls the foundational covenant passage in Exodus 19:5-6, where God defines the identity and mis-sion of his people Israel as "a priestly kingdom and a holy nation." As a *kingdom* people, the church both shares in God's reign and bears witness to that rule, which stands as an alternative to the "kingdom of this world" (Rev 11:5). As a *priestly* people, the church stands in the middle, mediating between God and the world.

For Israel, this priestly role moved in two directions.[14] On the one hand, Israel's priests taught the people and brought them God's blessing. In a simi-lar way, Israel as a whole was called to mediate the presence and knowledge of God to the surrounding nations. On the other hand, even as priests brought sacrifices and offerings to God for the people, Israel represented the nations to God. Their vocation was to serve God on behalf of the nations, living in such a way that others are attracted to worship Yahweh.

Now God says to people redeemed by Christ's blood: "Just as Israel was marked out to be a light to the Gentiles, you are to mediate my presence to people from every nation through a faithful witness of word and life." Christopher Wright puts it well: "We are a representative people. Our task

---

[14]See Christopher J. H. Wright, *The Mission of God's People: A Biblical Theology of the Church's Mission* (Grand Rapids, MI: Zondervan, 2010), 121-22.

is to represent the living God to the world, and to bring the world to acknowledge the living God."[15] This calling as a royal and priestly people flows not from God's act of deliverance from Egypt, but from a new Exodus, a rescue operation from bondage to the sinful powers, purchased through Christ's blood. And as Christ mediated his liberating, life-giving presence to others through his sacrificial death, we become a priestly community, through whom Christ brings life to the peoples of the world.[16]

A creational calling. Revelation anchors the church's role as a kingdom and priests not only in God's act of redemption in the exodus but also in creation itself. I noted in chapter two that when God creates humans in his image, he gives them the job of "ruling" (Hebrew *radah*, Gen 1:26, 28) over the fish of the sea, the birds of the air, and every other living thing. This is kingdom language. Part of what it means to bear God's image—what it means to be human—involves participating in God's rule over creation, as understudies to the King. This has nothing to do with dominating or exploiting God's creation. Rather, it involves exercising dominion, on God's behalf, in a way that brings God's good and gracious purposes to bear on creation.

Likewise, Genesis 2:15 announces that God put humans in the Garden "to work it and take care of it" (NIV). The verb that's often translated "to work" or "to till" essentially means "to serve" (*'abad*). In one sense, the Garden of Eden represents a kind of cosmic temple, where God's life-giving presence dwells.[17] As the priests of Israel cared for and served God's temple, we are called to exercise that servant role toward the earth, helping it to flourish and burst with life. Revelation is quite clear that God hasn't canceled that role. Rather, God has splendidly restored it through the redeeming death of Christ. Our missional calling, then, includes "reflect[ing] the Creator's wise and loving stewardship into the world."[18] Our care for God's earth now anticipates God's final purpose for the world. In the new creation, God's people from every nation "will reign on the earth" (Rev 5:10; cf. Rev 20:6;

---

[15]Wright, *Mission of God's People,* 122.

[16]Andy Johnson, *Holiness and the* Missio Dei (Eugene, OR: Cascade, 2016), 159.

[17]See T. Desmond Alexander, *From Eden to the New Jerusalem: An Introduction to Biblical Theology* (Grand Rapids, MI: Kregel, 2008), 20-31.

[18]N. T. Wright, *The Day the Revolution Began: Reconsidering the Meaning of Jesus' Crucifixion* (New York: HarperOne, 2016), 99.

22:5). God's original intention for humanity—to bear his image by ruling and serving his world—will come into its fullness.

Sealed and redeemed. The complementary texts of Revelation 7:1-18 and 14:1-5 stand as Himalayan peaks for grasping the mission of God's people in Revelation. There is much we could say about these intriguing passages, but I will focus on their implications for the church's participation in the mission of God. In both chapters, John pictures God's people as a company of 144,000, who belong to God (Rev 7:1-8; 14:1-5). In Revelation 7:1-8, two aspects of their identity stand out. First, Revelation portrays them as *members of the tribes of Israel* (Rev 7:4-8), not literally but in a symbolic sense. John envisions God's people as the restored Israel in the time of the Messiah. Moreover, the number 144,000 is the product of 12 x 12, representing the fullness of Israel's twelve tribes, multiplied by 1000—symbolically, a huge number. 144,000, then, stands for completion and fullness. It tells us that all of God's promises to restore Israel are realized in the redeemed followers of the Lamb.[19]

Second, God's people bear the seal of God on their foreheads (Rev 7:3, 4). This visible seal signals both God's protection (see Ezek 9:3-10) and his ownership. As God's "servants" (Rev 7:3, literally "slaves"), they belong exclusively to God. In chapter 14, John identifies this seal more specifically as the name of the Lamb and of the Father (Rev 14:1). Both the seal and the divine name are emblazoned on the foreheads of God's servants—*the most visible place possible.* These public marks enable Christians to fly their colors of allegiance to God and the Lamb, in bold contrast to those whose foreheads bear the number and name of the beast (Rev 13:16-18).

What is more, twice in chapter 14, John identifies God's faithful as the "redeemed" (Rev 14:3, 4). In Revelation, the redeemed church stands in closest relationship with the Lamb. Not only do they bear his name (Rev 14:1) but they "follow the Lamb wherever he goes" (Rev 14:4). Where is the Lamb going? His trail of tears leads to the cross. After all, he is the *slaughtered*

---

[19]Some interpreters take the 144,000 specifically as martyrs and not the whole people of God. See Mitchell G. Reddish, *Revelation* (Macon, GA: Smyth and Helwys, 2001), 152; Bauckham, *Theology*, 77-79. But this is unlikely. The terms *servant* (Rev 7:3; cf. Rev 1:1; 22:6) and the *redeemed* (Rev 14:3, 4; cf. Rev 5:9) refer to all followers of the Lamb, not a special group within God's people.

Lamb. Following the Lamb involves sharing in the Lamb's story—his faithful witness and suffering, his death and resurrection. Before this scene, in chapter 13, the beast launches an assault against God's people, defeats them, and kills them (Rev 13:7, 15). But now they stand together with the Lamb on Mount Zion, raised and vindicated by God (Rev 14:1).[20] In Revelation, the church's identity and mission are defined by their relationship to the slaughtered Lamb. Like the Lamb they follow, their cross-shaped mission comes with a price tag attached. It is "the way of conquering through suffering, victory through defeat, overcoming through cruciform love."[21]

And yet, their Lamblike witness *will bear fruit*. John calls the redeemed community the "first fruits" of God and the Lamb (Rev 14:4). Israel offered the first fruits of the harvest to God, demonstrating God's claim over the entire harvest that followed (Ex 23:19). For John, first fruits anticipate "a far greater harvest to come from among the mass of human beings from whom the 144,000 have been redeemed."[22] John shows us a screenshot of that great ingathering later in the chapter, when Christ returns to reap the harvest of the earth (Rev 14:14-16). Like a farmer blessed with a bumper crop, Christ will gather to himself an abundant harvest of people for God from all the earth's nations in the end (cf. Mk 4:29).

Uncountable and multinational. *A magnificent vision.* The second part of John's vision of God's people in chapter 7 pictures an uncountable multitude in heaven, standing before God and the Lamb (Rev 7:9-17).[23] Because they "have come out of the great ordeal" (Rev 7:14), some interpreters, from the church fathers on, have seen them as a special group of martyrs *within* the larger people of God.[24] But the text leads to a different conclusion.

---

[20]Johnson, *Holiness and the* Missio Dei, 166.

[21]Dean Flemming, "'On Earth as It Is in Heaven': Holiness and the People of God in Revelation," in *Holiness and Ecclesiology in the New Testament*, ed. Kent E. Brower and Andy Johnson (Grand Rapids, MI: Eerdmans, 2007), 355.

[22]Johnson, *Holiness and the* Missio Dei, 167.

[23]This section draws on Dean Flemming, "Following the Lamb Wherever He Goes: Missional Ecclesiology in Revelation 7 and 14:1-5," in *Cruciform Scripture: Cross, Participation, and Mission*, ed. Christopher W. Skinner et al. (Grand Rapids, MI: Eerdmans, 2021), 265.

[24]E.g., Andrew of Caesarea, *Commentary on the Apocalypse* 7.9–10, cited in William C. Weinrich, ed., *Revelation*, Ancient Christian Commentary on Scripture, New Testament (Downers Grove, IL: IVP Academic, 2005), 12:111; Tertullian, *Scorpiace* 12 (ACCS 12:114); Richard Bauckham, *The Climax of Prophecy: Studies on the Book of Revelation* (London: T&T Clark, 1993), 226-29.

Figure 4.4. Manuscript illumination of the adoration of the Lamb on Mount Zion (Rev 14:1-5) from the Facundus Beatus, 1047

Revelation envisions them as the same group as we find in Revelation 7:1-8—
all followers of the Lamb—from a different perspective. Once again, it's
important to notice both what John *hears* and what he *sees*.[25] John *hears* "the
number of those who were sealed" from every tribe of Israel (Rev 7:4), but
he *sees* a vast multitude from every tribe of humanity (Rev 7:9). Like a
Medieval altarpiece in which the pictures on two panels are hinged together,
chapter 7 paints a double vision of God's people. The first scene shows the
suffering church on earth, sealed and protected by God in the midst of their
trials. Scene two unveils a portrait of the triumphant church in heaven, a
community that already tastes some of the blessings of the new creation to
come (Rev 7:15-17; cf. Rev 21–22). Or, using another analogy, the two visions
function like before and after photos of the same people, projected on the
same video screen.

Are these simply pictures of what God's people will be in the end time?
Not at all. Although both visions show facets of the church's future, both
reveal who God's people must *be* in the present. The church lives as a trailer
of what is to come. Revelation portrays God's people simultaneously as the
restored Israel, marshaled for war against the powers of evil, *and* the global
community of God's people, worshiping God and the Lamb day and
night (Rev 7:15).

The "great multitude" represents every nation, tribe, people, and language
(Rev 7:9). This international company of the redeemed fulfills God's covenant promise that through Abraham and his descendants "all the families of
the earth shall be blessed" (Rev 12:3). God's promise to Abraham in
Genesis 12:1-3 comes in the context of, and as a response to, God's dealing
with all nations in Genesis 10–11.[26] These nations were initially "spread
abroad on the earth" (Gen 10:32). But when they try to join forces against
God in the infamous tower of Babel episode, God spreads them across the
face of the earth (Gen 11:1-9). Christopher Wright notices "a great trajectory—
from the 'tribes, languages and nations' of Gen 10, who stood in need of
redemptive blessing, to that 'great multitude that no one could count,

---

[25]Remember that in chapter 5, John *hears* about a fearsome lion, but he *sees* a slaughtered Lamb
(Rev 5:5-6).
[26]Wright, *Mission of God's People*, 70-71.

from every nation, tribe, people and language,' who will constitute the redeemed humanity in the new creation (Rev. 7:9)."[27]

Missional implications. Revelation's vision of the ethnically diverse multitude in Revelation 7:9-17 just might represent one of the most important images of the church in the New Testament. For now, let's consider three ways this hope-filled vision sculpts the identity and mission of the church today.

First, in a world teeming with ethnic, religious, and racial divisions, Revelation calls us *to embody a consciously multinational, multicultural, multiracial identity as God's people.* This is not some pie-in-the-sky dream about how all God's children will get along someday when we sit around the heavenly throne singing "Kum ba yah." Rather, it shows us precisely what God is up to in the world and how we, as God's people, are called to live into that. John's vision of the multitude reveals that diversity is baked in to our identity as God's people. Esau McCaulley explains, "These distinct peoples, cultures, and languages are eschatological, everlasting. At the end, we do not find the elimination of difference. Instead the very diversity of cultures is a manifestation of God's glory."[28]

But does the vision match the reality? More than sixty years ago, Martin Luther King Jr. famously observed that eleven o'clock on Sunday morning is the most segregated hour in Christian America. Sadly, that reality has not changed significantly in the decades since. Yet, I see signs of hope. One is a local church I know in Michigan, which found itself in a community that had received an influx of refugees and immigrants from around the world. In response, this traditionally White congregation, under the leadership of their pastor and the prodding of the Spirit, transformed itself into an intentionally international fellowship. Their ministries shifted dramatically to offer English classes for immigrants and employment assistance for refugees. When I visited the church on a Wednesday evening, I witnessed people dressed in a variety of traditional attire studying English at various levels. Sunday worship services became celebrations where people from

---

[27]Wright, *Mission of God's People*, 71.
[28]Esau McCaulley, *Reading While Black: African American Biblical Interpretation as an Exercise in Hope* (Downers Grove, IL: IVP Academic, 2020), 116.

twenty-plus national backgrounds came together to worship the one God on the throne.

"God's eschatological vision for the reconciliation of all things in his Son requires my blackness and my neighbor's Latina identity to endure forever. . . . [God] is honored through the diversity of tongues singing the same song. Therefore inasmuch as I modulate my blackness or neglect my culture, I am placing limits on the gifts that God has given me to offer to his church and kingdom. The vision of the kingdom is incomplete without Black and Brown persons worshiping alongside white persons as part of one kingdom under the rule of one king."[29]

ESAU MCCAULLEY

Second, Revelation's vision of the church as an international chorus of worshipers means that *the people of God must expel all forms of racism, nationalism, tribalism, and ethnocentrism (our way is better!) from their midst.* Wherever I have served in the world, I've encountered Christian communities that were divided over those who were "in" and those who were "out." But isn't it typical for people to "flock together" with "birds of the same feather" and to fear those whose feathers look different? *Typical,* yes. But *Christian,* no. Too often congregations are molded more by the values of their social experience than by the vision of the slaughtered Lamb. Gorman puts it well: "If Christians around the globe truly understood themselves as part of this international community, and fully embraced that membership as their primary source of identity, mission, and allegiance, it is doubtful that so many Christians could maintain their deep-seated national allegiances or their suspicions of foreigners."[30] Not only are such attitudes inconsistent with the New Testament vision of the

---

[29]McCaulley, *Reading While Black*, 116.
[30]Gorman, *Reading Revelation*, 134.

church; they also erect a towering barrier that impedes the church's witness to people in its world.

My own country, the United States, struggles particularly with deeply ingrained structures and values that privilege Whites over people of color. Far too often, the American church has *reflected* such power inequalities, rather than *resisting* them. African American theologian Drew Hart speaks uncomfortable words the American church surely needs to consider. He spotlights the need to subvert racial hierarchy in the church, including that which "normalizes white values, experience, and perspectives as the objective and universally right way." He continues,

> Instead, the church must subversively embrace the new humanity and the diverse gifts and varied perspectives that exist within it. It must intentionally privilege the voices and perspectives of those in society who are most neglected, forgotten, ignored, and silenced. . . . Practically, this . . . means that things like job descriptions, church food and meal choices, book selections, curriculum structures, money allocation, meeting times, and the composition of decision-making groups like the church board must be radically reconfigured. These things must become signposts of faithfulness to the God who sustains all of life, and whom every tribe, nation, and tongue will one day worship.[31]

Circumstances will vary, but such small "signposts" broadcast the beauty of God's new creation to a splintered and self-promoting culture.

Third, John's vision of the unnumbered multitude in heaven *extends hope to the church in mission*. It surely would have encouraged the marginalized and persecuted churches in Asia. Not only the sheer size of this throng but also its makeup of people from every tribe, language, and nation would stretch their imaginations almost to the snapping point. John's picture of the vast multinational community of worshipers still holds the power to energize and encourage churches facing persecution from their opponents or indifference from their cultures. It shouts, "Despite present setbacks or pushback, your faithful witness *will* produce a rich harvest in the end." At the same time, John's vision hands us a vocation—to share in the task of

---

[31]Drew Hart, *Trouble I've Seen: Changing the Way the Church Views Racism* (Harrisonburg, VA: Herald Press, 2016), 100.

global evangelization and to serve as agents of reconciliation in and among the world's peoples, at every level of human need.

Holy and blameless. *Holiness—a gift and a calling.* Twelve times in Revelation, God's people are called *saints*, literally, "holy ones." Given the popular perception of a saint as either a near–perfect Mother Theresa figure or as someone long dead to whom some Christians direct their prayers, we need to ask what this means. Above all, "holy ones" signifies the church's relationship to God. Like Israel of old, the church is holy because it is set apart by a holy God for himself (Lev 22:31-33; Deut 7:6; 14:2). For John, *saints* are not a collection of especially holy individuals or martyrs. "Saints" are *us*—the whole people of God. We are holy because we participate in the holiness of a holy God. It's who we *are*.

At the same time, holiness is not only God's gift; it is also the church's *calling.* People who are set apart by a holy God must reflect that holiness in their character and lifestyle (Rev 22:11). Consequently, in Revelation, holiness carries a strong ethical component.[32] To see this, we need look no further than at what the saints are wearing. Revelation's clothing metaphor weaves its way through the book like a white thread. Early on, Christ commends the faithful remnant in Sardis whose clothes are not soiled, but who will walk with him "dressed in white" (Rev 3:4-5). In Revelation, white robes symbolize both victory and purity (Rev 3:18; 6:11). Later, John reports that the great multitude of God's people "have washed their robes and made them white" (Rev 7:14). When the saints "do their laundry," the only cleansing agent that is able to whiten their garments is, paradoxically, "the blood of the Lamb." Here the blessings that flow from Christ's self-giving death include lives of integrity, love, and justice. As David deSilva explains, they have forsaken "the sins of the culture and attached themselves to the Lamb in holiness."[33] The church, as the bride of the Lamb, wears clean, bright linen, woven from the *righteous deeds* of God's holy ones (Rev 19:8). Ultimately, robes that are washed and clean become the required dress code for entering the new Jerusalem (Rev 22:14). What the saints wear on the outside represents their holy character and actions.

---

[32]The rest of this section draws significantly on Flemming, "Following the Lamb," 273-75.

[33]David A. deSilva, *Honor, Patronage, Kinship and Purity: Unlocking New Testament Culture* (Downers Grove, IL: IVP Academic, 2000), 303.

Holy virgins? The holiness of God's people shows up in another striking image in chapter 14. John pictures the redeemed as those "who have not defiled themselves with women, for they are virgins" (Rev 14:4). Virgins? *Really?* Not surprisingly, interpreters have struggled mightily over what to do with this passage. It's been read as anything from an endorsement for male celibacy[34] to a smear against women.[35] But this is not a *literal* description; rather, Revelation likely is drawing on the image of Israel's holy warriors from the Old Testament. John's point seems to be this: "Even as Israel's warriors practiced *ritual* purity by abstaining from sexual relations during battle (Deut 23:9-10; 1 Sam 21:5), so the church needs *moral* purity in order to overcome the enemies of the Lamb."[36] In fact, the church represents an even *higher* standard of holiness. As "virgins," they have *never* been defiled.[37] This picture of the church as a holy army carries missional implications, as Andy Johnson rightly notes: "They have been missionally faithful in their costly battle with the beast, actively participating in the saving, reconciling, life-giving purposes of the missional God."[38]

John's image of the redeemed as "virgins" may also anticipate the church's identity as the Lamb's pure and faithful bride (Rev 19:7-8). Further, they are morally pure and "blameless," and no lies or deceit leave their mouth (Rev 14:5). The church's integrity of word and life couldn't stand out more from Revelation's roll call of deceptive actors: Jezebel (Rev 2:20), fake apostles (Rev 2:2; cf. Rev 3:9), the false prophet (Rev 13:14; 19:20), the harlot Babylon (Rev 18:23), and Satan himself (Rev 12:9; 2:3, 8, 10). In contrast, God's people are like the Lamb they follow (Rev 14:4), holy and propelled by self-giving love (Rev 3:3; 12:11).

Missional implications. Revelation super-glues together *the church, holiness,* and *mission.* Character matters. Only when we fulfill our calling as the Lamb's holy bride, only when we publicly speak and live the truth, only when

---

[34]Especially among the church fathers. See, e.g., Augustine, *Holy Virginity* 12, 14.26–29 (*ACCS* 12:219–21); Cyprian, *The Dress of Virgins* 4–5 (*ACCS* 12:217).

[35]E.g., Tina Pippin, *Death and Desire: The Rhetoric of Gender in the Apocalypse of John* (Louisville, KY: Westminster/John Knox, 1992), 70, 80.

[36]Flemming, "Following the Lamb," 267; see also Bauckham, *Theology,* 77-78; Marianne Meye Thompson, "Reading What Is Written in the Book of Life: Theological Interpretation of the Book of Revelation Today," in Hays and Alkier, ed., *Revelation and the Politics of Apocalyptic Interpretation,* 167.

[37]Thompson, "Reading What Is Written," 167.

[38]Johnson, *Holiness and the* Missio Dei, 167.

we are conformed to the way of the crucified Lamb, can we live as the "first fruits" of a greater harvest to come. Mission flows out of who we *are*.

"Because the formation of a 'people' with distinctive character is so central in this understanding of the missio Dei, *I believe that we should talk about Christian mission as ecclesial holiness. . . . In fact, it is the very existence of this called-forth people that constitutes the offer to the world and foretaste in the world of God's purpose for the world."*[39]

BRYAN STONE

Perhaps the gap between what we say and who we are stands as the greatest barrier to the church's witness in the world. My heart breaks each time a media headline spotlights yet another clergy sex-abuse scandal, a church leader misappropriating funds, or a Christian organization using its financial and political muscle to "win back the culture" by force. My soul aches whenever I see Christians of different political persuasions or theological traditions ripping one another apart on social media. The church in mission's greatest need today is not better strategies for *reaching* the world but better character and conduct *before* the world. They'll know we are Lamb-followers by our cross-shaped love.

CONCLUSION

We can't talk about mission in Revelation without talking about the church. The mission is God's. But this missional God has chosen to accomplish his saving purposes largely through a people who become both the pulpit and the pattern of God's new creation in the world.[40] Revelation projects its images of God's people on a split screen, which displays both who we *are*

---

[39]Bryan Stone, "Christian Mission as Ecclesial Holiness" (paper presented at the Global Theology Conference, Church of the Nazarene, Guatemala City, Guatemala, April 2002), 1-2.

[40]See John Howard Yoder, *For the Nations: Essays Public and Evangelical* (Grand Rapids, MI: Eerdmans, 1997), 41.

and *who we will be*. On the one hand, we find ourselves in Christ's messages to the seven churches in Asia. *We* are the suffering, often-compromising congregations, embedded in a variety of circumstances. *We* are the churches who must repent and be transformed, if we want to get caught up in God's life-giving purposes for the world.

On the other hand, *we* are the community of people from every tribe and tongue, united in our worship of God and the Lamb. *We* are the redeemed people of God, who represent God to the world and reflect God's loving stewardship over all creation. *We* are the community of integrity and holiness, who follow the Lamb in his mission of self-giving love.

But *are* we? Isn't that simply about "when we all get to heaven," when the saints will be once and for all released from the ravages of sin, suffering, and the powers of this world? As Shakespeare's Hamlet famously put it, "Aye, there's the rub." Yes, Revelation's pictures of the victorious church project on a cosmic screen a vision of who we *will be* in the coming new creation. Yes, we cannot help but mourn over the gap between that vision and the church's present conduct in the world. But Revelation gives us, as clearly as anywhere in the Bible, a picture of who we must become *here and now*. It's both our future goal and our present calling. John invites us to lean into this vision of the church until it transforms who we are and how we live. Revelation energizes the church, by the Spirit's power, to *be* a foretaste of the future in the midst of the dark places of our world.

CHAPTER FIVE

MISSION AS WITNESS

*They have conquered [Satan] by the blood of the Lamb and by the word
of their testimony, for they did not cling to life even in the face of death.*

REVELATION 12:11

WHEN I WAS A TEENAGER, I had a clear view of what it meant to be a
witness for Christ. Witnessing was about *telling* the gospel to nonbelievers—
preferably, in short, well-packaged sound bites. I participated in various
workshops and training sessions, after which we were sent into city parks,
shopping malls, or public beaches to witness to complete strangers. Armed
with a crisp evangelistic pamphlet, our aim was to get them to listen to a set
gospel presentation and then "leave the results to God." As a natural intro-
vert who struggled to speak to strangers, the whole experience *terrified* me.
Now don't get me wrong. I'm not saying that God couldn't or *didn't* use this
type of approach. I'm sure he did. But such a one-size-fits-all strategy also
had the potential of turning people *off* to the faith. And it certainly didn't
do justice to the rich biblical understanding of what it means to *be* a
witness (Acts 1:8).

More recently, I've discovered that one of the Bible's most important, and
most challenging, portrayals of Christian witness is found, of all places, in
Revelation. In fact, bearing faithful witness comprises *the church's fundamental calling* in the Apocalypse. It is both central to Revelation's message
and vital to John's purpose to energize Christian communities to participate

in the mission of God. In this chapter, we will begin by looking at Jesus as the supreme faithful witness. Then we'll explore various dimensions of the church's testimony to God and the slaughtered Lamb. Finally, we will focus on the key passage for John's portrait of faithful witness, the story of the two witnesses in Revelation 11.

THE FAITHFUL WITNESS

In Revelation, the church's testimony is firmly anchored in the witness of Jesus himself. In his opening greeting to the churches in Asia, John describes Jesus Christ as "the faithful witness" (Rev 1:5). Later, the exalted Christ speaks as "the faithful and true witness" (Rev 3:14; cf. Rev 19:11) to the church in Laodicea, a congregation in which *both* faithfulness *and* truth were in short supply! What does it mean to call Jesus a "faithful and true witness"?

First, it has to do with the complete reliability of what Christ *says*. The notion of witness is closely linked to the word of God in Revelation (Rev 1:2, 9; 6:9), and God himself testifies that his words are faithful and true (Rev 21:5; cf. Rev 22:6). It surely follows that Jesus' faithful witness includes his testimony to the truth of God during his earthly life. But Jesus continues to bear witness as the living Lord. Near the end of Revelation, he claims, "It is I, Jesus, who sent my angel to you *with this testimony* for the churches" (Rev 22:16, italics added). As if to confirm this role, Jesus' final words to the churches ring out, "The one who testifies to these things says, 'Surely I am coming soon'" (Rev 22:20). In one sense, the entire book of Revelation serves as the exalted Jesus' testimony to himself and to the truth of God's redeeming mission on behalf of the world.[1] Christ is *the* trustworthy and true witness, the source and the model for the church's witness in every generation.

Making this practical, the church's claim to bear witness to a message that is reliable and *true* seems quite audacious in today's world. False teaching continues to subvert the church's authentic witness in many global contexts. Often it takes the form of watered-down versions of the gospel, which offer

---

[1]See Richard B. Hays, "Faithful Witness, Alpha and Omega: The Identity of Jesus in the Apocalypse of John," in *Revelation and the Politics of Apocalyptic Interpretation*, ed. Richard B. Hays and Stefan Alkier (Waco, TX: Baylor University Press, 2012), 78.

maximum blessings at minimum cost. In the West, postmodern perspectives reduce truth to a matter of personal preference. Truth is sacrificed at the altar of "tolerance," which can become an idol in itself. What's more, powerful people and news outlets frequently fashion their own version of "truth," simply by posting it on social media or by saying it often or loudly enough. In contrast, Revelation claims to tell the one true story for the entire world. That witness to the truth is anchored in an all-embracing vision of a God who reigns over cosmic history and of a victorious, slaughtered Lamb who has redeemed all people to himself and who will return, bringing judgment and restoration. The church's testimony in the world must flow out of that bedrock truth about God and Christ.

But Christ's faithful witness cannot be limited to *words* alone. Jesus also *embodied* that testimony in his earthly life and death. His steadfast witness in word and deed set him on a course that meant suffering, and ultimately dying on a cross. In Revelation 1:5, John pictures Jesus not only as the faithful witness but also "the firstborn of the dead," which surely implies that faithfulness to his testimony cost Jesus his life. Jesus' true witness, then, bears the wounds of the slaughtered Lamb. Even when Christ the exalted Lord bears prophetic testimony to the churches, he does so *as the crucified one*, who "was dead and came to life" (Rev 2:8). Jesus offered the world a "show-and-tell" witness, a testimony that was both spoken and embodied.

A WORD-AND-LIFE WITNESS

Jesus' word-and-life testimony cuts the pattern for how the church bears witness in the world. In the first place, God's people are called to offer a *verbal* witness to the truth of God. Revelation closely links witness to proclaiming "the word of God" (Rev 1:2, 9; 6:9; 20:4; cf. Rev 12:11) and to prophesying (Rev 10:11; 11:3). At the same time, followers of the Lamb *live out* their witness, in part by keeping God's commandments (Rev 12:17).

Above all, Christians hold firmly to the "testimony of Jesus" (Rev 12:17; 19:10; cf. Rev 1:2, 9)—one of the most intriguing and ambiguous phrases in all of Revelation. Debates swirl among interpreters over the meaning of this phrase. Does it refer to the church's testimony *about* Jesus, that is, its proclamation of the gospel, or is it primarily about Jesus' *own* witness to the truth? Trying to decide between the two is a bit like choosing whether a healthy lifestyle involves *either* a good diet *or* regular exercise. Surely it includes *both*. In the first place, displaying the "testimony of Jesus" calls us to prophetically bear witness *to* Jesus. We find this nuance in the angel's assurance to John that "the testimony of Jesus is the Spirit of prophecy" (Rev 19:10 translation mine). But this richly textured phrase also involves embracing Jesus' *own* testimony—both his prophetic witness to the truth and his embodied witness of a life spilled out for others. As a result, God's people "follow the Lamb wherever he goes" (Rev 14:4), even when that takes them on a journey of suffering, self-giving love. Like their Lord, the church bears a testimony of both prophetic word and poured-out life.

WITNESS AND SUFFERING

In Revelation, the church's faithful witness inevitably involves suffering. John provides a series of examples of those whose costly testimony bears the marks of the wounded Lamb. That list includes a martyred believer in Pergamum, named Antipas. Christ, in his message to this compromising church, calls him "my witness, my faithful one, who was killed among you" (Rev 2:13). John also spotlights the faithful ones in heaven who were "slaughtered for the word of God and for the testimony they had given" (Rev 6:9). These persecuted Christians are intimately bound to Jesus. Like the Lamb they follow, they have been "slaughtered," and their location "under the altar" demonstrates that they, too, are sacrifices whose blood was shed (Rev 6:9; cf. Rev 5:9). Later, we see the great prostitute Babylon, who symbolizes Rome and the earthly powers that oppose God, drunk with "the blood of the witnesses of Jesus" (Rev 17:6 translation mine). Finally, when describing Christ's defeat of Satan, John envisions victorious martyrs "who had been beheaded for the testimony of Jesus and for the word of God" (Rev 20:4 ESV). In Revelation, "witness" (*martys* in Greek) doesn't always entail martyrdom, but John leaves us in no doubt that God's people *must be willing* to lay down their lives, even as Jesus, the faithful witness, laid down his life for the sake of others.

"Do not fear what you are about to suffer."

REVELATION 2:10

For Revelation's first readers, such pictures represent more than mere theory. For them, resisting the idolatry and the false stories of the empire comes with a steep cost attached. It might cost them their social status, their jobs, their security, even their lives. Richard Hays wisely notes that embracing "the testimony of Jesus" becomes "an act of countercultural resistance through public prophetic proclamation of Jesus as Lord, an act of resistance that leads to persecution and (ultimately) martyrdom."[2] For John's readers, the message about Christ, the slaughtered Lamb, merges with lives that "preach" that message—lives shaped by the cross. But through this word-and-life testimony, God's witnesses share in the Lamb's victory over Satan and evil: "they have conquered him [Satan] by the blood of the Lamb and by the word of their testimony, for they did not cling to life even in the face of death" (Rev 12:11).

John's own name is inscribed on the tablet of those who suffer on behalf of Christ. Right out of the starting gate, John identifies himself as the one "who testified to the word of God and to the testimony of Jesus Christ" (Rev 1:2). Then he speaks directly to his audience, saying, in effect, "I am John, your brother, your partner in the suffering we share in Jesus. I was exiled on the rough rock of Patmos on account of the word of God and the witness of Jesus" (Rev 1:9). From John's prophetic perspective, as well as his personal experience, faithful witness sparks pushback and suffering. Indeed, John could hardly imagine the church bearing authentic witness to the gospel *without* suffering. Kenyan theologian Elias M. Githuka captures John's perspective in his sober reflection: "Persecution is an inescapable part of the true Christian's journey of faith."[3]

It is little different today. Christians throughout the world continue to feel the scorpion sting of suffering for proclaiming and embodying the lordship

---

[2]Hays, "Faithful Witness," 78.
[3]Elias M. Githuka, "Persecution," in *Africa Bible Commentary*, ed. Tokunboh Adeyemo (Grand Rapids, MI: Zondervan, 2006), 1564.

Figure 5.1. Statues of twentieth-century martyrs on the west façade of Westminster Abbey, London

of Jesus in settings that are unfriendly to the gospel. What does bearing witness for Christ look like in such places? For some, it still means martyrdom. Thousands of unnamed Christians each year continue to pay the ultimate cost by choosing not to "cling to life even in the face of death" (Rev 12:11).[4] Other faithful witnesses suffer. My understanding of costly witness has been shaped by humbling encounters with fellow believers in the Middle East, Asia, and the former sphere of Soviet power, who, like the first apostles, "rejoiced that they were considered worthy to suffer dishonor for the sake of the name" (Acts 5:41).

I cannot forget two encounters with faithful Chinese Christians who were severely persecuted during the repressive period of the "Cultural Revolution" in the 1960s and '70s. One humble Christian doctor I met was seized by the

---

[4]Estimates vary widely about how many Christians are martyred worldwide each year, in part depending on how martyrdom is defined. At the low end, the organization Open Doors' "World Watch List 2021" estimates that 4,761 Christians were martyred during the year prior to November 2020; https://odusa-media.com/2021/01/WWL2021_Booklet-digital.pdf.

authorities, forced to kneel with a dunce cap on his head, his body beaten repeatedly for bearing the name of Christ. This attempt to humiliate and injure him turned into an opportunity to identify with the suffering and shame of the slain Lamb. On another occasion, an aged Chinese pastor told me the story of his incarceration in a prison labor camp for twenty-two years for refusing to declare loyalty to the state over Christ. During that period, he endured freezing temperatures, crushing labor, and meager provisions. He had no Bible, no Christian fellowship, and little contact with his wife and children at home. Later he endured ten more years of house arrest. But rather than breaking him, this experience pressed him closer to Christ. Undaunted, his face beamed as he testified of the privilege of suffering for and with his Lord.

But what about those of us who do not experience such direct persecution and suffering because of our witness to Christ? How should we read Revelation's emphasis on suffering witness? This is too big a question to address fully in this context. Let me, however, raise two points to ponder.[5]

First, even if we don't face overt persecution at the hands of the beastly powers, we are called to stand in solidarity with those who do. Like John, we can say to persecuted Christians, we share with you "in the suffering and kingdom and patient endurance that are ours in Jesus" (Rev 1:9 NIV). At a minimum, this involves praying and offering practical support, by whatever means we can.

Second, if we took Revelation's perspective on power, wealth, and civil religion more seriously—not to mention the teaching of Jesus—we might experience more pushback from our own culture than we do. Stephen Fowl prods, "The question . . . becomes whether Christians in America or elsewhere testify in word and deed to a faith substantial enough to provoke opposition from powers that are either indifferent or hostile to the triune God."[6] Far too often, the church in the West has settled for Thyatiran accommodation or Laodicean complacency, rather than a prophetic witness that resists the idolatries of our age and refuses to compromise with them.

---

[5]See Dean Flemming, *Philippians: A Commentary in the Wesleyan Tradition* (Kansas City, MO: Beacon Hill, 2009), 92-94.
[6]Stephen E. Fowl, *Philippians* (Grand Rapids, MI: Eerdmans, 2005), 71.

To this point, our discussion has made it clear that a witness that triggers pushback and suffering is a *prophetic* witness. Let's further unpack what that means.

A PROPHETIC WITNESS

In chapter 19, when John blunders by attempting to worship an angel, the divine messenger reminds him that the two of them are "fellow servants," united in their testimony to Jesus the faithful witness. The angel goes on to clarify that "the witness of Jesus is the Spirit of prophecy" (Rev 19:10 translation mine). Although the phrase "the Spirit (*pneuma*) of prophecy" remains somewhat ambiguous in Greek, here it likely emphasizes that the church's prophetic witness is inspired and animated by the Holy Spirit. This intimate connection between the testimony of Jesus and the prophetic Spirit shouldn't surprise us. We've already seen that Jesus' messages to the seven congregations in Asia in chapters 2 and 3 also represent "what the Spirit is saying to the churches" (Rev 2:7; cf. Rev 14:13; 22:16-17). And the same Spirit who speaks Christ's word to the churches empowers the church's prophetic witness to Jesus in the world. When God's people participate in the "witness of Jesus," both in the sense of testifying *to* Jesus and living out Jesus' *own* Lamblike witness, that testimony "is fueled by the Spirit of prophecy."[7]

I noted in the introduction to this book that "prophecy" in Revelation is more about *proclaiming* God's word than *predicting* the future. Indeed, John sees the Apocalypse itself as Spirit-inspired prophecy (Rev 1:3; 22:7, 10, 18-19). As a prophet, John belongs to a specific group of Christian prophets through whom God speaks to the church (Rev 11:18; 16:6; 18:20, 24; 22:6, 9). But he also believes in, as Eugene Boring puts it, the "prophethood of all believers."[8] Three times John pictures the two witnesses, who symbolize the whole church, engaged in prophetic testimony (Rev 11:3, 6, 10). All Christians may not be prophets in the narrow sense, but every

---

[7]John Christopher Thomas and Frank D. Macchia, *Revelation* (Grand Rapids, MI: Eerdmans, 2016), 337.

[8]M. Eugene Boring, *Hearing John's Voice: Insights for Teaching and Preaching* (Grand Rapids, MI: Eerdmans, 2019), 142.

follower of Jesus is called to participate in the church's prophetic witness in the world.[9]

The prophetic witness of God's people shimmers the brightest in Revelation 10 and 11. Near the end of chapter 10, an angel tells John to eat an open scroll (Rev 10:8-9). This is likely the same scroll that God on the throne gave to Jesus in chapter 5, the scroll that contains God's sweeping purpose for all creation. By ingesting and internalizing the scroll, John is able to bear witness to its message in his own prophetic ministry (Rev 10:11). The visions that follow (Rev 11:1-13) then reveal the scroll's message about the role of *the Lamb's followers* in God's intention to bring the nations to repentance.

Just as the angel promises, the scroll tastes sweet in John's mouth, but bitter in his belly (Rev 10:9-10). For the Seer and his audience, this sweet and sour scroll operates on two levels. First, John's *message* is sweet because it announces God's salvation and victory, accomplished through the sacrifice of the slain Lamb and the sacrificial mission of the Lamb's followers. At the same time, it makes John sick to his stomach because it is also a message of judgment for those who refuse to repent and worship God. Second, for John and his audience, the *task* of bearing faithful witness is bittersweet. It's bitter because it will call them to suffer, perhaps die, in solidarity with the slain Lamb (see Rev 11:7-10). But it is also sweet, in that those who are faithful will be vindicated by God in the end (see Rev 11:11-12).

Chapter 10 ends with a call to mission. John is commissioned to prophesy "about (or "to" *epi*) many peoples and nations and languages and kings" (Rev 10:11). As Bauckham frames it, "John is commanded to prophesy *to* the nations, so that his own prophetic role is paradigmatic for the churches' prophetic witness to the nations, or to prophesy *about* the nations, in a prophecy to the churches enabling them to prophesy to the nations."[10] This mandate goes beyond merely warning the rebellious nations of God's judgment. John, and the church with him (see Rev 11:3), are called to bear faithful witness to the Lamb, so that people of "every nation and tribe and language and people" will come to worship and give glory to God (Rev 14:6-7).

---

[9]Richard Bauckham, *The Theology of the Book of Revelation* (Cambridge: Cambridge University Press, 1993), 120.

[10]Bauckham, *Theology*, 120.

THE TWO WITNESSES

What is only implied to this point becomes explicit in Revelation 11:1-13: the task of bearing prophetic witness applies to *the whole church*. This crucial passage, positioned at the very center of Revelation, reveals the surprising message of the open scroll. The nations will come to repentance not by God's warning judgments but through the Lamb's loving sacrifice, publicly proclaimed and embodied in the lives of God's witnesses, the church.

Measuring the temple. As the vision begins, John is told, "Come and measure the temple of God and the altar and those who worship there" (Rev 11:1). The "temple" or "sanctuary" functions here "as a symbolic way of referring to the faithful, holy people of God" (see Rev 3:12; 1 Cor 3:16-17; 2 Cor 6:16; Eph 2:21; 1 Pet 2:5).[11] In the Jerusalem temple, the inner court included the court of the priests and the altar where Israel's priests sacrificed on behalf of the people. This temple/sanctuary, then, represents the church as a community of priests (Rev 1:6; 5:10), people who have been redeemed to serve God and mediate on behalf of the world.[12] In contrast, the nations, symbolized by the outer court, will trample on the holy city (also a symbol of God's faithful community Rev 11:2). Although God's people will face hostility from the unbelieving world as a result of their faithful witness, they hold the assurance that God will preserve them during their trials and vindicate them in the end.

Following the true witness. In verse 3, "the two witnesses" come on stage. Interpreters, past and present, have had a proverbial field day trying to pinpoint the identity of these two witnesses. Candidates range from Enoch and Elijah (because neither tasted death, see Rev 11:11-12) to the Evangelists Matthew and John to Methodist founders Wesley and Whitfield to the Old and New Testaments.[13] More recently, the supernatural TV drama *Sleepy Hollow* cast the two witnesses in the roles of the show's heroes, Ichabod Crane and Lieutenant Abbie Mills. Within the context of Revelation, however, the two witnesses symbolize the prophetic witness of

---

[11] Andy Johnson, *Holiness and the* Missio Dei (Eugene, OR: Cascade, 2016), 163.

[12] Johnson, *Holiness and the* Missio Dei, 163.

[13] See Judith Kovacs and Christopher Rowland, *Revelation: The Apocalypse of Jesus Christ* (Malden, MA: Blackwell, 2004), 126-30.

the whole Christian community in an unfriendly world; in other words, *the church in mission*. It's noteworthy that the two witnesses are called "lampstands" (Rev 11:4), a picture that John has already identified with the church (Rev 1:12, 20).

The story of the two witnesses in Rev 11:3-13 recalls a collage of Old Testament passages. In particular, the image of the witnesses as olive trees and lampstands (Rev 11:4) points us to Zechariah 4. There Joshua the high priest and Zerubbabel the anointed king are pictured as two olive trees that flank a golden lampstand. It's therefore likely that Revelation's olive tree and lampstand images symbolize the witnessing church in its role as "a kingdom and priests," mediating God's presence in the world (Rev 5:9; cf. Rev 1:6). And there's something else that informs the church's mission. In Zechariah 4, the lamps on the lampstand represent God's Spirit that was to empower God's people to complete the building of the temple. This will happen "not by might, nor by power, but by my Spirit, says the LORD of hosts" (Zech 4:6; cf. Rev 4:5; 5:6). In Revelation, the church, God's new temple on earth, will draw its power from the Holy Spirit to bear faithful witness in the face of opposition.[14] As shining lamps, God's people will fulfill their calling to bear God's light to the nations (Is 42:6; 49:6; cf. Matt 5:14). Finally, in Revelation 11:4, God's witnesses "stand before the Lord of the earth" (an allusion to Zech 4:14), suggesting not only that the actions of the witnesses are the actions of God but also that the church's universal mission is inseparable from the lordship of God and Christ.[15] John, therefore, pictures the two witnesses in a way that highlights their prophetic, Spirit-empowered testimony to all nations.

In addition to the connections with Zechariah 4, the story of the two witnesses reminds us of the prophetic ministry of Moses and Elijah, both of whom confronted pagan idolatry with deeds of power, like bottling up the

---

[14]G. K. Beale, *The Book of Revelation: A Commentary on the Greek Text* (Grand Rapids, MI: Eerdmans, 1999), 576-77. Note that Revelation identifies the seven lamps burning before God's throne as the "seven spirits of God" (Rev 4:5), a symbol of God's Spirit. Later the seven spirits are "sent out into all the earth" (Rev 5:6) as the active presence and power of God in the world. John, then, draws an intimate connection between the church, God's Spirit, and the church's prophetic witness in the world. Bauckham, *Theology*, 111-15.

[15]Bauckham, *Theology*, 113.

heavens from sending rain, turning water into blood, and striking the earth with manifold plagues (Rev 11:5-6). The prophetic anointing of the Spirit is present in the powerful witness of the church.

Above all, John goes out of his way to superimpose the saga of the witnesses onto the story of Jesus. As Joseph Mangina observes, this drama unfolds in three scenes.[16] First, like Jesus in his earthly ministry, the two witnesses display miracle-working power and uncommon authority in their prophetic testimony (Rev 11:4-6).[17] The consuming fire issuing from their mouths stands for the word of God (Rev 11:5; cf. Jer 5:14), reminding us of the triumphant sword of the word that proceeds from the mouth of Christ (Rev 19:13, 15; cf. Rev 1:16; 2:16; 19:21). This is not a literal consuming fire, but rather a symbol of the powerful testimony of the church, which is able to overcome and convict those who try to snuff out that witness. The two witnesses therefore resemble Jesus in his earthly ministry, "in which he enjoyed unparalleled success against his foes . . . and in which he was widely celebrated for the liberating, authoritative power of his preaching."[18]

Figure 5.2. Manuscript illumination of rejoicing over the bodies of the two witnesses (Rev 11:9-10) from the Dyson Perrins Apocalypse, 1255–1260

[16]Joseph L. Mangina, *Revelation* (Grand Rapids, MI: Brazos, 2010), 137-39. The following paragraphs draw heavily from Dean Flemming, "Revelation and the *Missio Dei*: Toward a Missional Reading of the Apocalypse," *Journal of Theological Interpretation* 6 (2012): 173.

[17]Mangina, *Revelation*, 138.

[18]Mangina, *Revelation*, 138.

The second scene (Rev 11:7-10) signals a dramatic reversal of fortunes. Even as Jesus was shamed and slain at the hands of his enemies, so God's witnesses are killed by the beast and humiliated by its followers—all in the very city "where also their Lord was crucified" (Rev 11:8). As it was on Golgotha's hill, once again it appears that the beastly powers have triumphed. The story of the two witnesses takes the downward path of the Lamb.

But another plot twist awaits. The vision reaches a rousing climax in verses 11-13, where the faithful witnesses follow the pattern of Jesus' resurrection and ascension. After "three and a half days" of utter shame, God raises their dead bodies with the "breath of life" (Rev 11:11). The God who breathed life into Adam's nostrils in the Garden (Gen 2:7) and whose breath raised dead bones to life in Ezekiel's vision (Ezek 37:1-10), this God, once again, breathes into his witnesses, and they come alive (Rev 11:11). The victims become victors. What is more, like Jesus, they ascend to heaven in a cloud at God's own calling (Rev 11:12).

It is not only the witnesses, however, who are saved. Their faithful testimony, along with God's judgment in a great earthquake, draws people from every tribe and nation to give "glory to the God of heaven" (Rev 11:9, 13). The costly witness of God's people results in a global mission.

An embodied, public witness. The story of the two witnesses functions as a kind of parable for the witnessing church in every generation.[19] How does this story help to shape the missional church, both in John's day and our own? Let's consider three ways that it might.

First, *the church's witness is both verbal and embodied.* The pattern we have seen throughout Revelation comes into sharp relief in the story of the two witnesses. On the one hand, God's witnesses "prophesy" (Rev 11:3; cf. Rev 11:10). They enter the scene wearing sackcloth, signaling repentance and mourning (Rev 11:3). It follows, then, that the words of fire that issue from their mouths call the earth's inhabitants to repent and turn to God (Rev 11:4). In a time when the church's *verbal* proclamation of the gospel is sometimes downplayed in favor of a witness of deed and lifestyle, we cannot forget that the good news is precisely that—good *news*. Could it be that a

---

[19]Bauckham, *Theology*, 84.

Figure 5.3. Stained glass of the two witnesses ascending to heaven (Rev 11:12) from the Great East Window, York Minster, 1405–1408

courageous, costly, prophetic testimony to God's truth has never been needed more from the people of God?

On the other hand, it is not the church's proclamation alone that draws people from the world's nations to worship God. Above all, the faithful witness of God's people, even to the point of death, enables their *lives* to broadcast the gospel of the crucified Lamb. Mangina has it right: "The apostolic preaching must be performed in the key of the cross, so that there is a real congruity between the message and the messenger."[20] The church is not only a community of prophets but also a fellowship of priests, who, like Jesus before them, offer *themselves* as a faithful sacrifice to God on behalf of others.[21] This sacrificial, Lamblike witness bears fruit in mission, drawing people from the world's nations into the worship of God (Rev 11:13).[22] *How* the church goes about its mission remains no less important than the content of its witness. Our testimony to the truth is powerful, but only because it is vulnerable and noncoercive. We *become* the gospel of suffering love, traveling the path of the slaughtered Lamb.

> *"The fate of the two witnesses . . . reminds us that throughout history God's people are not spared from suffering or tribulation. . . . Prophets, as witnesses of God, can expect suffering and even death. Whenever Christians resist evil, they will come under pressure to conform. If they refuse to conform, they may find themselves the target of the anger and retribution of those who seek to maintain the world as it is."[23]*
>
> ONESIMUS NGUNDU

Second, *the church's witness is public—out there for all the world to see.* John goes out of his way to spotlight the *public* character of the church's testimony, symbolized by the two witnesses. The witnesses "stand before the Lord of the earth," and their testimony targets all "the inhabitants of the

---

[20]Mangina, *Revelation*, 141.

[21]Johnson, *Holiness and the* Missio Dei, 164.

[22]As Andy Johnson notes, Revelation's pattern of God's people fulfilling their missional vocation through suffering and death "is precisely the opposite of the logic of a 'secret rapture' theology," in which God saves his people "by whisking them out of a rebellious world so that he can then extinguish all the rebels." Johnson, *Holiness and the* Missio Dei, 165.

[23]Onesimus Ngundu, "Revelation," in *Africa Bible Commentary*, ed. Tokunboh Adeyemo (Grand Rapids, MI: Zondervan, 2006), 1561-62.

earth" (Rev 11:4, 10).[24] As the narrative of the witnesses unfolds, it takes a somewhat different path than the story of Jesus, who was buried after his public crucifixion and appeared only to his followers after his resurrection. In contrast, the fate of the witnesses remains on display to the world throughout. First, people of every tribe and nation gaze on the dead bodies of God's prophets and throw a citywide party to celebrate their demise (Rev 11:9-10). The entire global community casts a shadow of shame on them. Then as God both raises and exalts the two witnesses, the whole world is watching (Rev 11:11, 12). Finally, just in case someone has missed the point, a thunderous voice sends out a global bulletin, announcing the witnesses' ascension to heaven (Rev 11:12). John connects the dots between the enemies of God's people "watching" God's vindication of his witnesses and those same enemies changing sides to become worshipers of God (Rev 11:13).

John's vision of the two witnesses drives home that Christian mission happens in the public square. By its very nature, "witness" isn't a private affair. The good news of the slaughtered and risen Lamb goes on parade before a watching world, through what we say, how we act, and who we are. What form that public witness takes in practice will vary significantly, depending on the context. In places where evangelistic witness is restricted by law or the social control of a majority religion, witness may involve embodying the story of the slain Lamb in ways that look visibly different from those of the prevailing culture. Historian Alan Kreider makes a strong case that the remarkable expansion of the vulnerable Christian community in the Roman Empire during its first few centuries didn't happen primarily because of a planned evangelistic strategy. Rather, the church grew "because the Christians and churches lived by a habitus (pattern of life) that attracted others. The Christians' focus," he writes, "was not on 'saving' people or recruiting them; it was on living faithfully—in the belief that when people's lives are rehabituated in the way of Jesus, others will want to join them. . . . The church's growth was the product, not of Christians' persuasive powers, but of their convincing lifestyle."[25]

---

[24]Craig R. Koester, *Revelation: A New Translation with Introduction and Commentary* (New Haven, CT: Yale University Press, 2014), 507.

[25]Alan Kreider, *The Patient Ferment of the Early Church: The Improbable Rise of Christianity in the Roman Empire* (Grand Rapids, MI: Baker, 2016), 129, 155.

"Beloved brethren . . . we do not speak great things but we live them."[26]

CYPRIAN, BISHOP OF CARTHAGE, 256

Yet in societies in which the options for public Christian witness are greater, a testimony that goes beyond words alone is still essential. I have told this story elsewhere, but it bears telling again:

A pastor friend in the US told me about an anti-Muslim rally that was being planned in his city. Social media angrily proclaimed that protesters would gather outside of a mosque on a certain Friday evening to oppose and insult the worshipers, many of whom were recent refugees. Protesters were encouraged to bring guns, ratcheting up the potential for violence. After my friend expressed his concern on Facebook, a woman from his church commented, in effect, "We can't just *say* that we oppose this. We need to *do* something about it!" In response, with some fear, their congregation organized a gathering of Christians from throughout their city to stand as a prayerful presence at the mosque and show that the Christian message was one of love, not hate. They met with the mosque president ahead of time to discuss what they had planned. Then these Christians gathered before the protesters arrived, lining the sidewalk in front of the mosque. As angry protesters assembled with signs and semi-automatic weapons, shouting obscenities and burning holy books, this band of Christ-followers formed a human shield of protection for their Muslim friends. They prayed, sang worship songs, and held up signs that said, "Love your neighbor." Some of the Christians, including teenagers, engaged in conversations with the protesters, listening to their fears. They explained that Jesus had called them to love their neighbors, not vilify them. The anger of the situation soon deflated. Some of the protesters even seemed to experience a change of heart during the evening. The media picked up on the event, and what began as a demonstration of hatred turned into a loving witness to that religious community and the wider public in their city and literally around the world.[27]

---

[26]Cyprian, *On the Good of Patience*, 3, citied in Kreider, *Patient Ferment*, 13.

[27]Drawn and adapted from Dean Flemming, *Self-Giving Love: The Book of Philippians* (Bellingham, WA: Lexham, 2021), 46-47. For a fuller account, see Michael W. Goheen and Jim Mullins, *The*

Third, *the church bears witness to Christ not for its own sake but for the sake of the world.* The climax of the story of the church's witness in Revelation 11 pictures not only vindication for Christ's followers but also global mission. The testimony, death, and public vindication of God's faithful witnesses, along with God's judgment in the form of an earthquake, lead to something quite astounding. According to John's "theological mathematics," only one-tenth of the city, which symbolizes all the world's people that oppose God's rule (see Rev 11:9-10), perish in the earthquake (Rev 11:13). That means that *nine-tenths* of the earth's inhabitants repent and give glory to God! This represents a "merciful reversal" of the judgments announced by the Old Testament prophets, in which a remnant of one-tenth of the people are spared and the rest are judged by God (Is 6:13; Amos 5:3).[28]

Likewise, the seven thousand people who die in the earthquake recalls the ministry of the prophet Elijah in the Old Testament. But John flips the numbers on their head. In 1 Kings, God preserves a remnant of seven thousand worshipers who don't bow to Baal (1 Kgs 19:18). But here, precisely the opposite happens. Only seven thousand perish and the rest, the vast majority of those who dwell on earth, worship the true God of heaven (Rev 11:13). These converts represent people from every tribe, language, and nation (Rev 11:9). Revelation's symbolic arithmetic pushes the envelope of our imaginations almost beyond fathoming. I agree with Felise Tavo that John demonstrates a "remarkable sense of optimism" that a vast number of the world's people will turn to God through the faithful prophetic witness of the church.[29]

This hope-full vision ought to give profound encouragement to Christian communities today, especially those who feel the pain of persecution or who toil in the deserts of spiritual apathy. My own experience of doing ministry in western Europe for over a decade has taught me what it means to cling to such a hope. John assures God's people that despite their present circumstances, the church's faithful witness will not wither in vain; that it will contribute to those of all nations turning to

---

Symphony of Mission: Playing Your Part in God's Work in the World (Grand Rapids, MI: Baker Academic, 2019), 95-100.

[28]Johnson, *Holiness and the* Missio Dei, 165; cf. Bauckham, *Theology*, 86-87.

[29]Felise Tavo, *Woman, Mother and Bride: An Exegetical Investigation into the "Ecclesial" Notions of the Apocalypse*, BTS 3 (Leuven: Peeters, 2007), 217.

the Maker of heaven and earth, as God's universal mission reaches its goal.

> *"I have come to feel that the primary reality of which we have to take account in seeking for a Christian impact on public life is the Christian congregation. How is it possible that the gospel should be credible, that people should come to believe that the power which has the last word in human affairs is represented by a man hanging on a cross? . . . The only answer, the only hermeneutic of the gospel, is a congregation of men and women who believe it and live by it."[50]*
>
> LESSLIE NEWBIGIN

CONCLUSION

What does it mean for Christians to "witness" in their world? In Revelation, the church's ministry of witness entails something far richer than simply confronting unbelievers with a prepackaged "gospel presentation." John seeks to shape communities of mature disciples who bear faithful witness to their Lord. At the very least, Revelation calls us to a witness that

- shares in the mission of Jesus, the one "faithful and true" witness

- is fueled by the empowering Spirit

- embraces both what we say and how we live

- chooses faithful witness over a safe "holy isolation" from the world

- announces and embodies God's truth in the public square

- isn't passive but active; it prophetically resists the powers and idolatries of the culture

- is vulnerable and noncoercive, conformed to the pattern of the crucified Lamb

---

[30]Lesslie Newbigin, *The Gospel in a Pluralist Society* (Grand Rapids, MI: Eerdmans, 1989), 227.

- carries a cost, including loss of security and status, persecution, and for some, death

- leads to ultimate victory, sharing in the Lamb's triumph over Satan and evil (Rev 12:11)

- bears fruit in mission, as people from the world's nations are drawn to worship God

This brief summary underscores that the call to embrace the "testimony of Jesus" in our world isn't for the faint of heart. The powers, cosmic and material, that oppose the way of the slaughtered Lamb are all too real, not only in John's world but our own, as well. John Dickerson evokes an analogy from J. R. R. Tolkien to describe our situation:

> We can feel a bit like Frodo the hobbit in *The Lord of the Rings*. We are tiny creatures entrusted with an impossible task—to rescue humanity from unthinkable evil. . . . I think of the moment when a discouraged and distraught Frodo looks to the Christ-figure, Gandalf, and whimpers, "I wish the Ring had never come to me. I wish none of this had happened." To which Gandalf replies, "So do all who live to see such times; but that is not for them to decide. All we have to decide is what to do with the time that is given to us. There are other forces at work in this world."[31]

Our response to the powers that oppose Christ's lordship over the world is not to cave in and accommodate to their alternative truth claims, but to actively resist by bearing *witness*—Spirit-infused, cross-shaped, Lamblike witness. It was this kind of witness that landed John on an island of exile and made Antipas a martyr (Rev 2:13). It was this kind of witness that led Martin Luther King to oppose the evils of racism and injustice through nonviolent resistance, a witness that ultimately cost him his life. It is this kind of witness that I recently saw embodied by humble church leaders and ordinary Christians in a creative access area, in which their very act of meeting together bore the risk of reprisal. Sharing the testimony of Jesus is still a risky business. But should that amaze us? It has always been the way of the slaughtered Lamb.

---

[31]John S. Dickerson, *The Great Evangelical Recession* (Grand Rapids, MI: Baker, 2013), 126.

CHAPTER SIX

MISSION AND JUDGMENT

*All nations will come and worship before you, for
your judgments have been revealed.*

REVELATION 15:4

I TEACH A CLASS FOR COLLEGE STUDENTS on John's writings. Near
the end, I ask them to describe their main impression of Revelation *before* we
studied it in class. I consistently hear comments like, "I avoided it because it
was too hard to understand," or "It was so violent and scary that I was afraid
to read it." In fact, the giant word on their mental word cloud is *FEAR*. Let's
face it. It's not the messages to the seven churches (chapters 2 and 3) that generally frighten or confuse readers of Revelation. Nor is it the scenes of heavenly
worship in chapters 4 and 5. Nor the dazzling vision of New Jerusalem in
Revelation 21 and 22. What confounds most readers are John's graphic pictures
of judgment and violence in chapters 6–20. (Full disclosure: When I talk about
Revelation's "readers," I'm not simply projecting this discomfort on *other* readers. This is the part of Revelation that most unsettles *me*!) Visions of wars and
plagues, earthquakes and famines, plains of blood, and lakes of fire. My aim
in this chapter is not to solve all the riddles of John's judgment imagery. This
is a *missional* reading of Revelation. But that raises its own concerns. How
does God's loving mission to redeem all people and restore the whole creation
connect with Revelation's pictures of destruction, violence, and death? Can we
even speak of *judgment* and *mission* in the same breath?

I believe we can. Without grasping this connection, we simply won't hear the story of God's mission in Revelation rightly. This chapter seeks to place the theme of judgment in Revelation within the framework of the mission of God and of God's people. To do that, I'll start by taking a bird's eye view of Revelation's judgment scenes, followed by a closer look at several key passages that highlight the connection between judgment and God's purpose to redeem people of all nations. Then I will tackle the question of whether the violence in Revelation's visions negates God's loving purpose for the world. Finally, I'll reflect on what the theme of judgment reveals about the patient persistence of God.

REVELATION'S JUDGMENT SCENES: AN OVERVIEW

Let's begin with a panoramic view of Revelation's judgment visions in chapters 6–20, like someone might see a parade from a blimp high above it. Just before the scenes of judgment start, John unveils his defining visions of God on the throne and of the slaughtered Lamb in chapters 4 and 5. I noted earlier that these two chapters form the theological and liturgical heart of the book. They reveal not a picture of some far-off future, but rather a reimagining of the world in which the readers of Revelation live. These visions invite beleaguered communities of Christians to grasp the way things really are, as they join all creation in the worship of God and the Lamb, "on earth, as it is in heaven." If these Lamb-followers steadfastly endure as communities of witness and worship, they will share in the new Jerusalem, which John pictures in chapters 21 and 22. In this stunning final vision, we see the full and final realization of the universal worship pictured in chapters 4 and 5. God's enemies are utterly vanquished. The Lamb and his followers reign in total victory. People from every nation unite with creation itself in perfect worship of God and the Lamb. God makes *everything* new.

These two realities, the defining vision of God and Lamb in the heavenly throne room (Rev 4 and 5) and the final vision of the new heaven and the new earth provide the crucial context for the long series of judgment scenes in chapters 6–20. Beginning with chapter 6, "The seals are removed from the scroll, one by one, unleashing a sequence of divine judgments, which are necessary in order to overthrow and abolish the ingrained and powerful evil that has taken root in the world through human sin and its sinister empowerment."[1] Revelation's visions of judgment unfold in three sets of seven: seven seals, seven trumpets, seven plagues or bowls. *Seven* symbolizes completion in Revelation. Seven seals, then, point to God's purpose for the world in its fullness. We will miss the point of these visions if we expect them simply to unroll in chronological order, like episodes of *Downton Abbey*. Rather, Revelation's judgment scenes overlap and repicture earlier happenings. In different ways, the seals, trumpets, and bowls tell the same story, driving home the reality that God *will* defeat all powers of evil in the end. At the same time, the three cycles of judgment build in intensity as they move toward the final goal of new creation.

But even the emptying of the seventh bowl, which is extended in the destruction of Babylon in chapters 17 and 18, does not signal the end of sin and evil. In chapter 19, Christ appears on a white horse, flanked by the armies of heaven, and fully vanquishes the beast and its worshipers (Rev 19:11-21). Then in Revelation 20, the "unholy trinity" of Satan, the beast, and the false prophet meet their doom, while those who worship them face God's final judgment. At long last, the closing curtain drops on all opposition to God and Lamb, whether cosmic or human. Satan and evil must meet utter and ultimate defeat for the new creation to arrive.

Chapters 6–20, however, are not *only* about God's judgment on the sinful powers. Each segment of judgment is interrupted by an intermission that pictures God's people worshiping God and the Lamb (Rev 7:1-17; 10:1–11:14; 14:1-20; 19:1-10; 20:1-6). These interludes not only assure followers of the Lamb that God will preserve them through suffering and vindicate them in the end. They also reinforce the church's participation in the universal worship that starts in chapters 4 and 5 and reaches its climax in the new Jerusalem. God's just judgment, then, makes possible the goal of God's mission—a victorious, worshiping community sharing in the reign of the Lamb who has redeemed them (Rev 22:5) and the healing of the world's nations (Rev 22:2). Revelation's judgment scenes signal that *nothing*—evil, Satan, sin, empire, Babylon, or the beast—can abort God's saving purpose for his people.

---

[1] N. T. Wright, "Revelation and Christian Hope: Political Implications of the Revelation to John," in *Revelation and the Politics of Apocalyptic Interpretation*, ed. Richard B. Hays and Stefan Alkier (Waco, TX: Baylor University Press, 2012), 113.

Figure 6.1. Woodcut of *The Four Horsemen* (Rev 6:1-8) by Albrecht Dürer from *The Apocalypse of Saint John*, 1496–1498

JUDGMENT AND THE WORSHIP OF THE NATIONS

Zooming in from this widescreen picture, how does the specific connection between divine judgment and the divine mission play out? Although not always recognized, that bond surfaces again and again during Revelation's story of judgment in chapters 6–20.[2]

Earthquakes and praises. Take, for example, the climax to the story of the two witnesses that we explored in chapter 5. Recall that the beast tries its best to snuff out the prophetic ministry of the two witnesses by killing them and shaming them before the world's people. God, however, vindicates them by raising them from the dead in full view of people from every tribe and nation (Rev 11:7-12). John continues: "At that moment there was a great earthquake, and a tenth of the city fell; seven thousand people were killed in the earthquake, and the rest were terrified and gave glory to the God of heaven" (Rev 11:13).

The "great earthquake" represents a divine act of judgment on the inhabitants of the earth who oppose God's rule.[3] But this judgment cradles mercy. Only *one-tenth* of the people perish, which means that a massive majority of those on earth not only respond with fear but also glorify God.

What should we make of the survivors' response to God's judgment? Is their "fear" simply an expression of terror? Does "giving glory to God" mean that sinners are forced, against their wills, to acknowledge God's sovereignty?[4] If that's the case, this passage is only about God's judgment *on* the nations and *not* repentance *from* the nations. I think that's unlikely. Although at times in Revelation, "fear" can arise from the prospect of judgment (Rev 18:10, 15), elsewhere it represents genuine reverence for God (Rev 11:13; 14:7; 15:4; 19:5). In Revelation 11, both sides of "fear" seem to be present—terror at the

---

[2]The following section draws significantly from my essay, "Divine Judgment and the *Missio Dei* in Revelation," in *Listening Again to the Text: New Testament Studies in Honor of George Lyons*, ed. Richard Thompson (Claremont, CA: Claremont Press, 2020), 171-91.

[3]The "city" of Revelation 11:13 is the "great city" (Rev 11:8), which Revelation elsewhere identifies with Babylon (Rev 17:18). For John's readers, the "great city" of Babylon in the first place symbolizes imperial Rome, but ultimately represents all powers that oppose the life-giving purposes of God. In chapter 11, residents of the city include all those who dwell on earth, all "peoples and tribes and languages and nations" (Rev 11:9-10) who refuse to worship God.

[4]For this reading, see G. K. Beale, *The Book of Revelation: A Commentary on the Greek Text* (Grand Rapids, MI: Eerdmans, 1999), 603-7; Eckhard J. Schnabel, "John and the Future of the Nations," *Bulletin for Biblical Research* 12 (2002): 247-57.

destructive force of the earthquake *and* an authentic turning to the "God of heaven" (Rev 11:13). Likewise, the language of "giving glory to God" functions almost as shorthand for true repentance and conversion in Revelation (Rev 14:6-7; 15:4; 21:26). People from all nations grasp the truth of who God is and act on it.

This passage, then, displays a close link between God's judgment in the earthquake and the turning of survivors from all nations to God. But nowhere in Revelation does judgment *on its own* lead to repentance. On the contrary, when unbelievers meet the fire and fury of God's wrath, they do *not* "repent and give him glory" (Rev 16:9; cf. Rev 16:11). They do *not* quit their evil actions or their worship of idols (Rev 9:20-21). What appears to make all the difference in Revelation 11 is the faithful, Lamblike witness of the two prophets, who represent the church. When unbelievers hear the words of truth and witness the poured-out lives of God's people, they change directions. The earth-dwellers' theme song turns from "glory to the beast" (see Rev 13:4) to "glory to the God of heaven" (Rev 11:13).

Growing up in the church, I heard preachers thunder warnings about the perils of hell and God's impending judgment. I watched apocalyptic movies that ratcheted up the terror of being "left behind" when true believers were secretly transported to heaven. Although such messages scared me, they did not in themselves attract me toward a life of faithful discipleship. Rather, it was the consistent, Christlike testimony of word and life that I observed in my parents and other faithful believers that drew me to follow Christ. The Lamblike, faithful witness of God's people remains the most compelling endorsement for the transforming power of God.

Judgment and the eternal gospel. Nowhere does the connection between judgment and mission surface more visibly than in Revelation 14:6-7. The passage lies within one of Revelation's intermissions (Rev 14:1-20), just before seven bowls of judgment are unloaded on the earth (Rev 15:1–16:21). Here we've just seen a picture of the church, the "redeemed from the earth" singing a new song before God's throne (Rev 14:2-3). This new song first rang out in chapter 5, announcing that the slain Lamb is worthy because he has ransomed those "from every tribe and language and people and nation" (Rev 5:9-10). In chapter 14, then, this is not simply a song of praise but a song of witness, calling the nations of the earth from their idolatrous worship into the adoration of the Lamb.[5]

In the next scene a heavenly messenger echoes this universal witness:

> Then I saw another angel flying in midheaven, with an eternal gospel to proclaim to those who live on the earth—to every nation and tribe and language and people. He said in a loud voice, "Fear God and give him glory, for the hour of his judgment has come; and worship him who made heaven and earth, the sea and the springs of water." (Rev 14:6-7)

Here the angel's gospel proclamation directly targets unbelievers—the "earth-dwellers" from every tribe and nation. Lifted with a booming voice, the invitation is heard by all the world's peoples. As commentator Ian Paul recognizes, "This triple bidding to *Fear God, give him glory* and *worship him* is an unambiguous call to repentance."[6] The angel's call to worship reflects a wider battle for worship in Revelation, which pits worship of the God who made all things against the idolatrous worship of the beast (e.g., Rev 5:9-14; 13:4, 12-15; 14:9, 11; 20:4).[7] Now beast-worshipers from every nation are invited to change sides and join the choir of those who sing the song of the redeemed (Rev 14:3-4). The Creator of heaven and earth hasn't given up on his creation.[8]

Once again, *judgment* plays a crucial role in God's mission. In verse 7, the gospel-bearing angel gives unbelievers a specific motivation for turning to the Creator: "for the hour of judgment has come." So certain is the arrival of God's end-time judgment on those who persist in their wickedness, that Revelation speaks of it as though it has already taken place. People who refuse to repent have good reason to *fear God*. At the same time, the angel's announcement holds out hope. The reminder of God's judgment functions *both* as a warning *and* as a call to receive the good news of salvation. The

---

[5]Simon Woodman, *The Book of Revelation* (London: SCM, 2008), 205.

[6]Ian Paul, *Revelation* (Downers Grove, IL: IVP Academic, 2018), 149.

[7]For John and his readers, such good news stands in barefaced contrast with Rome's "gospel," which is bound up with the birth, rule, or victories of the emperor. For example, the well-known Priene inscription celebrates the birth of Caesar Augustus as "the beginning of good tidings [εὐαγγέλια] to the world," cited in J. Nelson Kraybill, *Apocalypse and Allegiance: Worship, Politics, and Devotion in the Book of Revelation* (Grand Rapids, MI: Brazos, 2010), 57.

[8]Craig R. Koester, *Revelation and the End of All Things*, 2nd ed. (Grand Rapids, MI: Eerdmans, 2018), 137.

Figure 6.2. Manuscript illumination of the eternal gospel (Rev 14:6-7) from the Cloisters Apocalypse, c. 1330

earth's inhabitants must decide between two alternatives: either repent and give glory to the Maker of everything or continue your pig-headed pursuit of worshiping the beast.

This choice not only confronts rebellious sinners; it also targets John's audience in the churches of Asia. But just *how* they hear the angel's message depends on their spiritual condition. For the faithful oppressed (Rev 2:8-11; 3:7-18), it serves as a call to worship and revere God, as well as an assurance that the Creator will rid his creation of all evil in the end. But for the proud and lukewarm Laodiceans, the command to *Fear God* conveys a stern warning to repent of their consumerist lifestyle; otherwise, they place *themselves* in danger of falling under the shadow of divine judgment.

At the same time, this passage offers a call to mission. As the church father Primasius noted many centuries ago, the proclamation of the gospel in the context of God's end-time judgment drives home the urgency of the church's mission to people in every enclave of the earth (Mt 24:14).[9] It's noteworthy that the invitation to worship and glorify God goes out to "every nation and tribe and language and people" (Rev 14:6)—the very demographics that earlier in Revelation assemble before God's throne in joyful worship of the slain and risen Lamb (Rev 7:9; cf. Rev 5:9). By repeating the same categories of people in chapter 14, John gives us hope that God's universal mission, and our participation in it, ultimately will yield an abundant harvest.

Judgment and the end-time harvest. John pictures that harvest later in the same chapter. In Rev 14:14-20, we find two back-to-back visions of reaping. First the Son of Man, carrying a sickle, descends on a cloud to gather the grain harvest of the earth (Rev 14:14-16). Then an angel, also with a sickle in his hand, garners a grape harvest, the vintage of the earth, tossing it into the wine press of God's wrath (Rev 14:17-20). Virtually all commentators worth their salt agree that the second image, the gathering of grapes, represents God's end-time judgment. The prior grain harvest, however, is more controversial. Although some interpreters think that this vision also symbolizes divine judgment on the wicked,[10] there's good reason to see the grain harvest as a positive, missional image. Earlier in the chapter, John calls the redeemed from the earth the "first fruits" of a greater harvest to come (Rev 14:4). That harvest is now realized in the gathering of people into God's kingdom at the time of Jesus' return. Who carries out this harvest? The "one like the Son of Man," someone we have already seen as the risen Christ, the one who stands among the churches (Rev 1:12-20). Like his counterpart in Daniel 7, the Son of Man comes not to judge the nations but to gather people from every nation into his kingdom. The fields are ripe; it's harvest time (Rev 14:15; cf. Mt 9:37-38; Jn 4:35-38).

John therefore sets, side by side, two contrasting images of harvest: the gathering of grain, symbolizing the great ingathering of people for God when Jesus returns (Rev 14:14-16), and the grape harvest of God's fearsome

---

[9]Primasius, *Commentary on the Apocalypse.* 14.7, cited in William C. Weinrich, ed., *Revelation,* Ancient Christian Commentary on Scripture, New Testament (Downers Grove, IL: IVP Academic, 2005), 224.

[10]See, e.g., Beale, *Book of Revelation,* 772-74; David E. Aune, *Revelation 6-16,* WBC 52B (Nashville: Thomas Nelson, 1998), 801-2, 842-45. Perhaps the strongest argument in favor of this interpretation is that both images draw from Joel 3:13, which only portrays eschatological judgment: "Put in the sickle, for the harvest is ripe. Go in, tread, for the wine press is full. The vats overflow, for their wickedness is great."

judgment (Rev 14:17-20). These dueling visions confront John's first-century readers—and readers today—with a stark choice: you can "hold fast to the faith of Jesus" (Rev 14:12), and so participate in the great end-time harvest when Christ gathers his own. Or you can reject the "eternal gospel" (Rev 14:6), persist in worshiping the beastly powers, and ultimately share the fate of those who are crushed in the winepress of judgment (Rev 14:19).

Figure 6.3. Manuscript illumination of the eschatological harvest (Rev 14:14-20) from the Escorial Beatus, 950–955

Revelation 14:6-20 reminds us that "the overarching purpose of God's judgment in Revelation is not *revenge* or *retribution* but *repentance* and *restoration*."[11] God's just judgment represents the flip side of God's missional love. Perhaps as a reaction against a former generation's one-sided "hell fire and brimstone" preaching, many Christian communities today refuse to broach the topic of end-time judgment altogether. Revelation offers a needed corrective to that pendulum swing, one that preserves both the perfect justice and the lavish love of a missional God.

Judgments and worship songs. Revelation's vision of a heavenly victory party in Revelation 15:2-4 pictures a fourth key link between judgment and the mission of God. John strategically locates this vision between the announcement of the final series of judgments in Revelation 15:1 and the releasing of the seven bowls of God's wrath (Rev 15:5–16:21). As a result, this short scene provides a crucial context for the judgments that immediately follow.

John paints this canvas in the party colors of celebration. We see a company of conquering worshipers, standing beside a sea of glass, harps in hand, singing a song of praise to God and the Lamb (Rev 15:2-3; cf. Rev 5:8-9; 14:2-3). Outward appearances might suggest that the beast has triumphed by killing the saints (Rev 11:7; 13:7), but God's faithful aren't fooled. The people of the Lamb have "conquered the beast and its image" (Rev 15:2), not by sheer force, but by their nonviolent witness to the slaughtered Lamb (Rev 12:11).

The song they raise is none other than the song of Moses and of the Lamb:

Great and amazing are your deeds,
    Lord God the Almighty!
Just and true are your ways,
    King of the nations!
Lord, who will not fear
    and glorify your name?
For you alone are holy.
    All nations will come
    and worship before you,
for your judgments have been revealed. (Rev 15:3-4)

---

[11]Flemming, "Divine Judgment," 187.

This scene echoes the Bible's story of the exodus from Egypt. Even as Israel, rescued from the talons of Pharaoh, extolled God's deliverance along the shores of the Red Sea (Ex 15), God's redeemed people lift a new song beside the fiery sea. But this hymn transposes the melody from the key of M(oses) into the key of L(amb). Instead of focusing on *Israel's* rescue when God overpowers the pagan nations, as the original song of Moses, the *Lamb's* song celebrates *the nations* coming to worship their true King. This is the Lamb's song not only because the redeemed conquer the evil powers through the blood of the Lamb but also because, in a new and greater exodus, the Lamb has liberated people from every tribe and nation.

John unpacks the song's missional message by interpreting the original song of Moses with "a patchwork quilt of OT phrases."[12] God is "King of the nations" (Rev 15:3), and the goal of God's mission is that people of all nations would adore him. But once again, divine *judgment* plays a crucial part in the mission of God. The song ends by exclaiming, "For all nations will come and worship before you, *for your righteous judgments have been revealed*" (Rev 15:4 translation mine, italics added). Similar to Rev 14:7, God's just judgments act as both a motivation and a reason for the nations turning to God. In this case, God's "righteous judgments" likely include both his saving acts on behalf of his people and God's judgments against a rebellious world (e.g., Rev 16:5-7).[13] The song's lyrics assume that "when the rebellious nations truly recognize the greatness of God's deeds, the truth of God's ways, the holiness of God's character, and the justice of God's judgments, they will be magnetically attracted to join the chorus of worshipers who sing the song."[14] John's song is planted in the Old Testament hope that when other nations observe God's blessing, power, and judgments, both toward his people and the whole creation, they will be drawn to know and worship such a God (1 Kings 8:41-43; Ps 67:1-4; 96; 98; Ezek 36:20-23). But, as Gordon Fee rightly notes, the song "also serves as another reminder to [John's] readers that even in the midst of their present difficulties, they themselves . . . must

---

[12]Ben Witherington III, *Revelation* (Cambridge: Cambridge University Press, 2003), 206. E.g., Deut 32:4; Ps 86:8-10; Ps 98:1-2; 111:2; 139:14; 145:17; Jer 10:6-7.

[13]Koester, *Revelation*, 633.

[14]Flemming, "Divine Judgment," 184.

continue to bear witness to these nations about their king, whom the nations have yet to acknowledge as Lord of all."[15]

What's more, the breathtaking image of *all nations* coming to worship God resonates with the sweeping hope of the Old Testament prophets, who envision a global, end-time pilgrimage of the nations to Jerusalem (Is 2:2-4; 60:1-9; 66:20-23; Zech 8:22). John's vision of all nations worshiping their true King anticipates the full realization of God's mission in the new Jerusalem. There the nations will walk by the light of God and the Lamb and bring the glory of their worship into the new creation (Rev 21:24).

VIOLENCE, JUDGMENT, AND MISSION

But we still have a problem, don't we? How do we square the grisly, gruesome, and seemingly vengeful images of divine judgment in Revelation with the loving mission of God? First, let's be honest. Revelation *is* violent. It starts in chapter 6, when the notorious "four horsemen" gallop across the stage, launching a deadly assault of war, famine, pestilence, and death on the earth's people. In chapter 8, trumpets of judgment unleash cosmic chaos, bringing ecological devastation to the earth's trees, seas, and living creatures, not to mention the celestial bodies. Before the trumpet blasts silence, a horde of "mutant Ninja" locusts streams from the abyss to torture people (Rev 9:1-11), and a demonic cavalry two hundred million strong kills a third of humankind (Rev 9:13-19). In chapter 14, rebellious humans are forced to drink the wine of God's wrath, suffering the torment of fire and sulfur in the presence of the holy angels and the Lamb (Rev 14:9-11). Later, disobedient humanity itself *becomes* the wine, trampled in the wine press of God's wrath. The result? A flash flood of human blood on the earth (Rev 14:19-20).

By chapter 16, the bowls of God's wrath pour out judgment on sinful humanity in the form of devastating earthquakes, imploding cities, disappearing mountains and islands, and boulder-sized hailstones. The vision that follows shows Babylon the whore, drunk with the blood of God's people. Then the beast and its cronies turn on the harlot like a starving carnivore, devouring her flesh and consuming her with fire (Rev 17:6, 16). In

---

[15]Gordon D. Fee, *Revelation: A New Covenant Commentary* (Eugene, OR: Cascade, 2013), 213.

VENITE. BENEDICTI. PATRIS. MEI. IN. REGNVM. ÆTERNVM. *Compt ghy ghebenedyde mijns vaders hier*
ITE MALEDICTI. PATRIS. MEI. IN. IGNEM. SEMPITERNVM. *En ghaet ghy vermaledyde in dat eewighe vier*

Figure 6.4. Woodcut of *The Last Judgment* (Rev 20) by Pieter Bruegel the Elder from *The Seven Vices*, 1558

chapter 19, we witness a gruesome "great supper of God," where a swarm of ravenous vultures tear into the flesh of captains and kings, slave and free (Rev 19:17-21). By the time we reach the end of chapter 20, all those whose names are not found in the book of life, along with Satan their commander, are flung into the lake of fire, where they anguish in torment that never ends (Rev 20:10, 15).

Whew! It's little wonder that critics have railed against Revelation's violence. Psychologist Carl Jung scorned it as an "orgy of hatred, wrath, vindictiveness, and blind destructive fury,"[16] while biblical scholar Dominic Crossan claims that Revelation turns "the nonviolent resistance of the slaughtered Jesus into the violent warfare of the slaughtering Jesus."[17] Are Revelation's judgment scenes simply too monstrous to salvage? Is God's redemptive mission ultimately subverted by John's vindictive violence?

---

[16]Carl H. Jung, *Answer to Job*, 2nd ed. (Princeton, NJ: Princeton University Press, 2011 [1969]), 76.
[17]John Dominic Crossan, *God and Empire: Jesus Against Rome, Then and Now* (San Francisco: HarperSanFrancisco, 2007), 224.

"There is far too much destroying in the Apocalypse.
It ceases to be fun."[18]

D. H. LAWRENCE

These are massive questions, and I can't fully solve them. But I want to lay out several perspectives that might help us to better understand what is going on in Revelation's violent judgment scenes and to place them within God's sweeping missional purpose in this book.

First, John's visions of destruction are *symbols* of God's complete victory over sin and evil, not literal descriptions of how that happens. "The violence in the text," says Chilean scholar Pablo Richard, "is more literary and rhetorical than real."[19] We have no more warrant for reading these vivid images literally than we do for insisting that Jesus is actually a wooly lamb or that the woman in chapter 17 in fact sits on many waters, a scarlet beast, and seven mountains, all at once!

Second, John deploys this over-the-top, highly rhetorical language for a purpose. In the first place, it targets, not the unbelieving world, but *the church.* As Michael Gorman explains, "Taken individually or together, these visions of judgment create a literary, rhetorical, and emotional experience of shock and awe. Their primary purpose . . . is not to instill fear but to provide a wake-up call for those who are sleeping, not merely through life, but through empire."[20] John's judgment visions in Revelation 6–20, then, piggyback on the function of Christ's messages to the seven churches in chapters 2 and 3. Both sets of visions warn complacent Christians against compromising with the beastly powers; both summon the church to repent.

Third, Revelation's judgment scenes draw on traditional images, but those images are transformed by the mission of the slaughtered Lamb. John's

---

[18]D. H. Lawrence, *Apocalypse* (London: Penguin Books, 1980 [1931]), 135.

[19]Pablo Richard, "Reading the Apocalypse: Resistance, Hope, and Liberation in Central America," in *From Every People and Nation: The Book of Revelation in Intercultural Perspective,* ed. David Rhoads (Minneapolis: Fortress, 2005), 149.

[20]Michael J. Gorman, *Reading Revelation Responsibly: Uncivil Worship and Witness: Following the Lamb into the New Creation* (Eugene, OR: Cascade, 2011), 141.

language of destruction is not some impromptu concoction. Overwhelmingly, he adopts and adapts it from the Old Testament and the Jewish apocalyptic tradition. As Eugene Boring helpfully points out, "Almost everything in the violent pictures of the seals, trumpets, and bowls of chapters 6–19 is derived from biblical pictures and is described in biblical language."[21] For example, John transposes the plagues against Egypt in the exodus into a new key (Rev 8:6–9:11; 11:6; 16:1-21). In Revelation, the plagues morph into cosmic disasters that wreak judgment on the current idolatrous empire, Rome, as well as *any* empire that shakes its puny fist in God's face.

At the same time, John reinterprets traditional images of apocalyptic terror in light of the story of the crucified Lamb. We can't forget that the judgment scenes in chapters 6–20 *flow out of* the central vision of God on the throne and the Lamb who is slain in chapters 4–5. And that changes everything. Again, Boring comments: "The *Lamb* is the controlling image throughout. The Messiah is still clothed in the bloody garments (Rev 19:13) of the eschatological victory, but the blood is his own (Rev 1:5). The scenes are scenes of 'wrath,' but it is the 'wrath of the Lamb' (Rev 6:16)."[22] The Lamb is worthy to open the seals of God's warning judgments (Rev 5:9), revealing their horror, precisely because he is the *slaughtered* Lamb. In his suffering and death, the Lamb has experienced the deathly effects of what God allows humans to bring upon themselves.

This transformed perspective, as Gorman rightly observes, guards us against a common misinterpretation of Revelation's visions of cosmic war (see Rev 12:7-12; 16:12-16; 19:11-21; 20:7-10).[23] The thinking goes like this: God and the Lamb are engaged in a sacred battle to judge the wicked and wipe out evil from the earth, *now* as well as in the final reckoning. Therefore, God's people ought to sign up as recruits in this holy war against evil, even when that involves violence. So runs a popular interpretation of the American Civil War anthem "The Battle Hymn of the Republic," which draws heavily from the language of Revelation 14:14-20 and 19:11-20. Notice the present tense verbs:

---

[21]M. Eugene Boring, *Revelation* (Louisville: John Knox, 1989), 115.
[22]Boring, *Revelation*, 118.
[23]Gorman, *Reading Revelation*, 154.

Mine eyes have seen the glory of the coming of the Lord.
He *is* trampling out the vintage where the grapes of wrath are stored;
He hath loosed the fateful lightning of His terrible swift sword.
He has sounded forth the trumpet that shall never call retreat;
He *is* sifting out the hearts of men before His judgment-seat:
Oh, be swift, my soul, to answer Him! be jubilant, my feet! (italics added)[24]

Sometimes this call to arms has been used to justify military action against nations or groups who are considered evil as a form of divine warfare. Presumably, that violence is justified because it leads to a good end. But such appeals to join God in a campaign of sacred violence completely misread John's images. Throughout Revelation, *God's people are never called to acts of violence*. Not once do they engage in battle. In fact, Revelation never pictures a *literal* war or final battle against the forces of evil. Yes, Christ decisively defeats God's enemies in Revelation 19, but he does so with the sword of the word of God and with a robe stained in *his own blood!* God's people *do* join him in this mission, but they do so through costly, nonviolent witness, "by the blood of the Lamb and by the word of their testimony" (Rev 12:11). The God who justly judges is none other than the crucified Lamb!

THE PATIENT PERSISTENCE OF GOD

Discussions about judgment in the Apocalypse sometimes miss an important theme—the *patience* of God. Throughout the piling up of judgment scenes in Revelation 6–20, we encounter God's persistent patience, a divine restraint that gives opportunity for rebellious people to repent. We find it in

- the chilling observations that sinful humanity did *not* repent in the face of God's judgments (Rev 9:20-21; 16:9, 11), which surely implies that they still had an opportunity to do so.

- the picture of God's two witnesses wearing sackcloth, the symbol of humility and repentance (Rev 11:3).

- the unspoken call to repent in the appeal, "Fear God and give him glory," in view of the hour of judgment (Rev 14:7; cf. Rev 11:13).

---

[24]Julia Ward Howe, *Battle Hymn of the Republic* (Oliver Ditson & Co., Boston, 1862), www.loc
.gov/item/ihas.200000858/.

- the very structure of Revelation's judgment visions, which are strung out over three sets of seven plagues, with growing intensity (Rev 6, 8-9, 15-16). This suggests that time still remains for humans to heed their message, repent, and glorify God.[25]

- the fractional nature of God's destruction of evil (e.g., "a fourth of the earth" Rev 6:8; "a third of the ships" Rev 8:8; "a tenth of the city" Rev 11:13). Throughout the cycles of judgment, God never completely writes off a rebellious world.

According to the church father Tertullian, God "endures ungrateful peoples" who worship idols, persecute Christians, and practice greed and godlessness; "by his patience He hopes to draw them to himself."[26]

What is more, God's patient judgment becomes an expression of the Creator's just and loving sovereignty over creation. Throughout Revelation's judgment scenes, God allows humans to experience the disastrous consequences of their idolatrous lifestyles. In the case of the disasters unleashed by the four horsemen (Rev 6:1-8), judgment comes largely as a consequence of human sin. People are allowed to experience the war, chaos, violence, economic injustice, and death that results from lives that refuse to give glory to God, with the hope that they might awaken out of their stupor and turn to their Creator (Rev 9:20-21; 16:9, 11). In Revelation, God refuses "to allow human beings to go on indefinitely treating others as less than the images of God they are and thereby become more and more beastly and dehumanized themselves."[27] In fact, this outworking of God's judgment could almost serve as a commentary on Paul's indictment of rebellious humanity in Romans 1:18-32, where God hands people over to the consequences of their self-destructive behavior. Judgment in Revelation, then, represents not the

---

[25]Richard Bauckham, "Judgment in the Book of Revelation," *Ex Auditu* 20 (2004): 7.

[26]Tertullian, *Patience* 2.3, in *Tertullian: Disciplinary, Moral, and Ascetical Works*, trans. Edwin A. Quain, Emily Joseph Daly, and Rudolphus Arbesmann (Washington, DC: Catholic University Press), 195.

[27]Andy Johnson, *Holiness and the Missio Dei* (Eugene, OR: Cascade, 2016), 160.

revenge of an angry God against sinners but the passionate pursuit of a just God who seeks repentance, worship, and wholeness for people from every nation.

PRAYERS OF THE OPPRESSED

It is from this perspective that we can begin to hear the haunting cries of the martyrs under the altar, begging for divine judgment on their enemies: "Sovereign Lord, holy and true, how long will it be before you judge and avenge our blood on the inhabitants of the earth?" (Rev 6:10; cf. Rev 18:20).

In John's first-century context, such calls arise from a vulnerable, marginalized community, which knows well the mighty engines of injustice, wielded by the power of Rome. These prayers do not vent personal vengeance, but rather desperately appeal to a God who is perfectly just and is able to set things right.[28] They echo the cries of God's oppressed people throughout the centuries (see Ps 13:1-2; 94:3; 119:84), prayers for God to enact justice and truth that echo into the present day. Listen to South African pastor and anti-apartheid activist Allan Boesak's moving meditation on the plea, "How long, O Lord?"

> In the face of nameless suffering and unnameable gods this cry is a confession: "The Lord reigns!" At the moment of detention; in the long dark hours of incarceration; as the footsteps of your interrogators come down the passage to your cell; above the harsh voices and the scornful laugh; through the blows of fists on tender flesh, the blinding pain of electric shocks, through the hazy, bloody mist of unwanted tears; above the roar of guns and tanks and armoured vehicles; in the nauseating sting of tear gas and the tearing, searing burn of the bullet through your body—the words are shouted or whispered: "How long, Lord?" It is in the cries of the suffering and the oppressed that the church will hear the voice of God.[29]

But in Revelation, God does not answer the martyrs' prayers immediately. God's final judgment on the oppressive powers doesn't come at once. They are "told to rest a little longer" (Rev 6:11). The longing for justice will be

---

[28]Bauckham, "Judgment," 9.
[29]Allan A. Boesak, *Comfort and Protest: The Apocalypse from a South African Perspective* (Philadelphia: Westminster, 1987), 69.

fulfilled, but only after the church's suffering and even dying witness to the world is finished, giving opportunity for the nations to repent (Rev 6:11). Between "How long, Lord?" (Rev 6:10) and the renewed heaven and earth (Rev 21–22) lies the costly mission of God's people to every tribe and nation. God patiently, graciously postpones the righting of all wrongs, allowing time for the church, through word and deed, to convince others to turn to their Creator instead of encountering God's judgment.[30] In the words of Peter's letter, the Lord "is patient with you, not wanting any to perish, but all to come to repentance" (2 Pet 3:9).

> *"The oppressed do not see any dichotomy between God's love and God's justice. . . . God takes up the cause of the poor and the oppressed precisely because in this world their voices are not heard—not even by those who call themselves Christians. . . . Christians who enjoy the fruits of injustice without a murmur, who remain silent as the defenseless are slaughtered, dare not become indignant when the suffering people of God echo the prayers of the psalms and pray for deliverance and judgment."[31]*
>
> ALLAN BOESAK

But that patience is not without limit. In Revelation, God's love isn't flabby. His grace isn't cheap. God's love remains a holy love that conquers evil through redemptive justice. John reveals God's love as "an all-powerful redemptive force that casts a dark shadow of judgment over those who continue to oppose its liberating work in the world."[32]

Ultimately, those who persist in spurning the mercy of their Creator, both the oppressive powers and those who attach themselves to them, must fall

---

[30]Bauckham, "Judgment," 10.

[31]Boesak, *Comfort and Protest*, 72.

[32]John Christopher Thomas and Frank D. Macchia, *Revelation* (Grand Rapids, MI: Eerdmans, 2016), 411.

under judgment's shadow. Those who seek to destroy the earth will be destroyed (Rev 11:18). Those who drink the wine of Babylon's passion, participating in her sins, must in turn drink the wine of *God's* passion, sharing Babylon's judgment (Rev 14:8, 10).[33] As theologian Miroslav Volf frames it, "After God's patience with chaotic powers who refuse to be redeemed by the cross has come to an end, God inflicts violence against the stubbornly violent to restore creation's original peace."[34]

Does judgment get the final word in God's world? It does not! Revelation's *last* word comes not with the lake of fire (Rev 20:7-15) but with the new creation (Rev 21–22), which represents the perfect realization of God's justice. Judgment in the Apocalypse isn't itself an end, but rather a *means* to an end. Beyond the destruction of evil lies the holy city, where a holy people of every tribe and tongue will dwell in the presence of a holy God (Rev 21:3). God's mission is fully realized in the "healing of the nations" (Rev 22:2), a holistic restoration that penetrates every corner and crevice of human need. Even judgment can't exhaust God's loving purpose for the world.

CONCLUSION

This chapter hasn't answered all the unsettling questions that Revelation's visions of judgment raise. Any effort to tie up the Apocalypse in a neat bow will fail. What we *have* tried to show is that divine judgment is not opposed to the gracious, patient mission of God. On the contrary, judgment and mission are inseparable partners. Let me summarize some ways in which that plays out in Revelation.

1. *Judgment in Revelation always happens in the context of God's mercy and love.* Judgment does not deny the redemptive love of God but functions as a necessary dimension of that love. God's love for his people and all creation

---

[33]Bauckham, "Judgment," 20. Some interpreters argue that in Revelation, final judgment is reserved only for the *systems* that oppress the innocent, not unrepentant sinners, who in the end will enter New Jerusalem. See Simon P. Woodman, "Fire from Heaven: Divine Judgment in the Book of Revelation," in *The Book of Revelation*, ed. Garrick V. Allen et al., WUNT 2.411 (Tübingen: Mohr Siebeck, 2015), 179-80, 186-90. This interpretation may be theologically attractive, but ultimately it strains the clearest reading of texts like Rev 20:7-15; 21:8, 27; 22:11, 15.

[34]Miroslav Volf, *Exclusion and Embrace: A Theological Exploration of Identity, Otherness, and Reconciliation* (Nashville, TN: Abingdon, 1996), 300.

means that *nothing, absolutely nothing* will be allowed to derail God's missional purpose to make everything new.

2. *Revelation's story of judgment (chapters 6–20) flows out of the defining vision of the slaughtered Lamb (chapter 5).* John never lets us forget that the wrath of God is the wrath of the crucified Lamb (Rev 6:17), the Lamb who overcame evil by his own self-giving death.[35]

3. *The focus of judgment in Revelation is not punishment or, even less, revenge, but rather repentance and restoration.* God's redemptive justice is intended to lead people to revere and worship the God who reigns over all. But *judgment alone* doesn't accomplish that. Only when the nations see the church living out its costly, Lamblike witness do they move from fear to faith in their Creator.

4. *Judgment serves as a warning alarm.* Revelation's weird, scary, and violent images of judgment are not literal descriptions of future events. Instead, they primarily function as a kind of theological "shock therapy," which demands a response. John says, in effect: "You can take the path that leads to death and destruction, or you can follow the way of the Lamb that ends in a new creation. It's your choice!"

5. *Revelation's warning, in the first place, targets the church.* Both in the first and the twenty-first centuries, Christian communities must let Revelation's visions address their current spiritual condition and need. Faithful communities will hear an assurance of God's final triumph over all injustice but compromising "Laodiceans" must confront the danger of flirting with the evil powers.

6. *Revelation's theology of judgment encourages the church to fulfill its missional calling.* John shows us a God who delays judgment and refuses to write off a rebellious world. This persistent patience, which is rooted in the character of God and revealed in the slaughtered Lamb, must shape *our* mission as well. It leaves us an open door for bearing witness to the "eternal gospel," in word and deed, among the nations.

7. *Finally, divine judgment offers a vision of hope to the suffering and the oppressed.* God's unstoppable, unflappable, unconquerable love assures us

---

[35]Mitchell G. Reddish, *Revelation* (Macon, GA: Smyth and Helwys, 2001), 318.

that God will not ignore the cries of people or of creation itself for liberation from sin's devastating effects (see Rom 8:18-25), that the powers that inflict pain, traffic children, exploit women, and destroy creation will be extinguished forever.[36] God's judgment makes possible a perfectly just world. This is good news indeed!

---

[36]Reddish, *Revelation*, 318.

CHAPTER SEVEN

MISSIONAL WORSHIP

Worship God!

REVELATION 19:10, 22:9

HOW COULD I HAVE MISSED IT for so long? For years, I read Revelation primarily as a prophecy of the future and failed to recognize that, as much as anything else, it has to do with *worship*. From one standpoint, Revelation is one big act of worship that invites God's people to participate in worship. Worship courses through the pages of Revelation like blood runs through our bodies.

The Apocalypse unfolds in a worship context and John is our worship leader. Revelation begins with a blessing on those who "read aloud" and "hear" its prophetic words in a worship setting (Rev 1:3). When John receives his visions, he is caught up in worship, "on the Lord's day" (Rev 1:10). This worship context forges a link with gatherings of believers who hear these words being read "on the Lord's day." Then, near the end of Revelation, John is commanded *twice* to "Worship God!," not any inferior being (Rev 19:10; 22:9). As it began, the book closes in a worship setting. Jesus himself promises, "Surely I am coming soon." The worshipers, with John as their leader, exclaim a collective liturgical response: "Amen. Come, Lord Jesus!" (Rev 2:20; cf. Rev 1:7).

In between this liturgical framework, Revelation is peppered with ritual acts (e.g., Rev 4:1–5:4; 7:9-12; 19:1-4) and worship hymns and songs, some of which congregations still sing today (Rev 4:8-11; 5:9-14; 7:10-12; 11:15-18; 12:10-12; 15:3-4; 16:5-7; 19:1-8). In fact, worship provides the background for everything that happens in chapters 4–22. These visions all originate from the throne room of God almighty, which is a worship setting. The twenty-four elders and four living creatures praise God day and night (Rev 4:8), and that praise continues as a kind of musical accompaniment to the visions that follow.[1] What's more, throughout the Apocalypse, the issue of true and false worship plays out as a signature theme. Eugene Boring hasn't over-stated things when he observes, "the language of the Apocalypse is the language of worship."[2] Writing to churches that face stern opposition and are tempted to compromise their witness, John calls them back to genuine worship of God on the throne and the Lamb who is slain.

There is much to say about worship in Revelation. However, I will focus on the connection between worship and mission. We will discover that for John and his audience, both then and now, worship

- announces

- reimagines

- confronts

- reveals

- invites

Like the different features of someone's face, together these various perspectives form a portrait of Revelation as a book of imaginative, missional worship.

Worship Announces

Revelation declares God's saving purpose for creation in the context of worship. Revelation's eight worship songs not only offer praise to the Almighty and to the Lamb; they also sing the story of salvation. More than simply background music, they serve as a commentary on God's character and

---

[1]Mitchell G. Reddish, *Revelation* (Macon, GA: Smyth and Helwys, 2001), 102-3.

[2]M. Eugene Boring, "Revelation 19–21: End Without Closure," *The Princeton Seminary Bulletin* Supp 3 (1994): 82.

actions in the Apocalypse. Further, they interpret the events and the symbols that surround them.

The singing starts in the magnificent throne room scene of Revelation 4 and 5. These chapters not only comprise the theological heart of the book but also function as Revelation's "worship center." The first worship hymn (Rev 4:8-11) proclaims the entire sweep of God's activity: he has always been, is now, and is soon to come with transforming power (Rev 4:8). The song's climax highlights the *beginning* of God's mission. It sings: "You are worthy" of honor and praise because "you created all things" and gave them their being (Rev 4:11).

The worship of God extends to Jesus, the Lamb, in chapter 5. The four living creatures and twenty-four elders announce that he alone is worthy to open the seven-sealed scroll, which reveals God's missional purpose for humanity and all of creation (Rev 5:9-14). Why? Because he is the

Figure 7.1. Manuscript illumination of the Adoration of the Lamb on Mount Zion (Rev 14:1-5) from the Cloisters Apocalypse, c. 1330

slaughtered Lamb, whose atoning death has redeemed people from every nation and given them a vocation as a kingdom and priests in service of God.

In the third hymn (Rev 7:9-12), a multitude from every tongue, tribe, and nation acclaim God and the Lamb as the sole source of salvation, even as they fall on their faces in worship. Then, at the climax of the seven trumpets of judgment, we hear a heavenly bulletin, in words that fly off the page: "The kingdom of the world has become the kingdom of our Lord and of his Messiah" (Rev 11:15).

This hymn (Rev 11:15-18) makes explicit what up to this point has only been implied. God's end-time kingdom has arrived; God's eternal rule has begun. In their antiphonal response (Rev 11:16-18), the twenty-four elders praise God as the one who *was* and who *is*. But the line about God's *coming* has been dropped from the song's lyrics. From the perspective of this hymn, *he has already come.* The fulfillment of God's mission is *here.* It's time to grab a partner and celebrate! The rest of Revelation will show in more detail, how this fundamental reality unfolds. This hymn also introduces the theme of God's righteous judgment of the powers that oppose him, which will feature in the rest of the worship songs.

The fifth hymn (Rev 12:10-12) celebrates the utter defeat of Satan and his minions. It echoes the arrival of God's salvation and God's messianic kingdom from previous hymns, and it proclaims that God's persecuted people will share in his triumph over Satan. But not by their own might. They will conquer the accuser "by the blood of the Lamb and by the word of their testimony" (Rev 12:11). Victory comes only by participating in the Lamb's suffering, even to the point of death.

The song of Moses and of the Lamb (Rev 15:2-4) spotlights the universal character of God's work in the world, as we saw in the last chapter. A chorus of redeemed conquerors celebrates God as "king of the nations" and foreshadows the fulfillment of God's mission in the new creation, when "all nations will come and worship before you" (Rev 15:4).

Then, in the thick of the bowls of judgment that follow, the angel of the waters declares the flip side of God's salvation (Rev 16:5-7). For God's restoring mission to be realized, he must judge those who have persecuted his servants. The oppressors are force-fed the very blood they have shed.

Immediately, the altar affirms: "Your judgments are true and just!" (Rev 16:7). "God's devastating blow is so fiercely appropriate," writes Brian Blount, "that even the furniture is compelled to sing."[3]

We hear the "grand finale" of the worship anthems in Revelation 19:1-8. Various groups in heaven erupt into a series of "hallelujah choruses," creating an antiphonal effect. First, a heavenly multitude extolls God's salvation, which is linked to judgment on the bloodthirsty prostitute Babylon and liberation from her corrupting power (Rev 19:1-2; cf. Rev 18:20). Once again, "praise is not simply for what God has done or is doing, but for what he is going to do when his justice is fully revealed at the End."[4] Then the twenty-four elders and four living creatures fall down in worship and add their "Amens." Finally, a mighty chorus of God's people shouts its praise of the God who reigns over the world and rejoices in the relationship that now may develop between Christ and his church, the bride of the Lamb (Rev 19:6-8).[5]

As this brief survey shows, it's in the context of worship that Revelation most explicitly bears witness to God's missional purpose for the world. Like Israel's Psalms (e.g., Ps 67:3-5; 96; 138:5-6) Revelation's hymns *sing* the story of God's saving work. We might call this "music in the key of mission." Here are some of the themes that dominate the lyrics:

- God's lordship over all creation
- God's purpose to draw people of all nations to worship him
- God's triumph over the powers of evil and God's righteous judgments
- the eternal kingdom rule of God and Christ
- the Lamb's sacrificial death for people of every tribe and tongue
- the church as the redeemed, priestly community that shares both Christ's victory and his suffering

Revelation's hymns proclaim by praise. At the same time, they invite us to embrace these truths and participate in that worship. In Revelation, the

---

[3]Brian K. Blount, *Revelation: A Commentary* (Louisville, KY: Westminster John Knox, 2009), 97.
[4]Ian Paul, *Revelation* (Downers Grove, IL: IVP Academic, 2018), 311.
[5]Blount, *Revelation*, 97.

worship that takes place in heaven serves as a pattern for the worship of God's people on earth.

Making this practical, we might ask whether our own worship consistently bears witness to the loving, redeeming, and just mission of God and the Lamb. Worship declares the truth of God. It is more than simply an emotional response or a repetition of our love for God. As in Revelation, the sacred music of the church historically has instilled in God's people the truth about God and God's purposes in the world.

Christian communities in various cultures debate the relative value of singing "theological" hymns versus contemporary praise songs. But if we listen to the music of Revelation, this becomes a misguided choice. Revelation's hymns are drenched with "hallelujahs" and praise offerings to God. And rightly so. God is worthy of our exuberant praise. At the same time, those songs articulate the great truths of God's saving work through the slaughtered Lamb and his purpose for the nations and all creation in the end. Sacred music plays a crucial role in the church's calling to make disciples in the nations. The early Methodists learned their theology to a large extent by singing Charles Wesley's hymns. Whatever the music *style*, if our worship, which includes singing, fails to announce the great themes of Scripture, we squander a prime opportunity to disciple worshipers, enabling them to gain a deeper grasp of what God is doing in the world.

What is more, Revelation's hymns do not deal exclusively with "bright" subjects. They address themes like the power of Satan and evil in the world, the rebellion of humanity, the unjust suffering of God's people, and God's righteous judgment in the end. We may be tempted to include only "happy music" and uplifting themes in our worship gatherings. But in the process, we may shortchange the breadth of biblical teaching and human experience that we find in texts like the Psalms of lament and the more uncomfortable bits in Revelation's songs.

Unfortunately, the Revised Common Lectionary (the list of prescribed Scripture readings followed by many Protestant churches in their worship services), falls short precisely at this point. The lectionary's three-year cycle includes only six passages from Revelation, and even these carefully edit out anything that sounds strange or violent. As a result, congregations hear only passages of comfort, praise, and promise (among Revelation's hymns, only Rev 5:11-14 and Rev 7:9-17 appear, together with three readings from Rev 21 and 22). Nothing from Christ's words to the churches in chapters 2 and 3 makes the cut, nor does anything from Revelation's prophetic messages of judgment in Rev 6–20. We are left with a "sanitized, 'G-rated' version of Revelation," which may confuse congregations, who know that isn't *all* this book is about.[6]

Finally, Revelation *still* sings the story of God and the Lamb when the church gathers to worship. Revelation's worship hymns have inspired the church's music and ignited Christian imaginations across the centuries and continue to do so.[7] Consider, for example, Handel's exhilarating "Hallelujah Chorus" from *Messiah*, which includes the lines from Revelation 11:15: "The kingdom of this world has become the kingdom of our Lord and of his Christ. And he shall reign forever and ever." Recall the stirring hymn by Matthew Bridges (1800–1894), which lifts images from Revelation 5, 7, and 19:

> Crown him with many crowns, the Lamb upon his throne.
> Hark! How the heavenly anthem drowns all music but its own!
> Awake, my soul, and sing of Him who died for thee.
> And hail Him as thy matchless King through all eternity.

More recently, Andrew Peterson's "Is He Worthy?," based on Revelation 5, sings the brokenness of the present world, our deep longing for new creation, and our unshakable hope in a slain and risen Lamb, who alone is *worthy* to bring that new world into being. It pierces my imagination such that it brings me to tears almost every time I hear it.

Revelation's worship continues to shape the church's imagination, which brings us to our next point.

Worship Reimagines

In 2009, the British filmmaker Leslie Woodhead produced a BBC documentary titled "How the Beatles Rocked the Kremlin."[8] His thesis was both

---

[6]Richard B. Hays and Stefan Alkier, "Introduction," in *Revelation and the Politics of Apocalyptic Interpretation*, ed. Richard B. Hays and Stefan Alkier (Waco, TX: Baylor University Press, 2012), 2.
[7]See, e.g., Michael J. Gorman's fine discussion of this topic in *Reading Revelation Responsibly: Uncivil Worship and Witness: Following the Lamb into the New Creation* (Eugene, OR: Cascade, 2011), 112-15.
[8]Leslie Woodhead, "How the Beatles Rocked the Kremlin," British Broadcasting Company Storyville, 2009.

simple and compelling: the music of the Beatles, as much as any other factor, contributed to the collapse of the Soviet Union. Even as the Kremlin saw the popularity of the British Rock band as a threat to their power to control the minds of young people and banned it from the USSR, teenagers continued to listen to bootlegged Beatles albums. The band's music inspired hope for freedom and a culture of resistance among Soviet youth. Many in that generation grew up rejecting the repression of the dominant Soviet system and eventually helped to bring the system down. According to Woodhead's film, the mighty Soviet empire crumbled, at least in part, because the imaginations of a whole generation were shaped by songs.

Why is this not surprising? Because songs and stories can reshape our imaginations. And when we imagine a new reality, in time, we begin to live into that new reality. Old Testament scholar Walter Brueggemann shows how the Psalms carried out this role for ancient Israel. He writes, "The singing congregation describes, imagines, and evokes an alternative world," one that reconstitutes all of life.[9] Something similar happens in Revelation. The hymns and worship scenes of Revelation enable John's audience to reimagine the reality in which they live. Worship constructs a new world.

We see this above all in Revelation 4 and 5. John pictures a cosmos in which God and the Lamb occupy a throne at the very center. Surrounding the throne, all creation, in concentric spheres, offers the worship that God and the Lamb alone deserve. With this centering vision, Revelation reimagines the world. It gives the Christian communities in Asia an alternative *cosmology*; in other words, a new understanding of the whole universe.[10] This worldview, articulated in the praise and worship of God on the universal throne, collides with Rome's vision of how the universe was ordered. Rome's cosmology placed Caesar and the gods that gave him authority at the center of the world. Imperial Rome shaped and sustained the universe.

But in John's reimagined world, the myriads of angels are joined in their praise by "every creature in heaven and on earth and under the earth and

---

[9] Walter Brueggemann, *Worship in Ancient Israel: An Essential Guide* (Nashville, TN: Abingdon, 2005), 45.

[10] On Revelation's cosmology as an alternative to the imperial cosmology of Rome, see Ryan L. Hansen, *Silence and Praise: Rhetorical Cosmology and Political Theology in the Book of Revelation* (Minneapolis: Fortress, 2014), 2-10; Laszlo Gallusz, *The Throne Motif in the Book of Revelation*, LNTS 487 (London: Bloomsbury T & T Clark, 2014), 286-99, 334.

in the sea, and all that is in them" (Rev 5:13). "Augustus had claimed to rule the Roman world 'by universal assent' (*Res Gestae* 34.1); John declares that, if there is any genuinely *universal* assent, it undergirds the rule of God and the Lamb."[11] Revelation envisions nothing less than a complete regime change.

God's people, as well, are caught up in that heavenly worship. John pictures the church, through the image of the twenty-four elders (most likely derived from the twelve tribes of Israel and the twelve apostles), joining the angels and the rest of creation in worshiping the one on the throne. From an earthly vantage point, these churches in Asia may seem to be frail and marginalized communities of faith. But in Revelation's transformed imagination, they are part of the heavenly court; they will share in God's victory over the evil powers, as well as his eternal reign.[12] This is not simply a vision of the far-off future. Even now, they are called to bring God's reign to bear on his creation; even now they are invited to participate in unceasing worship (Rev 4:8; 7:15), a worship that embraces all of life.

Today we are also called to see our world through radically different lenses than those of the mainstream culture. In our everyday experience, brokenness, violence, and suffering dominate the headline news. How can we possibly sing about the victory of God's kingdom? Commentator Mitchell Reddish frames it well:

> We are a community that sees the world differently from the way others see it. Where others see brokenness, we see wholeness. Where others see death, we see life. Where others see hatred, we see love. Where others see a world in rebellion, we see a world transformed. Even when the events around us seem to argue against any belief that God will triumph, we keep singing our victory songs, confident that the love and mercy of God will ultimately bring healing to a fractured creation.[13]

Before that happens, we endure, bearing faithful and costly witness to what we know to be true. We live as agents of God's transforming work in

---

[11]David A. deSilva, *An Introduction to the New Testament: Contexts, Methods and Ministry Formation*, 2nd ed. (Downers Grove, IL: IVP Academic, 2018), 813.

[12]Simon Woodman, *The Book of Revelation* (London: SCM, 2008), 183.

[13]Reddish, *Revelation*, 225.

the present world, in anticipation of the final triumph of the kingdom of our Lord and of his Messiah that is to come.

WORSHIP CONFRONTS

Political worship. David deSilva hits the nail on the head: "The basic question undergirding Revelation is: Who is worthy of honor and worship?"[14] In John's world, this was not only a religious but also a *political* question. Wes Howard-Brooke and Anthony Gwyther explain,

> In our modern world of separation of church and state, most churchgoers have not been called upon to consider the inherently political nature of worship. In Revelation's world, though, this connection was obvious and went without saying. What is surprising is not that worship was political, but that worship of the One on the throne *excluded* worship of other gods or deified emperors.[15]

Worship is political because it declares ultimate allegiances. It concerns who or what holds power over people's lives and thereby demands their loyalty. Jesus' statement to Pilate, "You would have no power over me if it were not given to you from above" (Jn 19:11 NIV), challenges every human power that tries to usurp God's place on the throne.[16]

"Behind the activity of worship is the question of power: 'Who indeed is in charge of this world?' There is a worship that leads to life and a worship that is an instrument of death. Africans are a worshiping people; worship is integral to their life. Worship reaffirms the God-given cosmic order, and it fans the hopes for fullness of life."[17]

JAMES CHUKWUMA OKOYE

---

[14]deSilva, *Introduction to the New Testament*, 813.
[15]Wes Howard-Brooke and Anthony Gwyther, *Unveiling Empire: Reading Revelation Then and Now* (Maryknoll, NY: Orbis, 2003), 206.
[16]Paul, *Revelation*, 129.
[17]James Chukwuma Okoye, "Power and Worship: *Revelation* in African Perspective," in *From Every People and Nation: The Book of Revelation in Intercultural Perspective*, ed. David Rhoads (Minneapolis: Fortress, 2005), 124.

In Roman Asia, it was widely held that the gods had chosen Rome and that the emperor was the agent of the gods' rule over the world. The question, "Who is worthy of our praise and allegiance?" allowed only one answer: "Caesar, of course!" Forms of worshiping the emperor and praising Rome's power drenched John's world like the monsoon rains of India. Poets lauded Rome's eternity. Coins publicized Caesar's deity. Choral societies sang the emperor's praise.[18] This was the *normal* way of seeing the world.

But not for the Lamb's people. Their exclusive allegiance, their ultimate loyalty, their singular *worship* belonged to the one who sits on the throne and to the Lamb. When the congregations of Asia gathered to worship, they publicly announced to the world, "The God who made all things occupies the throne of the universe and Caesar does not!"

The same is true today. When we come together to worship, whatever our cultural setting, we declare our "political" allegiances to those around us. This isn't about partisan politics but rather our public acknowledgment that God alone is on the throne and the idols of our culture are not.

Revelation's worship war. Because worship involves declaring loyalties, it can take either a positive or a negative path. Worship of the true God in heaven is constantly defied by its evil twin, the idolatrous worship of the beast on earth (Rev 13:4, 8, 12-17; 14:9-11; 16:2, 19:20; 20:4). Consequently, Revelation envisions a "worship war" of cosmic proportions.

Nowhere is this clearer than in chapter 13, where "the whole earth" follows and worships the beast (Rev 13:3, 4). The earth's inhabitants, who have succumbed to the beast's spell, chant their own idolatrous liturgy: "Who is like the beast, and who can fight against it?" (Rev 13:4), mimicking the very question repeatedly asked about God in the Old Testament (e.g., Ex 15:11; Ps 35:10; Is 40:18). The beast seems invincible. As a result, it attracts peoples' allegiance. For John, worship of the beast is "antiworship," a demonic parody of the worship of God. As we will see in the next chapter, John's readers immediately would have associated the beast with Caesar and the empire, and its worship with the emperor cult. But John also perceives that behind Rome's demand for loyalty lies a cosmic battle with Satan, who is ravenous

---

[18]J. Nelson Kraybill, "The New Jerusalem as Paradigm for Mission," *Mission Focus Annual Review* 2 (1994): 129.

Figure 7.2. Wood cut of the beast worshiped by the nations (Rev 13) by John Bale from *The Image of Both Churches*, 1535

for human worship. Other *earthly* centers of power compete with the throne of God: Satan's throne (Rev 2:13) and the beast's throne (Rev 16:10), which is granted by the dragon Satan (Rev 13:2). The idolatry of the empire becomes none other than the worship of demons (Rev 9:20). As Brian Blount wisely notes, "John wants his hearers and readers to understand this critical point: to participate in the Roman imperial cult is to worship the draconian evil that lurks behind Rome."[19]

The question underlying Revelation is not only, Who is worthy of worship? but also, Who are *we* going to worship? By pitting the eternal throne of God in heaven against the earthly thrones of Satan and the beast, Revelation counters the human tendency to worship something less than God and the Lamb. John offers his readers a two-pronged strategy for resisting false worship: nonparticipation and praise.[20]

---

[19]Blount, *Revelation*, 249.

[20]Ryan L. Hansen characterizes this two-fold vocation as "silence and praise." See Hansen, *Silence and Praise*, e.g., 10.

Resisting through nonparticipation. Revelation calls the Christians in Asia to pledge their allegiance to God and the Lamb not only with words but also with their lifestyle. Part of the church's costly witness to Jesus before outsiders involves *not* worshiping the beast (Rev 20:4; cf. Rev 13:15). Practically, that meant refusing to participate in the state-sponsored idolatry of the imperial cult. As we have seen, the tentacles of emperor worship reached far and wide in Roman Asia, pervading everyday public and private life. Opting out wasn't easy. What's more, it could be dangerous. Just ask Antipas (Rev 2:13)!

According to Rome's worldview, the rule of Caesar and the gods over the world was maintained by the ritual, sacrifice, and images of the emperor cult. Ryan Hansen shows that engaging in Caesar worship functioned something like a social contract for maintaining a stable universe. The gods sustained the world through imperial Rome, and, in turn, people sacrificed and honored the divine emperor.[21] In other words, "Give Caesar his due and the

Figure 7.3. Temple of emperor Domitian in ancient Ephesus

[21]Hansen, *Silence and Praise*, 8-9, 63-66.

gods will take care of your security, peace, and prosperity." An appealing transaction.

Participating in the emperor cult, then, was both expected and necessary to maintain the world order. Christians who refused to join citywide festivals that celebrated the divine emperor or opted out of trade guild meetings that honored their city's patron gods could be singled out as both disloyal to Caesar and "a threat to the ongoing nature and stability of the world."[22]

Risky or not, Revelation asks Christians to resist Rome's claim over the world, not by force, but by *nonparticipation* in the liturgical practices that maintained it. It's hardly surprising, then, that John takes the matter of Christians eating food that's been sacrificed to the gods so seriously (Rev 2:14, 20). In John's eyes, this practice represents more than a harmless cultural custom; it signals their involvement in an entire idolatrous system, in which Caesar and the gods run the world. Ultimately, it sucks them into the work of Satan himself (Rev 2:20, 24; 9:20). The Christians in Asia must refocus their worship and resist cooperating in the idolatry that was embedded in their mainstream culture.

Similarly, Revelation calls Christians in every location and generation to resist the idols of their culture and the practices that sustain them. For example, Christians in the West might need to dismantle the idol of consumerism by resisting the cultural pressure to buy unnecessary luxury goods or to ring up massive debt to feed an unsustainable lifestyle. Or we may need to tune out the voices of the powerful that promise peace and security at the price of our unquestioned loyalty. Any time we direct our worship and allegiance to powers within creation itself instead of to the Creator (Rom 1:25), we traffic in what the Bible calls idolatry.

Songs of resistance. The other side of Revelation's strategy for resisting the false worship of the empire comes through its liturgy and hymns of praise. Earlier we saw that Revelation's worship songs transform the imaginations of its readers, helping them to see and experience a new world, where God reigns supreme. As a result, those hymns confront the

---

[22]Hansen, *Silence and Praise*, 64.

powers and idols of this world. Revelation's hymns give its readers a counter-imagination, which energizes them to resist the dominant stories of their culture.

> *"Revelation is a dangerous blend of memorable music and recalcitrant rhetoric. Its liturgical hymns witness to the promise that God is relieving Rome of its historical command. Right now."*[23]

BRIAN BLOUNT

Consider the opening praise songs of chapters 4 and 5. It's no coincidence that the same ways of describing God in Revelation 4:8-11 (Almighty, who was, is, and is to come, our Lord and God) were used to laud Caesar or a Greco-Roman god in John's day.[24] Nor is it by accident that the acts of worship extended to God on the throne (e.g., singing hymns, offering crowns) played a role in the rituals that signaled submission to Roman emperors. In John's world, when the heavenly choral groups shout "You are worthy" to God and the Lamb (Rev 4:11; 5:9; cf. Rev 5:12), it could only mean, "You, and *only* you!"[25]

Likewise, the daring proclamation in chapter 11, "The kingdom of the world has become the kingdom of our Lord and of his Messiah" (Rev 11:15), couldn't help but issue a poke in the imperial eye to Caesar, whose empire claimed to rule the world. Moreover, the line from the hymn's lyrics that sings, "and he will reign forever and ever" explodes Rome's arrogant eschatology, which celebrates its eternal rule. From the perspective of Revelation's worship, God's universal kingdom cannot happily coexist with the human empire and its claim to reign. As with Harry Potter and evil Voldemort, "Neither can live while the other survives."[26]

---

[23]Blount, *Revelation*, 95.
[24]Blount, *Revelation*, 95.
[25]Blount, *Revelation*, 95.
[26]J. K. Rowling, *Harry Potter and the Deathly Hallows* (New York: Scholastic, 2007), 737.

> *"Rome, queen of all, your power will never end."*[27]
>
> AN INSCRIPTION FROM AN ELEGANT HOUSE
>
> IN ANCIENT EPHESUS

When the congregations in Asia sing Revelation's hymns in their own context, they participate in its celestial worship. As they do, they are empowered to take heart and to resist any power or idol, human or cosmic, that competes for their worship. God's people respond to the worship call of the elders and the angels "with their own politically charged worship and witness to history's sole sovereign—to the Almighty God and to the Lamb."[28]

Today, worship, particularly the songs of worship, still offer resources for resisting the narratives, the powers, the idols that try to shape our world and demand our allegiance. Songs have always played a crucial part in resisting the powers of this age. They help us voice a confident hope that one day the infrastructure of present power will collapse and God's justice will reign. Richard Hays notes that the simple anthem of the US civil rights movement, "We Shall Overcome," was taken from the King James translation of the promise that ends each of the messages to the seven churches. "As freedom marchers from the black churches joined hands and sang, 'We shall overcome someday,' they were expressing faith that, despite their lack of conventional political power, their witness to the truth would prevail over violence and oppression."[29]

Alan Boesak expressed a similar hope during the darkest days of apartheid in South Africa, before that system of oppressing non-White peoples was abolished. Hear his poignant reflection:

> Black people in South Africa have made freedom songs part of the struggle; in fact, the struggle is inconceivable without them. . . . In jail, they sing— songs of defiance and faith and freedom. . . . In prison singing is not allowed, but political prisoners do it anyway, their voices blending as the song is picked up from cell to cell until the prison resounds with music that celebrates the

---

[27]Cited in Gallusz, *The Throne Motif*, 275.
[28]Blount, *Revelation*, 98.
[29]Richard B. Hays, *The Moral Vision of the New Testament: A Contemporary Introduction to New Testament Ethics: Community, Cross, New Creation* (San Francisco: HarperCollins, 1996), 183-84.

coming victory. Prison wardens, policemen, and heavily armed soldiers cannot understand how people can sing under such circumstances. . . . But we sing because we believe, we sing because we hope. We sing because we know that it is only a little while, and the tyrant shall cease to exist.[30]

Revelation's worship songs continue to ask Christian leaders and Christian communities, "Are you chaplains of the empire or prophets of the resistance?"[31]

WORSHIP REVEALS

In Revelation, worship reveals the goal of God's mission. The great worship scenes of the Apocalypse show us where the *missio Dei* is heading. God's loving purpose for the world is that people of every tribe and nation would come to love, glorify, and worship the triune God for all of eternity. John provides a series of stunning screenshots of that aim. In chapter 7, we encounter a cheering multinational choir of the redeemed standing before the throne, engaged in ceaseless worship of God and the Lamb (Rev 7:9-17). In chapter 5, that worship includes not only redeemed humanity, but "every creature in heaven and on earth and under the earth and in the sea, and all that is in them" (Rev 5:13). Our worship is caught up into something far bigger—God's purpose that the whole created order might unite to bring him glory and praise.

We see the goal of God's mission most vividly in John's dazzling vision of the new creation (chapters 21 and 22). There the river of the water of life flows freely, and the tree of life flourishes with leaves that heal the nations (Rev 22:1-2). Immediately John adds: "The throne of God and of the Lamb will be in it [the city], *and his servants will worship him*" (Rev 22:3 italics added). Revelation imagines new Jerusalem worship as the deepest flourishing of people created in the image of God, the joyful fulfillment of our human potential. Apart from an intimate relationship with God that leads to loving worship, we settle for something less than humanity in its fullness.

---

[30]Allan A. Boesak, *Comfort and Protest: The Apocalypse from a South African Perspective* (Philadelphia: Westminster, 1987), 60-61.

[31]See Michael-Ray Matthews, "Will You Be Chaplain to the Empire or Prophet of the Resistance?," *Sojourners*, February 17, 2017, https://sojo.net/articles/faith-action/will-you-be-chaplain -empire-or-prophet-resistance.

*"We are most fully ourselves as human beings when we are
in relationship with God in which God is glorified in and
through our enjoyment of that relationship. That is why
the biblical pictures of life in the new creation can combine
so seamlessly descriptions of human life in its richest
perfection and the worship of God in all his splendor,
for each will be part of the substance of the other
(Is 65:17-25; Rev 21-22)."*[32]

CHRISTOPHER WRIGHT

If this is God's ultimate purpose for humanity and all creation, then surely that should reinforce our calling as God's people to bring others from every nation into a relationship of love, trust, and worship of the God who created them.[33] Humanity will not discover fruitful life and true joy through technology, wealth, science, sports, sex, celebrity, power, or politics. It comes only by engaging in loving service and worship of God and the Lamb as part of a faithful community of worship. That reality shapes our mission in the world. This leads to our final observation about worship and mission in Revelation.

WORSHIP INVITES

Not only does worship unveil the goal of God's mission; it also becomes an *instrument* by which that purpose is accomplished. John extends the call to worship not only to the church but also to the unbelieving world. Repeatedly, Revelation pictures the world's nations worshiping and giving glory to God, or it invites them to do so (Rev 11:13; 14:7; 15:3-4; 21:24-25). Chapter 14 broadcasts this appeal on a wide-vision screen. Sandwiched between parallel visions of people worshiping the beast (Rev 13:1-18; 14:9-11), the redeemed of humanity stand on Mount Zion and thunder their praise to God

---

[32]Christopher J. H. Wright, *The Mission of God's People: A Biblical Theology of the Church's Mission* (Grand Rapids, MI: Zondervan, 2010), 244.
[33]See Wright, *Mission of God's People*, 245.

(Rev 14:1-5). At once, an angel begins cruising the heavens and proclaims the gospel to those who live on earth. His message calls them to "fear God and give him glory" and to worship the Maker of heaven and earth (Rev 14:6-7). Although those who currently worship the beast have not yet repented and switched camps, they are invited to join the throng of worshipers that surround God's throne (Rev 4:11; 5:11-14; 7:9-12).

Later the victorious church sings beside the glassy sea, accompanied by a stringed ensemble. The lyrics include: "For you alone are holy. All nations will come and worship before you" (Rev 15:4). This represents more than the church's hopes for the future. The church's worship leans out toward the world and invites outsiders to pick up their harp and join the Lamb's worship band. Michael Gorman puts it well: "As a call to join the ongoing heavenly worship of God, Revelation is simultaneously a presentation of the divine drama that is celebrated in worship, and therefore also a summons to enter the story and mission of God."[34] Revelation is missional to the core.

Praise, then, becomes an act of witness. Revelation's heavenly worship is anything but otherworldly. As Joseph Mangina insists, to the extent that Christian congregations worship the one God on the throne and sing the praises of the slaughtered Lamb, they participate in that heavenly worship.[35] As they do, they bear witness to God's missional purpose for all people. They publicly embody a preview of the new creation, in which every creature in the universe will fall prostrate in worship of God. It's as though their worship songs carry the subtitle, "Come and worship! Join the choir, both now and into the future!" This is not unlike Peter's picture of God's people declaring God's "mighty acts," at least, in part, through their public worship (1 Pet 2:9). Christopher Wright points out that "such declarative praise is not a private affair between God and the worshipers, but it spills out into the public arena as one of the means by which God draws the nations to himself."[36]

Finally, the worship scenes and songs of Revelation not only call outsiders into the sphere of worship; they also energize the church for a mission to all

---

[34]Gorman, *Reading Revelation*, 37.

[35]Joseph L. Mangina, "God, Israel, and Ecclesia in the Apocalypse," in Hays and Alkier, *Revelation and the Politics of Apocalyptic Interpretation*, 94.

[36]Wright, *Mission of God's People*, 250.

nations. When the worshipers encircling God's throne sing, "You are worthy . . . for you were slaughtered and by your blood you ransomed for God saints from every tribe and language and people and nation" (Rev 5:9); when a multitude from every tribe and tongue cries out, "Salvation belongs to our God" (Rev 7:9-10); when John pictures vast numbers of the earth's inhabitants giving glory to the God of heaven (Rev 11:13), such visions post an agenda for the church in mission. We cannot celebrate the Lamb's death for the sake of the nations without offering our lives as God's instruments to see that happen. We sing the world that God desires; we serve the world that God redeemed. Worship is married to witness. Praise participates in God's purpose to redeem all nations and to make everything new.

CONCLUSION

Christians sometimes drive a wedge between worship and mission. Worship, it is assumed, is something we do *within* the church, whereas mission happens *outside* the church. The Revelator knows better. John draws us into *missional worship*. In this chapter, we have seen that missional worship

- publicly announces God's loving purpose to redeem and restore all of creation to what God intends it to be through the shed blood of the Lamb. It trumpets that God's people are caught up in that mission as a kingdom and priests on behalf of the world God has made.

- empowers us to reimagine our world in light of God's future. In a broken and shattered world, God's people can celebrate in advance God's final victory over all the powers that "destroy the earth" (Rev 11:18).

- proclaims to the world that God is on the throne of the universe and the idols and ideologies of our various cultures are not. In worship, we "pledge our allegiance" to the one Lord who reigns supreme.

- articulates and energizes our righteous resistance to the narratives, powers, and practices of "the kingdom of this world" (Rev 11:15).

- reveals the goal of God's mission, that people of every nation might flourish in a relationship of love, trust, and worship of the triune God.

- declares God's mercy and power to unbelievers who are "listening in," inviting people of all nations to join the worship of almighty God.

- equips us to engage in a life of worship that offers the world a foretaste of God's coming kingdom. It calls us to bear witness to God's desire for all people to worship him with our words and with our lives.

Revelation's worship invites us not only to adopt its transformed vision of the world but to *embody* that vision—in our own worship gatherings and our daily interactions, in a "day and night" worship that embraces all of life (Rev 7:15).

I recently shared in a memorable worship gathering in which representatives of a dozen or so different nations and cultures sang a text from Revelation 5, declaring, "Worthy is the Lamb who was slain!" As each person or group came to the microphone and sang the same melody and lyrics in their distinctive languages, I caught a glimpse of the vast chorus of worshipers from all peoples and languages in Revelation 7. I joined in the celebration of the Lamb whose blood has purchased that global gospel choir. I begged God to help the church to live out that vision in ways that display the gospel's power to reconcile people and to break down barriers. I also prayed, "God, forgive us," for so often failing to reflect that vision in the ways that we treat and think about people who are different from us.

To participate in the *missio Dei* means that our cries of "Hallelujah" must lead to pleas of "Lord, have mercy," until, in its fullness, God's kingdom comes and God's will is done "on earth as it is in heaven."

CHAPTER EIGHT

MISSIONAL POLITICS

Alas, alas, the great city,
Babylon, the mighty city!
For in one hour your judgment has come.

REVELATION 18:10

I GREW UP LARGELY IN CHRISTIAN CIRCLES that didn't trust mixing religion and politics. We lived our lives on the spiritual side of life. Let others, like the elected officials, worry about the political sphere. Our main goal was to get to heaven and take some other souls with us along the way. Effectively, we surrendered the world of politics, society, economics, and culture to the worldly powers in favor of a pious, privatized faith.

What we failed to grasp was the profoundly *political* nature of the gospel. I'm not talking about *partisan* politics. The gospel is political because politics relates to how we organize our public life together. It concerns who or what has power over peoples' lives and how that power is used. Eugene Peterson reminds us that the very language of the "kingdom of God" that Jesus preached is "an altogether political metaphor" that "insists on a gospel that includes everything and everyone under the rule of God."[1] Years ago, when I began teaching ministry students in the Philippines, I was forced to

---

[1]Eugene H. Peterson, *Reversed Thunder: The Revelation of John and the Praying Imagination* (San Francisco: HarperSanFrancisco, 1988), 117.

rethink what the "good news" meant for issues like poverty, exploitation, and economic injustice. I came to see that if Jesus is Lord of *all* of life, not simply our private, spiritual lives, then we cannot avoid politics. A gospel without a public, political dimension makes about as much sense as an ocean without water!

No New Testament writer understood this better than John. In a world in which the lordship of Jesus over all of life was constantly under assault by the claims of other gods and lords, John didn't have the option of separating the spiritual from the political realm. Instead, he spotlights the fundamental difference between the politics of the Lamb and the politics of Rome. A key strategy for doing so involves deploying symbols that put the true nature of satanic politics on display, symbols that force his readers, then and now, to reimagine their world. This chapter will focus on two of John's bigger-than-life images, the symbols of *the beast* and *Babylon*. Revelation's "killer Bs."

But can politics be *missional*, as the chapter title suggests? Absolutely. God's mission seeks to establish his loving rule over every dimension of human life, including our public life in the world. Since Jesus is already Lord, those who follow the Lamb need to learn what it means to worship and testify to him in the face of other competing lords.[2] You'll find that this chapter reinforces some themes we encountered in chapter seven, since, as we saw there, worship is inherently political. Let us then explore Revelation's missional politics through the images of Babylon and the beast.

WHO IS LIKE THE BEAST?

As Revelation 13 opens, John sees "a beast rising out of the sea" (Rev 13:1). Perhaps no biblical symbol has sparked such intense efforts to decipher its "code." These speculations often equate Revelation's beast from the sea with the antichrist. Popular dispensationalism typically identifies this figure with an evil individual, like Nicolas Carpathian in the Left Behind novels, who will mastermind a satanic one-world government. But *the term* antichrist *never appears in Revelation*. Indeed, the biblical language of *antichrist* only

---

[2]N. T. Wright, "Revelation and Christian Hope: Political Implications of the Revelation to John," in *Revelation and the Politics of Apocalyptic Interpretation*, ed. Richard B. Hays and Stefan Alkier (Waco, TX: Baylor University Press, 2012), 106.

surfaces in John's letters, and there it refers, collectively, to false teachers within the church (1 Jn 2:18, 22; 4:3; 2 Jn 1:7). 1 John warns that "many antichrists have come" (1 Jn 2:18). Frequent attempts to connect the antichrist with the number 666, "the mark of the beast" (Rev 13:18), have only stoked the fires of speculation. Harry Maier quips that generations of Christians have "done the math and made their own nomination for the award of 'best hated.'"[3] The long list of public figures who have been called the antichrist includes various popes, Muhammad, Napoleon, Hitler, Stalin, Ronald Reagan, Saddam Hussein, Barack Obama, and Donald Trump. I once heard a well-known Bible scholar say with a twinkle in his eye, "If your favorite antichrist has died, don't worry. Another one will surely come along!"

Speculating on the antichrist's identity is not my concern in this chapter. I'm much more interested in what a missional reading of Revelation 13 reveals about "the *nature* of the beast." Recalling Daniel's terrifying vision of multiple beasts (Dan 7:3-7), the beast from the sea represents the powers of evil that stand opposed to God and God's mission in the world. John envisions the beast as an avatar of the dragon, Satan. Both have ten horns and seven heads, and Satan gives the beast his own throne of authority. But the beast "wears ten kingly crowns—even more than the dragon's seven (Rev 12:3; 13:1). If anything, the beast is more power hungry than its master."[4]

In Revelation, however, this symbol also carries a concrete political dimension. Christians in Asia Minor would have had little trouble identifying the beast from the sea with the awesome political, military, economic, and religious power of Rome, embodied in the emperor himself.[5] Later, John connects the dots even more clearly when he interprets the seven heads of the beast as the seven hills of Rome and seven emperors (Rev 17:9). For John, the empire demands total loyalty and worship (Rev 13:4). This beast may not be "the antichrist" in the popular sense, but it is certainly *anti-Christ.* The

---

[3]See Harry O. Maier, "A First-World Reading of Revelation Among Immigrants," in *From Every People and Nation: The Book of Revelation in Intercultural Perspective*, ed. David Rhoads (Minneapolis: Fortress, 2005), 62.

[4]Dean Flemming, "Revelation," in *Wesley One Volume Commentary*, ed. Kenneth J. Collins and Robert W. Wall (Nashville, TN: Abingdon, 2020), 923.

[5]"The sea" (Rev 13:1) not only symbolizes chaos and disorder in the Bible, but here it probably alludes to Rome as an outside power that crossed the Aegean Sea to reach Asia Minor.

Figure 8.1. Tapestry of the dragon giving a scepter to the beast from the sea (Rev 13:2-4) from *The Apocalypse of Angers*, 1375–1380

beast and the satanic empire it symbolizes oppose Christ and everything God is doing to bring redemption to the world.

John exposes the bankrupt politics of the empire by describing the beast as a parody of the Lamb:[6]

- Even as God shares his throne, power, and authority with the Lamb (Rev 3:21; 5:6, 12; 12:10), so the dragon gives its authority to the beast (Rev 13:2, 4).

- As the Lamb liberates a kingdom made up of followers from every tribe and tongue (Rev 5:9-10), so the beast rules over "every tribe and people and language and nation" (Rev 13:7).

- Like the Lamb, the beast was "slaughtered" (Rev 5:6, 9, 12; 13:3). But like the *risen* Jesus, the beast is now alive, because its mortal wound has been healed (Rev 13:3, 12, 14).

---

[6]See Flemming, "Revelation," 923.

John's audience couldn't miss the point. The beast is a crass counterfeit, a cheap imitation of the real thing. This in-your-face parody calls the question for the Christians in Asia. John asks, in effect, where do *your* loyalties lie? Will you join all creation in adoring God and the Lamb (Rev 5:13-14)? Or will you throw in your lot with "the whole earth" in following Satan and the beast (Rev 13:3, 4, 8)? Perhaps Revelation asks *us* the same questions today.

THE DEPARTMENT OF PROPAGANDA

The parody continues with a second beast, this one rising from the earth (Rev 13:11). Like the first beast, the beast from the land tries in vain to mimic Jesus. It has "two horns *like a lamb.*" But it's a fake lamb that speaks "like a dragon" (Rev 13:11)—a dragon in sheep's clothing. Along with the dragon and the beast from the land, the second beast rounds out a kind of demonic trinity.

The beast from the earth has one job: to promote the worship of the first beast. For the churches in Asia, the land beast likely recalled the various local institutions and groups that promoted emperor worship, including temple priests, local politicians, and provincial councils. As we saw in chapter 1, cities like Ephesus and Pergamum tried to "out-Rome" Rome in their devotion to the emperor cult.

In effect, notes Simon Woodman, the beast from the earth acts as the propaganda machine of the empire.[7] Like all agents of propaganda, its MO is deception. The second beast dupes the crowd by performing miraculous signs, similar to the ministry of the two witnesses in chapter 11 (Rev 13:13-14; 11:5-6). Unlike those faithful prophets, however, Revelation brands the land beast as a "false prophet" (Rev 16:13; 19:20; 20:10), whose mighty deeds amount to no more than smoke and mirrors. Like a circus huckster, it gives breath to the image of its master, the first beast, so that the idol "could even speak" (Rev 13:15). The false prophet's propaganda campaign only exposes his clumsy attempt to imitate God's power to breathe life into humans (Gen 2:7; Rev 11:11). Such propaganda has always been the stock and trade of beastly politics, whether Rome's promises of security and salvation or Hitler's monumental deception of "good" German citizens or today's

---

[7]Simon Woodman, *The Book of Revelation* (London: SCM, 2008), 169.

politicians who play fast and loose with the truth to promote their own image and political fortunes.

NAMING THE BEAST

Chapter 13 closes by linking the mark of the beast with its name and with its number, 666 (Rev 13:17-18). The meaning of this number, whom it might signify, and what form its mark might take have inspired a cottage industry of apocalyptic speculation. Conspiracy theories of microchip implants or beastly barcodes using the number 666 only distract from the power of John's symbolism. At its most basic level, 666 represents *imperfection*. It falls pathetically short of 7, the number of completion and fullness in Revelation. Triple six announces the beast's "triple failure" in its pretense to be like God.[8]

Figure 8.2. *The Number of the Beast Is 666* (Rev 13:18) by William Blake, c. 1805

At the same time, John invites his audience to "calculate the number of the beast," which he identifies with a person (Rev 13:18). For the Christians in Asia, the Roman emperor Nero represented the prime suspect. According to the ancient practice of adding up the numerical value assigned to letters in the alphabet, the name "Nero Caesar" totals 666, when written in Hebrew letters. Moreover, Nero fits the beast's profile in other ways. Nero was infamous as a persecutor of Christians (Rev 13:7; 17:6), and, like the beast's slaughtered head that bounced back to life, a popular legend had Nero returning from

[8]Peterson, *Reversed Thunder*, 126.

the dead to reclaim his throne. But this doesn't limit the significance of the beast to Nero or to the empire he represents. This beast rears its demonic heads wherever governments, political powers, or individuals oppose the lordship of Christ over all things and demand an allegiance that God alone deserves.

THE POLITICS OF THE BEAST TODAY

John, then, uses symbolism and scalding parody to confront his readers with a different way of seeing the world than the politics-as-usual of the empire. He urges them to model a counterpolitics to the prevailing political stories of their culture. How does this speak to the church in mission today? Let me suggest three ways that it might:

Civil religion. John closely links the beast to the state-sponsored idolatry of the empire. The beast is the focus of universal worship (Rev 13:4). The blasphemous names it wears on its heads recall titles given to emperors, like "lord," "god," "son of God" or "savior" (Rev 13:1, 5-6; 17:3). In John's world, piety and politics were hopelessly entangled in the form of the emperor cult and the worship of local gods that sustained the empire.

But this isn't simply ancient history. A "God-and-country" ideology is alive and well in the twenty-first century. I see it particularly in my own American context, not least in many American churches.[9] Civil religion gives "sacred status to secular power (normally the state and/or its head) as the source of divine blessing, requiring devotion and allegiance of heart, mind, and body to the sacred-secular power and its values."[10] A complex of myths, narratives, rituals, and media serve to reinforce such values. American Christians regularly embrace such myths (America as a *Christian nation*) and practice such rituals. Patriotism becomes synonymous with godliness. Patriotic services celebrating national holidays sometimes resemble political pep rallies. I recall attending a worship service on an Independence Day weekend in which, as the congregation

---

[9]See the excellent treatment of American civil religion in Michael J. Gorman's *Reading Revelation Responsibly: Uncivil Worship and Witness: Following the Lamb into the New Creation* (Eugene, OR: Cascade, 2011), 48-54. See also Gregory A. Boyd, *The Myth of a Christian Nation: How the Quest for Political Power Is Destroying the Church* (Grand Rapids, MI: Zondervan, 2005).

[10]Gorman, *Reading Revelation*, 46.

lifted a patriotic song, a massive digital image of the American flag was superimposed over a standing cross. One writer keenly observes that although "no Western nation has outright ruler worship today, we do have political, military, and economic powers to which millions give unquestioned allegiance."[11]

Civil religion often involves *nationalism*, an extreme devotion to one's nation, which exalts it as being superior to all other nations. "This devotion," remarks Michael Gorman, "is often based on the conviction that the nation is chosen, blessed, and commissioned by God, its power and wealth being signs of God's approval."[12] Naturally, it follows that other peoples and nations are *not* favored and blessed by God in the same way, which flies in the face of John's vision of a multinational throng of worshipers around God's throne (Rev 7:9-10). In its nationalistic form, civil religion regularly confuses the power and mission of a nation (America as "the greatest nation on earth," destined to transform the world) with the glory and mission of God.

How should we respond to the potent pull of civil religion? First, we need the courage and humility to call out civil religion for what it is: a form of *idolatry*. In the context of widely held national myths and narratives, American Christianity seems particularly vulnerable to "worshiping the beast" by confusing allegiance to country with allegiance to God, by mistaking support of a political party for loyalty to the slaughtered Lamb. No less than in John's time, Revelation urges us to break up with the god of nationalism and to abandon the idolatry of civil religion.

Second, we must humbly seek the Spirit's discernment in these matters. The line between patriotism and idolatrous nationalism isn't always easy to draw, especially when Christian Americanism seems *normal*. Gorman makes an important observation about the difference between civil religion today and that of John's world. For Christians in Asia Minor, civil religion combined Roman ideology and *pagan* religiosity. For Christians in the United States, civil religion blends American ideology with a form of

---

[11]J. Nelson Kraybill, *Apocalypse and Allegiance: Worship, Politics, and Devotion in the Book of Revelation* (Grand Rapids, MI: Brazos, 2010), 15.

[12]Gorman, *Reading Revelation*, 49.

Christian spirituality. This makes American civil religion all the more seductive and worship of the beast even harder to resist.[13]

In recent years, nationalism, in its various forms, undoubtedly has ascended in its profile throughout the world. It will likely prove to be increasingly costly to swim against the stream of civil religion not only in relation to society at large but also the church itself. Local congregations must courageously discover how to offer an alternative vision of their public life together. That may involve prayerful conversations about whether to continue patriotic worship services around national holidays or, as with one Christian community I know, about whether it remains appropriate to display a national flag at the front of the sanctuary next to the cross. These are not simply harmless cultural matters. They communicate to people where our identities and allegiances lie.

Lamb power, not beast power. John's use of parody in chapter 13 draws a stark contrast between two kinds of politics and two kinds of power. We might call them *beast power* and *Lamb power.*[14] Beast power achieves its aims through arrogance, lies, and domination. Lamb power displays humility, truth, and self-giving love. In John's world, beast power, the control of the mighty empire, seemed unbeatable: "Who is like the beast, and who can fight against it?" (Rev 13:4).

The church in every generation and culture is tempted to achieve its aims by the normal political means, that is, beast power. This happens, for example, when we try to push our agenda on the society as a whole through coercion ("Let's take America back for God"). Such methods sabotage the gospel of the crucified Lamb. We simply cannot engage in God's mission in the public square with merely human methods. Instead, we are called to embody *Lamb power.* Lamb power is prophetic, not passive. It's vulnerable. Sacrificial. Counterintuitive. *How* we publicly engage our culture and its politics must be consistent with the gospel we profess.

Are rulers "God's servants"? While preaching recently, a pastor I know mentioned a particularly egregious example of a political leader demonstrating, in word and deed, the dehumanizing values of the beast, rather than

---

[13]Gorman, *Reading Revelation*, 54.
[14]I owe the term *Lamb power* to Michael Gorman, *Reading Revelation*, e.g., 43.

those of God's kingdom. Almost immediately, he faced a flurry of criticism from some parishioners for being too political, for embracing a position they did not agree with, or for failing to support the government. This brings up an important question. How does Revelation's call to resist the beastly powers that be square with other New Testament perspectives that seem to support the political status quo? How do we reconcile Revelation 13 with Paul's teaching in Romans 13 that Roman political authorities are "instituted by God" (Rom 13:1) and act as "God's servants" for the church's good (Rom 13:4, 6; cf. 1 Pet 2:13)? Some Christians take such statements as the final and *only* word the Bible speaks on Christians' relationship to the state. Yet the same texts have been obscenely misused, for example, to rationalize the return of fugitive slaves in America or to justify Christians' support of Hitler's fascist regime in Germany.

The tension between Romans 13 and Revelation 13 reveals a classic example of the New Testament writers "contextualizing" the gospel.[15] Paul's attitude toward the governing authorities in Romans 13 assumes a kind of best-case scenario, when human rulers fulfill their God-ordained role of serving their citizens and executing justice in a generally responsible way. Further, Paul apparently is concerned that if the Roman Christians engage in antisocial behavior or refuse to pay taxes, they would bring reproach on the church and smear its public witness.[16] In other words, such disobedience could jeopardize the mission of this already marginalized Christian community in Rome.

Revelation 13 assumes a profoundly different situation, in which obedience to Christ sets Christians on a collision course with an idolatrous empire that has hijacked the authority that belongs to God alone. Given that John sees the beast's authority coming from Satan, not from God (Rev 13:2, 4), submission to the governing powers isn't an option. Romans 13, therefore, can in no way justify blind loyalty to a nation-state or any other political figure or entity. Recall that when Peter and the apostles were commanded to stop speaking the name of Jesus, they boldly announced, "We must obey God rather than any human authority" (Acts 5:29).

---

[15]See Dean Flemming, *Contextualization in the New Testament: Patterns for Theology and Mission* (Downers Grove, IL: IVP Academic, 2005), 288-91.
[16]Flemming, *Contextualization*, 289.

"Because governmental authority should be a servant of God for the good of God's people, it is inconceivable that a government can use the sword not to establish justice but to maintain injustice; not to secure liberation but to maintain slavery; not to break down but to maintain structures of oppression and inhumanity—and still be an agent of God. . . . When government no longer distinguishes between good and evil, between what is humanizing and what is not, it is no longer the servant of God but the beast from the sea."[17]

ALLAN BOESAK

Revelation 13 affirms that at times, a faithful response to human powers that act like the beast will be Lamblike resistance. What form that resistance takes will depend on the context, but it will never be cost free. When Christians like Dietrich Bonhoeffer, Martin Luther King Jr., and multitudes of persecuted Christ-followers throughout the world have chosen that courageous path, they have suffered the wrath of the beast. For others, resisting the beast may result in social exclusion or personal criticism. Commentator Mitchell Reddish reflects wisely on the biblical tension regarding our relationship to political powers:

> Between Romans 13 and Revelation 13, where does the modern Christian stand? Is submission to the state or civil disobedience the path which the follower of Christ should walk? In truth, at different times both responses may be appropriate. When the state works for peace, justice, equality, and the dignity of all humanity (including citizens of other countries), the state deserves our support. On the other hand, when the state becomes an instrument of oppression, greed, or injustice—when it confuses its role with that of God and demands ultimate allegiance or when it demands from its citizens

---

[17] Allan Boesak, *Comfort and Protest: The Apocalypse from a South African Perspective* (Philadelphia: Westminster: 1987), 99.

actions that are immoral or idolatrous—the state needs to be challenged and even opposed.[18]

Faithfulness to God's mission will at times place us at odds with politics-as-usual. Instead, Revelation 13 calls us to embrace a *theo-politics* (politics involving God) that "creates a public life together . . . that is an alternative to the status quo in the Roman Empire, the American empire, or any other body politic."[19]

BABYLON THE PROSTITUTE: REVELATION 17

A second key symbol unveils Revelation's missional politics: "Babylon the great" (Rev 17:5), pictured as both a woman and a city in chapters 17 and 18. Popular dispensationalist interpretation often reads "Babylon" as a code for a future worldwide religious system and government, headquartered in a literal, rebuilt city of Babylon in Iraq.[20] But that history-in-advance approach cuts the cord between this symbol and the theological and political realities of John's world. Once again, John uses a symbol, Babylon, to equip his audience to reimagine the way things are in their world.[21]

In chapter 17, "the great whore" (Rev 17:1, 4) dominates the stage. Eugene Peterson relates that the novelist Flannery O'Connor once was asked why she created such bizarre characters for her stories. She responded that "for the near-blind you have to draw very large, simple caricatures."[22] The whore Babylon represents such a large, unforgettable caricature. John makes no secret about her identity for the churches in Asia. Far from a code to be cracked by twenty-first-century bloggers, John's portrayal of Babylon fits Rome like a tailored suit. The empire was famous for its command of the seas ("many waters" Rev 17:1), its worship of emperors and the gods that stood behind them ("blasphemous names" Rev 17:3), and for flaunting its wealth and luxury (Rev 17:4). The harlot sits on "seven mountains"

---

[18]Mitchell G. Reddish, *Revelation* (Macon, GA: Smyth and Helwys, 2001), 267.

[19]Michael J. Gorman, *Reading Paul* (Eugene, OR: Cascade, 2008), 45.

[20]E.g., Tim LaHaye, *Revelation Unveiled* (Grand Rapids, MI: Zondervan, 1999), 260-85.

[21]The rest of this chapter draws extensively from Dean Flemming, "Locating and Leaving Babylon: A Missional Reading of Revelation 17 and 18 in Light of Ancient and Contemporary Political Contexts," *Missiology* 48 (2020): 112-26. Used with permission.

[22]Peterson, *Reversed Thunder*, 146.

Figure 8.3. Harlot of Babylon (Rev 17:1-8) from the Polyptych of the Apocalypse, 1360–1390

(Rev 17:9)—a clear allusion to Rome, traditionally the city set on seven hills. What's more, "the great city that rules over the kings of the earth" (Rev 17:18) points directly to the sole superpower in John's world.

John's picture of the prostitute demands an "imagination switch" from his audience. Rome is pictured as a woman. But she is *not* the goddess Roma, the mother figure who embodied Rome's might and dignity, who was worshiped in the temples of Asia, and whose image graced Roman coins. Creating a stinging parody of "mother Rome," John unmasks her as the "mother of whores" (Rev 17:5). She reeks of abominations from the immorality of her idolatrous worship. Flaunting her fancy clothes and flashy jewelry, Babylon is "dressed to kill."[23] She's besotted with the blood of the saints (Rev 17:4, 6). John announces, in effect, "This is the *true* picture of the great and glorious empire—a debauched whore, a cruel and violent murderer." As Craig Koester grasps, the image is utterly disgusting, and that is precisely John's strategy.[24] By co-opting and reworking a familiar symbol *from* his world, John asks his readers to *see* their world from a new end-time perspective.

At the same time, John positively shapes his readers' imaginations by providing alternate feminine symbols.[25] Babylon "the great whore," decked

---

[23]Craig S. Keener, *Revelation*, (Grand Rapids, MI: Zondervan, 2000), 406.

[24]Craig R. Koester, "Revelation's Visionary Challenge to Ordinary Empire," *Interpretation* 63 (2009): 17.

[25]See Craig R. Koester, *Revelation: A New Translation with Introduction and Commentary* (New Haven, CN: Yale University Press, 2014), 682-83. We must take seriously the feminist critique that Revelation uses feminine stereotypes, such as the whore, and more disturbingly portrays

Figure 8.4. Coin of emperor Nero (54–68) and the goddess Roma holding the image of Victory

out in her seductive luxury, stands in bold contrast both to the woman radiantly clothed with the sun (Rev 12:1-6) and the church as the virgin bride of the Lamb, adorned with righteous deeds (Rev 19:8; 21:2, 9).

BABYLON THE ECONOMIC EXPLOITER: REVELATION 18

In chapter 18, Babylon particularly represents Rome's wealth and prosperity, gained by exploiting the empire. Rome dominated "the kings of the earth" (Rev 17:18), not just politically, but also economically. Chapter 18 spotlights the economic networks that benefit the power brokers. The "kings" and "merchants of the earth" (Rev 18:9, 11) mourn their lost profits due to Babylon's abrupt fall. John's blistering critique of Babylon exposes Rome's thirst for luxury and obscene consumption, quenched at the expense of others (Rev 18:3, 7). The long list of cargo in Rev 18:11-13 reflects actual Roman imports, most of them aimed at satisfying the expensive tastes of the rich.[26]

---

graphic violence against this female image (Rev 17:16). See, e.g., Tina Pippin, *Death and Desire: The Rhetoric of Gender in the Apocalypse of John* (Louisville, KY: Westminster/John Knox, 1992), 65-68; Susan R. Garrett, "Revelation," *The Woman's Bible Commentary* (Louisville, KY: Westminster/John Knox, 1992), 381. Such images do not legitimate violence against women in any form. It is vital to see John's symbol of the whore/Babylon in the context of the ancient world, where it was common to represent cities with female images. In Revelation, this symbol functions both as a parody of the goddess Roma, who symbolizes Rome, and the antithesis of the Lamb's bride. The brutality against the whore in Rev 17:16 thus serves as a shocking warning "that the city that thrives on the violence its rulers use against others will finally fall victim to these same destructive practices." Koester, *Revelation*, 694.

[26]See Koester, *Revelation*, 702-5.

The last and least valuable item on the list is "slaves—and human lives" (literally, "bodies and human souls"). Rome gets rich by enslaving *human souls*, by treating persons as commodities. An estimated 10 million slaves populated the Roman Empire in the first century, many of them mined from Asia Minor.[27] John understands that Rome's consumption relies on the trafficking of human lives. Babylon's judgment shows that God refuses to turn away from economic oppression and injustice.

The language in chapter 18 draws heavily from the Old Testament prophets, especially their critiques of Tyre, the maritime power (Is 23; Ezek 27, 28), and ancient Babylon itself (Jer 52:24-58; Hab 2:4-13). Echoing Isaiah 47:7-9, John lambasts Rome's arrogance: "In her heart she says, 'I rule as a queen; I am no widow, and I will never see grief'" (Rev 18:7).

John also apparently confronts popular Roman myths. Notably, the *Pax Romana* (Roman Peace) uplifted Rome as the gracious benefactor of peace, order, and security for the empire. For John, however, those who consort with the harlot Babylon pay a steep price for the privilege. The empire delivers "peace" at the cost of tyranny and violence, the spear and the cross. John unmasks Babylon's taste for blood: "And in you was found the blood of prophets and of saints, and of all who have been slaughtered on earth" (Rev 18:24; cf. Rev 17:6). It's striking that John calls out Rome's violence not only against Christians but *all* people, whatever their religious commitments.

John, then, draws from a quiver full of cultural and traditional resources—popular symbols and myths, contrasting images, Scripture, and parody, among them—to give Christians an alternative vision of the world. He seizes the language and popular ideals of Rome precisely to subvert them. Readers must choose between the "gospel" of Caesar and the good news of the Lamb.

BABYLON TODAY

Although Babylon represented Rome and its corrupting influence on the empire for Christians in Asia, its meaning refuses to stay frozen in the past. Babylon is a *symbol*, not a code, and symbols offer different levels of meaning. John's portrait of Babylon recalls Old Testament forerunners, cities like

---

[27]Ryan L. Hansen, *Silence and Praise: Rhetorical Cosmology and Political Theology in the Book of Revelation* (Minneapolis: Fortress, 2014), 151.

Babel, Sodom, Tyre, and not least, ancient Babylon itself. For John, Rome may be the *current* embodiment of Babylon, but it's by no means the first or the last. Babylon and its sins address ultimate issues, which transcend ancient Rome. A versatile actor, Babylon is capable of playing multiple roles, wearing different costumes.

A missional reading of Revelation not only asks how a symbol like Babylon sought to reshape the imagination and practice of churches then but also how it might continue to do so in the present. We can't dodge the question: Where is Babylon *today*?

> *"I am concerned that the Babylon of the Apocalypse does not apply to Rome exclusively; but to the union of Religion with Power and Wealth, whereof it is found."*[28]
>
> SAMUEL TAYLOR COLERIDGE, 1797

BABYLON'S PORTRAIT

How might a missional reading of Revelation help contemporary Christians discern the presence and power of Babylon? On the one hand, we must not launch too quickly into drawing parallels between John's world and today's postcolonial context.[29] For example, Revelation simply doesn't imagine the possibility of transformation taking place through established political structures, such as the legislative changes that resulted from the costly actions of American civil rights marchers in the 1960s. On the other hand, we must follow John's lead in recognizing Babylon in our midst. As Onesimus Ngundu observes, "Babylon exists wherever there is idolatry, prostitution, self-glorification, self-sufficiency, pride and complacency, reliance on luxury and wealth, and violence against life."[30] A great deal could be said about

---

[28]Samuel Taylor Coleridge, *Poems*, ed. John Beer, 3rd ed. (London: Dent, 1993), 89, cited in Judith Kovacs and Christopher Rowland, *Revelation* (Oxford: Blackwell, 2004), 186.
[29]See the cautions by Wright, "Revelation and Christian Hope," 118-19; Richard Bauckham, *The Theology of the Book of Revelation* (Cambridge: Cambridge University Press, 1993), 163.
[30]Onesimus Ngundu, "Revelation," in *Africa Bible Commentary*, ed. Tokunboh Adeyemo (Grand Rapids, MI: Zondervan, 2006), 1572.

how Babylon flexes its muscles in a variety of global settings today. I will focus, however, on four areas in which Babylon's costume might fit the current American political and cultural setting in which I now live.

1. *Economic exploitation.* If Babylon symbolizes Rome's lust for luxury and its exploitive economic practices for John's first audience, it isn't hard to find the harlot's imprint on the consumer-driven economies of the world's richest nations today. The pursuit of wealth, luxury, and dominance of the world marketplace frequently leads to policies and practices that help create a world of "haves" and "have-nots," in which wealthy nations enjoy a standard of living vastly greater than the majority of the human population and consume most of the world's resources.

But at what price? Mitchell Reddish notes that multinational corporations, the new "merchants" and "magnates of the earth" (Rev 18:23) often are driven to boost profits by building factories in Majority World (non-Western) countries, employing cheap labor, accepting inadequate health and safety standards, and wreaking havoc on the environment. "Too often," he insists, "the controlling criterion in world economic matters is not what is best for all the people of the world, and certainly not what is best for the poor and disenfranchised, but what is best for the few who already possess and control the most."[31] When this happens, the frenetic "mission" to accumulate and spend wealth becomes an idolatrous power. John leaves no doubt that Babylon's consumer excesses will be *consumed* by God's judgment fire in the end (Rev 18:8-10).

2. *Arrogance.* Repeatedly, Revelation refers to Babylon as the "great city" (Rev 16:19; 17:18; 18:10, 16, 18, 19, 21), "the great Babylon" (Rev 16:19), or "Babylon the Great" (Rev 17:5). Such language plays on Rome/Babylon's hyperinflated self-image ("I rule as a queen," Rev 18:7). Popular myths extolled the imperial period as the long-awaited golden age, the fulfillment of humanity's hopes, eternal in its reign.[32] Nations throughout the world today cling to exalted visions of their own importance. The United States seems especially vulnerable to such pride. Historically, visions of being "the greatest country on earth" or a "light to the nations" have sprung from

---

[31]Reddish, *Revelation*, 351.
[32]Gorman, *Reading Revelation*, 42.

myths of American exceptionalism and divine election. In this generation, promises of a return to "America the Great" echo through the halls of government. "Greatness" is often defined in terms of political might, military supremacy, economic prosperity, individual rights and freedom, and nostalgia for a time when White churchgoing Americans held the keys to power. Sadly, multitudes of American Christians seem to have embraced that longing.

Rome's greatness was communicated to the masses through a variety of media, including coins, public inscriptions, monuments, statues, hymns and poetry, processions, and standards carried by soldiers.[33] Modern forms of media fulfill a comparable role, whether by cable news stations, partisan podcasts, or popular Facebook feeds.

3. Violence. I noted earlier that Rome maintained "peace" (the *Pax Romana*) ironically, through a pattern of sacred violence, which was supported by the gods (see Rev 17:6; 18:24). Today violence remains the preferred method of ensuring stability and order in many regimes throughout the world. The United States cannot plead innocence. "Divinely-approved" violence has too often undergirded America's mission of expansion or of promoting democracy and freedom (slaughtering native Americans, wars, invasions of other countries, support of repressive regimes that benefit national self-interests).[34] Tragically, patterns of official violence against vulnerable people continue into the present. As I edit this chapter, the nation is writhing over how to respond to highly publicized cases of police brutality against African Americans and the mobilization of military troops to break up peaceful demonstrations against that violence.

Violence and intimidation abound in personal relationships, as well, whether in the form of sexual harassment at the workplace, domestic abuse in the home, or cyberbullying on social media. Sadly, the church is not immune from such behavior. The appalling history of sexual abuse and coverup of that abuse in various Christian contexts reveals Babylon's insidious influence in the church.

---

[33]Gorman, *Reading Revelation*, 42.

[34]See Gorman, *Reading Revelation*, 50; see also Peter J. Leithart, *Between Babel and Beast: America and Empires in Biblical Perspective* (Eugene, OR: Cascade, 2012).

4. Dehumanization. The haunting demotion of "slaves" and "human souls" to the very bottom of the list of imported goods (Rev 18:13) spotlights Babylon's dehumanizing character. In striking contrast, Christ purchases humanity with his blood and dignifies it with a calling to reign with Christ (Rev 5:9-10).[35] Clarice Martin

Figure 8.5. Relief of the goddess Roma sitting on the armaments of defeated enemies from the *Ara Pacis* (Altar of Peace), Rome

sees parallels between Babylon and the American experience, whether the commodification of Black slaves or more recent treatment of refugees, immigrants, and people of color.[36] The very label *illegals*, which features prominently in current public discourse regarding immigration in North America, triggers an imagination shift from *persons* to a mere *category*.

A missional reading of Revelation invites us to perceive what we do not see; to prayerfully and humbly ask, "Where does Babylon ride the beast in *our* world?"

LEAVING BABYLON BEHIND

John isn't content simply to bring the portrait of Babylon into sharp focus for his audience. He calls God's people to "come out of her" (Rev 18:4). But what would that mean for Christians living *in the midst of* the empire?[37] This is not an appeal to *physically* depart Babylon. Instead, it's an invitation

---

[35]John Christopher Thomas and Frank D. Macchia, *Revelation* (Grand Rapids, MI: Eerdmans, 2016), 445.

[36]Clarice J. Martin, "Polishing the Unclouded Mirror: A Womanist Reading of Revelation 18:13," in Rhoads, *From Every People and Nation*, 82-109.

[37]For the rest of this paragraph, see Dean Flemming, *Why Mission?* (Nashville, TN: Abingdon, 2015), 119-20.

to leave behind Babylon's *ways of thinking and living*. Revelation not only unveils how Babylon is embodied in the power structures of Rome. It also boomerangs against his audience. For them, leaving Babylon would involve forsaking ordinary cultural practices, such as eating food sacrificed to idols (Rev 2:14-15, 20-21), with its connections to the idolatry of the imperial cult. Coming out of Babylon also would entail abandoning the kind of materialism and arrogance that boasts, "I am rich, I have prospered, and I need nothing" (Rev 3:17).

A missional reading of Revelation 17 and 18, then, compels us not only to reimagine our world in view of God's loving and just purposes for creation but also to respond to that transformed vision in our day-to-day practices, as we embody God's mission within our own circumstances. John doesn't prescribe in detail what coming out of Babylon means for his audience, and neither can we. Churches in every generation, culture, and missional context must wrestle with what it means to leave the city. But let me suggest two areas in which this task seems especially compelling in North America today.

The idol of greed. Exiting Babylon's greed and economic exploitation carries both a prophetic and a lifestyle dimension. Can we put on blinders when governments use economic coercion as a tool for self-seeking policies or divert funds from aiding the sick and oppressed in our world to increase their own wealth and security? Can we simply remain silent when corporations use sweatshops to produce our cheap sneakers or exploit natural resources and poor local workers to satisfy our thirst for high-end jewelry and technology?

At the same time, forsaking Babylon profoundly shapes our everyday lifestyles and practices, as persons and as Christian communities. Christians in many global settings confront daily choices about whether to participate in a system of bribery and corruption that benefits the rich and the powerful. In the West, Christian communities hear the siren call of the materialistic "good life." Reddish reflects that Christians "come out of the city" whenever they resist the driving impulse to consume goods and experiences, practice radical generosity with their time and money, and adopt a simpler lifestyle that does not devour a disproportionate measure of the world's resources.[38]

---

[38]Reddish, *Revelation*, 354.

Michael Goheen relates a story in which British theologian Lesslie Newbigin, after visiting the civil rights museum in Birmingham, Alabama, reflected on the complicity of Christians in the horrors and cruelty of slavery. Newbigin then mused, "'I wonder what later generations will identify as our biggest idol to which we are oblivious.' Immediately he offered an answer to his own query: 'No doubt it will be our economic idolatry and our blindness to consumerism. It will be our lives immersed in mindless consumption in a world where there is so much poverty and hunger.'"[39] Might leaving Babylon require Western Christians to confess that they have been seduced by the charms of a consumerist whore?

Rehumanizing the outsider. How might Christians come out of Babylon, in an American political and social context in which the most vulnerable of our world are often dehumanized; in which migrants as a group can be labeled as violent gang members or criminals; or where children, including toddlers, are separated from their asylum-seeking parents at the border?[40] Whatever our global context, we must begin by humbly confessing our own participation in any form of sexism, racism, ethnocentrism, and indifference toward victims of violence and oppression, hunger and homelessness. Second, Christian communities must seek ways to extend love and concrete service on behalf of marginalized and exploited people, whether victims of poverty, trafficking, abuse, discrimination, persecution, or violence.

This is not an easy path, given the extent to which large segments of the American church risk entanglement with Babylon. According to a 2018 Pew Research Center study, only one in four White evangelical Protestants thought the United States had a responsibility to accept refugees, the lowest percentage of any group identified in the survey, and significantly less than nonreligious persons.[41] A loving, missional response to frequently dehumanized groups like refugees may come with a cost.

---

[39]Michael W. Goheen, *The Church and Its Vocation: Lesslie Newbigin's Missionary Ecclesiology* (Grand Rapids, MI: Baker Academic, 2018), 206.

[40]Approximately 5,500 children were separated from migrant parents or guardians at the US southern border, mostly in the first half of 2018. See "Family Members Separated at Border May Each Get Up to $450,000," *New York Times*, October 28, 2021, www.nytimes.com/2021/10/28/us /politics/trump-family-separation-border.html.

[41]Hannah Hartig, *Pew Research Center Fact Tank*, May 24, 2018, www.pewresearch.org/fact-tank/2018 /05/24/republicans-turn-more-negative-toward-refugees-as-number-admitted-to-u-s-plummets/.

Revelation's picture of Babylon helps us to see that evil represents more than a collection of wrong acts by individuals but is structural as well. John saw evil and the work of Satan behind the systems of empire that promoted idolatry, fed the lust to consume by exploiting people and the earth, and maintained security through oppression and violence.[42] We must recognize that a prophetic response to Babylon today must address the *systems* that affect the lives of people, systems that sustain poverty, racial inequality, consumer excess, abortion-on-demand, harm to God's creation, and inequities in health of mind and body. Local congregations must ask, how can we promote patterns of "healing the nations" (Rev 22:2) in our governments, our companies, our media outlets, our schools, and our churches?

CONCLUSION

What can Revelation's use of the symbols of the beast and Babylon teach us about the task of reading the Bible missionally today, especially in light of the political and cultural realities of our own contexts? We could talk about a number of issues, but let's zero in on three.

First, Revelation models an approach that *is context-specific, but not context-bound*. It's clear that John fixes his crosshairs squarely on Rome. Babylon the whore wears Roman garments, drinks from a Roman cup, and rides a Roman beast. Yet John's targeted prophetic message draws from scriptural texts and themes that reach far beyond the cities of Roman Asia. In short, John has contextualized the one gospel story of the slain Lamb's triumph over evil and God's righteous judgments in light of the political and religious realities of his world.

Christian communities today can do no less. Recently, while reading Revelation with African students, I was struck by how perceptively they spotted Babylon's presence, not only in foreign heavyweight powers, but in their own political contexts in countries like Kenya, Ethiopia, and South Africa. The current political environment in the United States and elsewhere demands a revisiting and recontextualizing of Revelation's portrait of Babylon. We dare not sanitize such texts, either by turning them into

---

[42]Micah D. Kiel, *Apocalyptic Ecology: The Book of Revelation, the Earth, and the Future* (Collegeville, MN: Liturgical, 2017), 91.

first-century museum artifacts or by neutralizing them with a bland, "Well, after all, Babylon is everywhere." Granted. But Babylon is also *here*. And the *here* must profoundly shape our reading of these texts.

> *"When Africans hear about Babylon and the beast*
> *from the sea, their minds turn to the powerful*
> *international forces who grow fat on the blood of*
> *Africans, who foment wars and supply arms*
> *to keep servicing their selfish interests. . . .*
> *And Africa itself*
> *has produced merciless tyrants and*
> *despots—they are the beast from the land."*[43]
>
> JAMES CHUKWUMA OKOYE

Second, we can learn from Revelation that missional readings of Scripture *must challenge the church as well as the world*. John's portraits of the beast and the fallen city were not merely about "those bad Roman rulers and systems of power out there." Christians who share Babylon's perspective or that of its collaborators must recognize that they, too, stand in danger of sharing Babylon's judgment. Tragically, churches continue to submit to the harlot's seductions today. In the American political and commercial environment, distinctions between the kingdom of Christ and the empire of Babylon frequently blur beyond recognition. Christians' political imaginations too often are shaped more by cable news than by the biblical story. Modern-day Laodicean churches still build empires, based on models of success, power, and influence derived from the dominant culture. Many Christians in America and elsewhere seem ready to strike a pragmatic bargain with the beast, rationalizing public officials' falsehoods, corruption, and exploitation of the weak, let alone creation itself, in exchange for the promise of prosperity and political success.

---

[43]James Chuckwuma Okoye, "Power and Worship: *Revelation* in African Perspective," in Rhoads, *From Every People and Nation*, 114.

"The church cannot be the church in Babylon until it is the church out of Babylon."[44]

Michael Gorman

At the same time, the symbols of Babylon and the beast speak in different ways to different churches. A congregation largely made up of Central American migrants in urban Los Angeles will hear these texts differently than one embedded in an upscale suburb of Sydney. Each community of Lamb-followers must discover what it means to participate in the mission of God within their life circumstances, and, if necessary, repent of their collusion with Babylon.

Third, Revelation demonstrates that *a missional reading of Scripture is profoundly political.* No less than the Christians in western Asia Minor, *we* are called to unmask and exit Babylon, resist the beast, and reimagine who controls the power and the purse in our world. A missional reading of Revelation invites us to proclaim and embody God's new creation on the broad streets and dark alleys of Babylon, in all the messy places where the powers of greed, idolatry, and injustice shake their bony fists in the face of God.

But it's not enough simply to break out of Babylon. Revelation calls us *into* another city, a city of healing and hope. Let's explore that city now.

---

[44]Gorman, *Reading Revelation*, 185.

CHAPTER NINE

A NEW JERUSALEM MISSION

And I saw the holy city, the new Jerusalem,
coming down out of heaven from God.

REVELATION 21:2

FEW PASSAGES IN THE BIBLE have fueled the popular Christian imagination like Revelation 21 and 22. For many Christians, these chapters offer a description of "heaven," the new Jerusalem. Heaven is pictured as a realm beyond time and space, a land of golden streets, pearly gates, and happy reunions with family and friends (and, perhaps, favorite pets!). In my case, that image was reinforced by a parade of sermons, hymns, gospel songs, and even jokes, with Saint Peter employed as the bouncer at heaven's gates. Christians who see a "spiritual" heaven as their ultimate hope and final destination may even support the Bible's teaching about Christ's second coming and the resurrection of the dead. But practically, those events have little effect on how the Christian story ends, since the goal is for individuals to make it home to what one old hymn calls "the summerland above," the new Jerusalem.[1]

But is that really how the story ends? A closer look at Revelation's final chapters pictures New Jerusalem as a destination, all right, but one vastly different from "the home in the sky where I go when I die" of the popular

---

[1]"In the New Jerusalem," words and music by C. B. Widmeyer, 1911.

imagination. That vision is the subject of this chapter. We'll see that Revelation's New Jerusalem represents

- the goal of God's mission
- the fullness of God's presence
- a transformed creation
- an alternative to power-hungry Babylon
- the healing of the nations

But John's final vision also summons us to embody God's new creation and to get caught up in God's restoring mission for the world here and now. Join me in exploring this powerful and compelling finish to Revelation's story.

THE GOAL OF GOD'S MISSION

Where does it all end? Revelation 21 and 22 not only bring a climax to the book of Revelation; they also portray the grand finale of the entire biblical drama. It's as if John unfurls a banner that stretches from one corner of the cosmos to the other, announcing: "Mission accomplished!" The story that begins with God creating the heavens and the earth (Gen 1:1) comes to its fulfillment with God forming a new heaven and a new earth (Rev 21:1). These closing chapters are crucial for our understanding of what God's mission in the world is about and where it is heading. God's loving purposes involve more than simply getting individual people saved so that they can go to heaven when they breathe their last breath. God desires to bring all creation to the end he intended for it from the beginning.

In Revelation 21 and 22 we see the realization of that goal. John unveils a portrait of a magnificently restored creation that flourishes with beauty and abundant life. The powers of sin and death will never again threaten. Suffering and pain are forever banished. People of every nation dwell in the immediate presence of God and the Lamb, enjoying perfect harmony with each other and with God. All of creation unites in worship and service of God and the Lamb. What the angel announced in chapter 11 has come true in its fullest sense: "The kingdom of the world has become the kingdom of our Lord and of his Messiah" (Rev 11:15). In short, God's purpose to make *everything* new (Rev 21:5) is accomplished. God says, "It is done!" (Rev 21:6). Let's zoom in on some important dimensions of God's New Jerusalem mission and how that vision draws *us*, his people, into what God is doing to make that happen.

God's Presence Saturates the Earth

As chapter 21 begins, the new Jerusalem comes down from heaven and merges with a renewed earth (Rev 21:2). Immediately, a voice pierces the cosmos:

> See, the home of God is among mortals.
> He will dwell with them;
> they will be his peoples,
> and God himself will be with them. (Rev 21:3)

At its heart, New Jerusalem represents the unfiltered *presence* of the triune God with his people. The God who promised Israel that he would "dwell" among them and be their God (Ex 29:45-46; Lev 26:11-12) now does so without hindrance or constraint. Like Moses, *all* of God's servants will "see his face," and his name will be inscribed on their foreheads (Rev 22:4). Furthermore, *the whole city* becomes God's temple or sanctuary, the earthly place of his presence.[2] Perfectly cubed in its shape (Rev 21:16), the new Jerusalem functions as "a megasized analogue of the holy of holies in the tabernacle or temple."[3] Indeed, the very name *New Jerusalem* ties this city directly to the city of Jerusalem and its temple as the place of God's presence.

Revelation 21 and 22, however, complete a story that emerges long before the building of Solomon's temple in Jerusalem. The Bible pictures Eden itself as a sanctuary or temple-garden in which the presence of God dwells on earth, a place where the humans God created worship him.[4] God makes

---

[2]See Gregory K. Beale, *The Temple and the Church's Mission: A Biblical Theology of the Dwelling Place of God* (Downers Grove, IL: IVP Academic, 2004), esp. 23-26, 328-31, 365-73.

[3]J. Richard Middleton, *A New Heaven and a New Earth: Reclaiming Biblical Eschatology* (Grand Rapids, MI: Baker, 2014), 171.

[4]See G. K. Beale and Mitchell Kim, *God Dwells Among Us: Expanding Eden to the Ends of the Earth* (Downers Grove, IL: InterVarsity Press, 2014), 17-38; T. Desmond Alexander, *From Eden to the New Jerusalem: An Introduction to Biblical Theology* (Grand Rapids, MI: Kregel, 2008), 19-31.

humanity in his image and gives them a job: to "have dominion . . . *over the earth*" and to "be fruitful and multiply, and *fill the earth*" (Gen 1:26, 28 italics added). Although it isn't stated directly, this suggests that God intends for the sanctuary of Eden, and thereby his presence, to expand throughout the whole earth. And this will happen through God's image-bearers—people who are created to represent God's presence and rule in the world. In other words, our human calling is to extend God's presence throughout the entire world, in anticipation of the coming of the new creation, when the whole earth will be saturated with God's glory (Is 6:3), fully and forever. That's a *missional* calling.

But the story takes a tragic turn when the first image-bearers, Adam and Eve, rebel against God. Driven from the sanctuary of Eden, they are cut off from God's immediate presence. God, however, demonstrates his faithfulness to his people Israel by instituting the tabernacle (the tent of God's presence) and the Jerusalem temple. These structures represent the particular location of God's dwelling and glory on earth, where people encounter and worship God. Yet even Solomon, who built the temple, recognizes its inadequacy (1 Kgs 8:27), and the place of God's presence shifts from a building to a person. God the eternal Word becomes flesh and pitches a tent, or tabernacles, among us (Jn 1:14). Through his death and resurrection (Jn 2:19-21), Jesus becomes the cornerstone of the new temple of God, the church (Eph 2:19-22; 1 Pet 2:4-8; cf. 1 Cor 3:16-17). Now the church as the "dwelling place for God" (Eph 2:22) is called to extend God's presence throughout the earth. This dynamic spiritual temple "grows" (Eph 2:21) and expands through the church's faithful witness of word and life (Eph 1:13; Acts 1:8).[5]

The new Jerusalem in Revelation 21 and 22, then, brings God's persistent purpose to dwell among his people to a magnificent climax. The same verb that described the earthly presence of Jesus, the Word made flesh, in John 1:14 shows up in Revelation 21:3. In the new creation God will "tabernacle" among his people in an unhindered way. The presence of the slain and risen Lamb soaks the restored creation. Crucially, John extends the traditional Old Testament promise from "they will be his people," referring to Israel

---

[5]See Beale and Kim, *God Dwells Among Us*, 104-9.

(Lev 26:12; Jer 24:7), to "his *peoples*" (Rev 21:3 italics added), representing all peoples of the earth. In the new Jerusalem, people of every tribe and nation dwell and flourish in God's presence, with God and the Lamb at the very center of their shared life.

What's more, God's purpose to drench *the whole earth* with his presence, originating in creation, becomes a stunning reality in the new heaven and the new earth. Israel's prophets caught a fragmented glimpse of this hope when they envisioned a new end-time temple in a transformed Jerusalem, where God once again will dwell (Is 2:2-3; Ezek 40–48; cf. Zech 8:3, 7-8). But John's vision takes us by surprise. He reports: "I saw *no temple* in the city, for its temple is the Lord God the Almighty and the Lamb" (Rev 21:22 italics added). *No* temple? A temple in the future city would be as redundant as a lawn sprinkler during a hurricane. It's *all* God's temple. Old divisions between what is sacred and what is secular evaporate. God's glory fills all of heaven and earth (Rev 21:11)—a radiance so profound and pervasive that even the sun and moon receive a pink slip (Rev 21:23).

In the new Jerusalem God's people continue their role as priests who serve and worship God continually in his earthly sanctuary (Rev 22:4). And as kings, "they will reign forever and ever" (Rev 22:5). What does that mean? Will life in the new creation consist simply of perpetual harp jam sessions and praise choir practice? Perhaps we will still have a "mission" in New Jerusalem, one that restores God's original mandate for humans to extend his presence and rule as his representatives on earth. Andy Johnson suggests that those who share God's stewardship over the renewed creation will actively contribute to its flourishing, by engaging in human cultural life in all its fullness. Freed from sin, "such cultural activities . . . would be wholly for the sake of others, for creation as a whole, and for bringing honor to God."[6] He goes on to muse, "What if everyone who has ever played in any production of 'Les Misérables' joins together in a 'cosmic' production that celebrates God's liberating activity and human participation in it throughout history?"[7] Perhaps we will all do our bit in contributing toward extending God's healing, life-giving presence throughout a redeemed earth.

---

[6]Andy Johnson, *Holiness and the* Missio Dei (Eugene, OR: Cascade, 2016), 178.
[7]Johnson, *Holiness*, 178.

MISSIONAL IMPLICATIONS

John's vision of God's "mission accomplished" in the new Jerusalem is not only a picture of the church's future. It also shapes our participation in God's mission *now*. How does John's picture of New Jerusalem as an amphitheater of God's glory and presence speak into our present mission?

In the first place, it reminds us that mission begins with *being*, rather than doing or telling. Mission involves far more than a certain set of activities, a line item on a church budget, an annual mission trip, giving money to help support missionaries and ministries, or even witnessing to neighbors and colleagues. First and foremost, mission is about who we *are*. It flows out of our participation in the life of the triune God, not what we do *for* God. Unless we experience the intimate, transforming presence of God, our mission activities will remain shallow and self-serving.[8]

Second, if the goal of God's mission is for people of all nations to flourish in intimate communion with the triune God and loving fellowship with one another, then this aim ought to shape the church's mission today. As God's image-bearers, we are called to extend God's presence throughout the earth by our faithful witness, anticipating the day when the whole world shimmers with his glory.[9] Our task involves leading fellow humans from every tribe and culture into fellowship with God so that they, too, might be overwhelmed with his presence. Beyond simply "saving souls" for heaven, we are called to form disciples who reflect the abundant life of God in the world. Moreover, redeemed people don't experience God's presence solo. We must draw them into affirming, loving, worshiping communities, as citizens of God's kingdom and members of God's family (Rev 5:10; 21:7).

Third, local churches live as both a preview and the real presence of the new world to come. The new creation is emerging now in the mission of the slain and risen Lamb in and through the church. N. T. Wright reminds us that Christian communities serve as "advance signposts" of the time when God's presence will fill the whole earth.[10] Signposts, yes. But perhaps even

---

[8]For more on this point, see Dean Flemming, *Recovering the Full Mission of God: A Biblical Perspective on Being, Doing and Telling* (Downers Grove, IL: IVP Academic).

[9]Beale and Kim, *God Dwells Among Us*, 122.

[10]N. T. Wright, *Paul and the Faithfulness of God* (Minneapolis: Fortress, 2013), 437.

more. As communities that reflect the self-giving love and justice of the slaughtered Lamb, we also become the Spirit-enabled *embodiment* of the new world to come, imperfectly and incompletely, for sure, but in a real way, nonetheless.[11] If we are "on mission," shouldn't we be able to say with humility, "If you want to see the difference that God's healing, restoring presence makes in the world, look at our community, the people of the Lamb"?

HEAVEN COMES DOWN

It might surprise some of us that the final movement in the Bible's story does not go *up* to heaven but *down* to earth. John's concluding vision begins: "Then I saw a new heaven and a new earth; for the first heaven and the first earth had passed away, and the sea was no more. And I saw the holy city, the new Jerusalem, *coming down out of heaven from God*, prepared as a bride adorned for her husband" (Rev 21:1-2; cf. Rev 21:10 italics added).

Instead of the earth serving as a launching pad for "raptured" Christians to take flight to heaven, heaven comes down to earth. Heaven and earth, divided since creation, will undergo a divinely orchestrated merger. Up to

Figure 9.1. Tapestry of the new Jerusalem descending from *The Apocalypse of Angers*, c. 1375–1380

[11]See Michael J. Gorman, *Becoming the Gospel: Paul, Participation, and Mission* (Grand Rapids, MI: Eerdmans, 2015), 47.

this point in Revelation, the throne of God and the Lamb has been situated exclusively in heaven. Now that throne, which symbolizes God's sovereignty over the universe, relocates from heaven to earth (Rev 22:1, 3). God has a future for the earth, and this reality profoundly shapes our understanding of God's mission. What kind of future is it?

TRANSFORMED, NOT REPLACED

John sees "a new heaven and a new earth" (Rev 21:1). Later God speaks directly for the first time since chapter 1: "See, I am making all things new" (Rev 21:5). So how *new* is "new"? After all, John tells us that the first earth and heaven have "passed away" and the sea has vanished (Rev 21:1). Does this imply that the present earth must be destroyed before God ushers in his new creation? This is how many Christians picture the end of the world. Hal Lindsey's *The Late Great Planet Earth*, for example, predicts that "there will be a great roar and intense heat and fire. Then Christ will put the atoms back together to form a new heaven and earth."[12] But the notion of earth's obliteration doesn't fit John's picture of the new creation. John imagines an earth that is restored and transformed, not destroyed and replaced.

John's vision of New Jerusalem shows both continuity and discontinuity between the old creation and the new. The "passing away" of the first heaven and earth shows God's *faithfulness* to creation, not its destruction. *The earth itself isn't left behind.* What is ended is the world in which sin, death, and Satan seek to sabotage God's good purposes for creation (see Rev 20). In the new creation, all death and suffering have passed away (Rev 21:4). Even the sea, a symbol of chaos and evil in Revelation, abruptly disappears (Rev 21:1; cf. Rev 12:12; 13:1; 20:13). A "new" heaven and earth means the absence of every power that threatens to "destroy the earth" God has made (Rev 11:18).

At the same time, God does something new and revolutionary, even as the prophet Isaiah promised (Is 43:19; 65:17; 66:22). The same God who "created all things" (Rev 4:11), now is "making all things new" (Rev 21:5). As commentator Brian Blount puts it, "God is taking what is old and

---

[12]Hal Lindsey, *The Late Great Planet Earth* (Grand Rapids, MI: Zondervan, 1970), 179.

transforming it. Out of the destruction that occurs in the various plagues and battles for creation, God will weave God's new thing. The old will remain a constituent part of the new, but it will be fiercely transfigured."[13] In a sense, what happens to *people* in their resurrection will be true of *creation* in its restoration. Paul speaks of our present bodies dying and being raised to a qualitatively different kind of life when Christ returns (1 Cor 15:35-57). Similarly, John envisions that the present creation, diseased by sin and death, will pass away, only to be healed and transformed for a new kind of flourishing life.[14] In neither case does God simply scrap the old and start again. God must remake his creation in order to bring it to its intended goal.[15]

> *"This world is God's 'baby,' God's creation.*
> *Rather than discard it, God seeks to save it, to rid it*
> *of its beasts and its monstrous evils, to drive out its*
> *dragons, to purge it of its impurities. The climactic*
> *finale of the book [of Revelation] is God's creation*
> *of a new heaven and a new earth, transforming*
> *the old into something new."*[16]
>
> MITCHELL REDDISH

It's noteworthy that in Rev 21:5, God speaks in the present tense: "I am making all things new" (Rev 21:5). These words not only promise what God *will* do in the future but also announce what God *is* doing in the present.

---

[13]Brian K. Blount, *Revelation: A Commentary* (Louisville, KY: Westminster John Knox, 2009), 376.

[14]Mark B. Stephens, *Annihilation or Renewal? The Meaning and Function of New Creation in the Book of Revelation*, WUNT 2.307 (Tübingen: Mohr Siebeck, 2011), 257.

[15]Clearly, a tension emerges between Revelation 21 and a passage like 2 Peter 3:7-13, where we find statements like "the present heavens and earth have been reserved for fire" (2 Pet 3:7), "the heavens will pass away with a loud noise, and the elements will be dissolved with fire" (2 Pet 3:10), and "all these things are to be dissolved" (2 Pet 3:11). But Richard Middleton makes a plausible argument that the apocalyptic images in 2 Peter 3 envision the transformation, not the literal annihilation of the world. See Middleton, *A New Heaven and a New Earth*, 189-200; cf. Douglas J. Moo and Jonathan A. Moo, *Creation Care: A Biblical Theology of the Natural World* (Grand Rapids, MI: Zondervan, 2018), 153-61.

[16]Mitchell G. Reddish, *Revelation* (Macon, GA: Smyth and Helwys, 2001), 416.

God is already in the process of making everything new. The church in mission lives in its cultural circumstances as the embodiment of God's new creation (see 2 Cor 5:17), a foretaste of what is yet to come.

BACK TO THE GARDEN?

John spotlights God's remaking of creation by describing the holy city as a restored Eden. Nowhere is this clearer than in Revelation 22:1-2, which pictures the comeback of the tree of life (see Gen 2:9; 3:22, 24) and the river that "flows out of Eden to water the garden" (Gen 2:10): "Then the angel showed me the river of the water of life, bright as crystal, flowing from the throne of God and of the Lamb through the middle of the street of the city. On either side of the river is the tree of life with its twelve kinds of fruit, producing its fruit each month; and the leaves of the tree are for the healing of the nations."

John's vision represents more than the 1960s dream of the Woodstock generation that they could make a better world by somehow "getting back to the garden." Instead of some romantic notion of going *back* to the garden, John paints a picture of Eden expanded and transformed. Eden on steroids! The goal of God's mission is not a return to the way things were in some pristine paradise, as if everything that has come since then must be trashed. Rather, "Eden is brought forward to the end of history, and becomes a central park in the redeemed city, complete with the tree of life and water of life."[17] New Jerusalem represents not an escape from human history and culture but their *fulfillment*. This garden city nourishes the kind of flourishing human community that God intended the original humans to work toward, if only they had realized it.[18] In Eugene Boring's memorable words, "God does not make 'all new things,' but 'all things new' (Rev 21:5)."[19] John doesn't speak of "the new Eden," but "the new *Jerusalem*"—a city. But what kind of city?

---

[17]M. Eugene Boring, "Revelation 19–21: End Without Closure," *The Princeton Seminary Bulletin* Supp. 3 (1994): 74.

[18]N. T. Wright, "Revelation and Christian Hope: Political Implications of the Revelation to John," in *Revelation and the Politics of Apocalyptic Interpretation*, ed. Richard B. Hays and Stefan Alkier (Waco, TX: Baylor University Press, 2012), 112.

[19]M. Eugene Boring, *Revelation* (Louisville, KY: John Knox, 1989), 220.

"Many people want to go to heaven the way they want to go to Florida—they think the weather will be an improvement and the people decent. But the biblical heaven is not a nice environment far removed from the stress of hard city life. It is the invasion of the city by the City. We enter heaven not by escaping what we don't like, but by the sanctification of the place in which God has placed us."[20]

EUGENE PETERSON

A TALE OF TWO CITIES

Like the Dickens classic, Revelation tells "a tale of two cities." New Jerusalem embodies God's life-giving purpose for creation. Babylon the Great (see Rev 17–18) symbolizes human efforts to build arrogant and idolatrous empires that challenge God's loving reign over the world. John alerts us to the clash between these two alternative cities by giving them parallel settings:

Then one of the seven angels who had the seven bowls came and said to me, "Come, I will show you the judgment of the great whore." . . . So he carried me away in the spirit into a wilderness (Rev 17:1-3).	Then one of the seven angels who had the seven bowls . . . came and said to me, "Come, I will show you the bride, the wife of the Lamb." And in the spirit he carried me away to a great, high mountain (Rev 21:9-10).

This structural clue plows the ground for a whole series of parallels and contrasts between the harlot city of Babylon and the holy city of God:

- Babylon is a depraved whore; New Jerusalem a pure bride.

- Babylon is the haunt of demons (Rev 18:2); Jerusalem the dwelling of God (Rev 21:3).

---

[20]Eugene H. Peterson, *Reversed Thunder: The Revelation of John and the Praying Imagination* (San Francisco: HarperSanFrancisco, 1988), 174.

- The harlot is decked out in seductive luxury (Rev 17:4; 18:16); the bride wears the righteous deeds of God's people (Rev 19:8; 21:2).

- Babylon's splendor comes from exploiting others (Rev 18:11-14); New Jerusalem's glory radiates from God's dazzling presence (Rev 21:11-21).

- The wicked city stinks of abominations and deceptions (Rev 17:4; 18:23); the holy city bans everything false and unclean (Rev 21:27).

- The former city groans with mourning and darkness (Rev 18:15, 23); the new city is drenched with celebration and light (Rev 19:7; 21:23; 22:5).

- Babylon dominates and corrupts the world's nations (Rev 17:18; 18:3); New Jerusalem heals and reconciles them (Rev 22:2).[21]

These two starkly different visions of human community force John's readers, then and now, to decide: Which city will shape our present identity *and* our future destiny as God's people? New Jerusalem offers an alternative vision of what it means to be human. Casting our lot with New Jerusalem involves much more than somehow surviving Babylon now so that we can reach the happy shores of the celestial city someday. It calls Christian communities, whether in Roman Asia or modern Angola, Argentina, or America, to live out the life of the city to come, which is already our true home. We live as citizens of New Jerusalem *in the very midst of Babylon*.

But citizenship in New Jerusalem also gives us a mission. If God's purpose is to lead people and nations to abandon the power games of Babylon and to walk in New Jerusalem's light, then we must align ourselves with that purpose. David deSilva aptly describes this calling:

> As John uses this vision (and thus as we must use it), new Jerusalem is a proclamation of God's purpose for creation, and in light of this all human purposes and societies are judged, critiqued, weighed in the balance, and found wanting. Christians are challenged not only to *wait* but to *witness*, to proclaim and protest, to encourage and direct, in light of God's vision.[22]

Let's take a closer look at what that mission means for the world's nations.

---

[21]See Dean Flemming, *Contextualization in the New Testament: Patterns for Theology and Mission* (Downers Grove, IL: IVP Academic, 2005), 287.

[22]David deSilva, *An Introduction to the New Testament: Contexts, Methods and Ministry Formation*, 2nd ed. (Downers Grove, IL: IVP Academic, 2018), 819.

THE HEALING OF THE NATIONS

John invites us to see New Jerusalem as the fulfillment of something that has been in the works since God first chose a people to bear his name. When God initiated a covenant with Abraham, he promised that through this one person's descendants all nations on earth would be blessed (Gen 12:3; 18:18; 22:18). Throughout the biblical story, the God of mission relentlessly pursues that aim, through Israel, through Christ, and through the church. In New Jerusalem, however, God's redeeming purpose for the nations reaches its goal. In Revelation 22:1-2, John pictures the tree of life growing on either side of a river, bursting with an abundance of fruit. These images recall Ezekiel's vision of a river flowing from God's end-time temple, flanked by fruit-bearing trees (Ezek 47:1-12). But there's a difference. Ezekiel's trees bud leaves that are "for healing" (Ezek 47:12). John, however, gives these thera-peutic leaves a major upgrade. In John's vision, they "are for the healing *of the nations*" (Rev 22:2, italics added). *The mission of New Jerusalem is the healing of the nations.*

This should hardly surprise us. In chapter 5, the slaughtered Lamb's blood redeemed people from every tribe and nation (Rev 5:9; cf. Rev 7:9; 14:6). Later those who triumphed over the beast acclaim God as "King of the nations" and rejoice that "all nations will come and worship" before him (Rev 15:3-4). That promise becomes a reality in the new creation, where God dwells with his diverse "peoples" (Rev 21:3), and the nations walk by the light of God and the Lamb (Rev 21:24). The God of mission gathers a new creation community from every nation and people on earth.

But Revelation dangles an uneasy tension before us.[23] It holds out two possible outcomes, like alternative endings to a Hollywood movie.[24] One strain that plays out through chapters 6–20 appears to give the nations little hope of repenting and sharing in the new creation. They rage against God's kingdom and his wrath overwhelms them like a tsunami (Rev 11:18). The nations are deceived by the devil (Rev 20:3, 7, 10), fall under Babylon's spell (Rev 18:23), and bow the knee to the beast (Rev 13:4, 7-8). Faced with the

---

[23]The following paragraphs adapt material from Flemming, *Why Mission?* (Nashville, TN: Abingdon, 2015), 114-16.

[24]Andy Johnson, *Holiness and the Missio Dei*, 171-72.

Figure 9.2. Manuscript illumination of the river of life (Rev 22:1-2) from the Facundus Beatus, 1047

fury of God's judgments, rebellious humanity refuses to repent (Rev 9:20-21; 16:9, 11). Even after John has seen the new creation arrive, he seems to give little hope for the wicked to change: "Let the evildoer still do evil, and the filthy still be filthy" (Rev 22:11). Due to this dark thread in Revelation, some interpreters have concluded that John doesn't expect salvation for the disobedient nations, only the hammer of judgment.[25]

That isn't the whole story, however. Revelation offers another possible ending, the hope that the church's witness to the world's diverse peoples *will* bear abundant fruit. As we saw in chapter 6, Revelation repeatedly pictures the sinful nations fearing God, worshiping him, and giving God glory (Rev 11:13; 14:6-7; 15:3-4).

But it's only in the new Jerusalem that God's mission to the nations reaches its goal. The cast of characters that shows up in the holy city includes some rather unlikely actors—the nations and the "kings of the earth" (Rev 21:24-26). The last time we saw the nations in Revelation's unfolding narrative, they were allied with Satan, judged by God, and consumed by fire from heaven (Rev 20:7-15; cf. Rev 11:18; 16:19; 19:15). But in the final act, the nations promenade down "Main street" of the future city by the light of God and the Lamb (Rev 21:24). Even more astounding, the kings of the earth "bring their glory" into the new creation (Rev 21:24). Up to this point, these kings have played the role of God's enemies. In chapter 19, they wage war against Christ and are killed by his sword (Rev 19:19, 21; cf. Rev 6:15; 17:2, 18; 18:3, 9). In the new creation, however, the kings of the earth join the nations in offering glory and honor to their creator (Rev 21:24, 26).

This act of surrendering their glory and honor above all means that the nations and their rulers will worship God Almighty in the eternal city.[26] Throughout Revelation, the language of unbelievers giving glory to God implies genuine repentance (Rev 11:13; 14:7; 15:4). At the same time, John's vision recalls Isaiah 60, in which the nations and their kings make an endtime pilgrimage to Jerusalem, bringing their wealth and material treasures,

---

[25]See, e.g., Greg Carey, *Elusive Apocalypse: Reading Authority in the Revelation to John* (Macon, GA: Mercer University Press, 1999), 160-62.

[26]G. K. Beale, *The Book of Revelation: A Commentary on the Greek Text* (Grand Rapids, MI: Eerdmans, 1999), 1095.

like camels, silver, iron, ships, and pine trees to the City of the Lord (Is 60:5-17). It's plausible that Revelation sees the nations yielding not only their spiritual worship but also their material culture and the product of their labors as an offering to God and the Lamb. The nations, kings, and merchants of the earth once offered the "glory" of their cultural products in service to Babylon the whore (Rev 18:9-19; cf. Is 60:13). But now elements of human culture and workmanship are transformed and devoted to bringing glory to God.[27]

"The city of God is not a final escape from the troubles of historical existence along the road of life, a final retreat into the castle where the door is locked from the inside: it is a fulfillment in which the road traveled, the splendid variety of human culture developed in the toil of history is not neutralized but redeemed and glorified."[28]

EUGENE BORING

Revelation 21–22, then, gives us a picture of a redeemed humanity and the healing of the nations. For the marginalized, minority churches in Roman Asia, such a vision might push their collective imaginations almost to the breaking point, like someone who's never viewed the night sky through a telescope suddenly beholding Hubble's images of deep space. Revelation's last word on the nations is not the fearful fire of judgment in chapter 20; it is the healing of the nations (Rev 22:2) and their presence in the eternal city (Rev 21:24-26).

Revelation finishes with a mind-boggling vision of hope. This doesn't mean that John is a universalist who thinks that everyone will be saved in the end. That seems clear from the book's repeated warnings that those who persist in their sinful practices are not fit to enter New Jerusalem (Rev 21:8, 27; 22:15). John makes no attempt to sort out the tension between the visions

---

[27]Middleton, *A New Heaven and a New Earth*, 173; Stephens, *Annihilation or Renewal?*, 253-54.
[28]M. Eugene Boring, *Hearing John's Voice: Insights for Teaching and Preaching* (Grand Rapids, MI: Eerdmans, 2019), 126.

of the nations worshiping God on the one hand and of God judging the nations and shutting sinners out of the city on the other. Revelation seems to hold out both as real potential outcomes for the nations, depending on how they respond to the church's gospel witness (e.g., Rev 14:6-7). What Revelation *does* assure us is that the Bible's story of God's mission to the nations through his people will reach a glorious triumph in the end. Those redeemed from the diverse peoples of the earth will walk in New Jerusalem's light. This is a vision of exceptional hope for Christian communities today that labor in places where the weeds of spiritual apathy or outright hostility seem to overwhelm the seedlings of the gospel. The church's mission to disciple the nations (Mt 28:18-20) will ultimately lead to an unimaginable harvest. Amen!

A NEW CREATION IDENTITY

It's time to focus on what Revelation 21 and 22 mean for the church in mission today. New Jerusalem represents more than the church's magnificent hope for the future. For John, the future casts its light into the present. Revelation unveils a sneak preview of God's life-giving purpose for all of creation in the end so that, by the Spirit's enabling, *we* can live as a trailer of that future now.

This now and not yet perspective helps us avoid two misunderstandings of Revelation 21 and 22. The first views the new creation only as an otherworldly, future state that we aspire to, but which doesn't have much to do with our life in the world now. It's simply where we go when we die or when Jesus returns. The second misreading sees the new Jerusalem as something that can be fully realized in *this* world if we only work hard to build it. That misconception comes into sharp focus in William Blake's poetic text for the hymn "Jerusalem," still popular in the United Kingdom. Its final verse testifies:

I will not cease from mental fight,
Nor shall my sword sleep in my hand,
Till we have built Jerusalem
In England's green and pleasant land.[29]

---

[29]William Blake, "Jerusalem," 1804, music by Hubert Parry, 1916.

A nice thought, but John likely would have snapped his stylus in half at the notion of *humans* building the new Jerusalem. In contrast, John's future city reshapes our imaginations, enabling us to resist the pressure to conform to the ways of Babylon and to live as a contrast community that embodies the life of New Jerusalem in our world. New creation hasn't yet arrived, but it has begun to be true.[30] God is *already* "making all things new" (Rev 21:5)— through his people. Let's get more specific. If we let the goal of God's mission shape the character of the church now, we will be.[31]

Communities of healing. The river of life that erupts from the main street of New Jerusalem and the tree of life that sentinels its banks symbolize God's life-giving grace that never fails to sustain life (Rev 22:1-2). The church not only drinks from the water of life but is called to offer that abundant life to others. What's more, if the purpose of the tree of life is "the healing of the nations" (Rev 22:2), then our mission involves serving as instruments of healing in and among the world's nations. That restoring ministry is wide enough to embrace all the wounds that sin has inflicted on humanity— physical, relational, spiritual, emotional, political; in short, all of life. It seeks to reconcile at every level, whether enmity between nations, alienated groups within nations, like tribes, races, and political rivals, or fragmented families and Christian communities.

Communities of hospitality. New Jerusalem bristles with gracious hospitality. It's twelve gates never close. They only receive one-way traffic, welcoming those who want to leave Babylon and enter the city of God.[32] The city's gates face all directions of the compass, enabling the nations and peoples of the world to bring their glory into the city (Rev 21:25-26). The new creation is "inclusive, but . . . not homogenized."[33] It doesn't remove cultural differences; rather, it celebrates them. In a historical moment in which voices of nationalism and exclusion of the "other" screech throughout our world,

---

[30]Wright, "Revelation and Christian Hope," 111.

[31]The following section adapts some material from Dean Flemming, *Recovering the Full Mission of God: A Biblical Perspective on Being, Doing and Telling* (Downers Grove, IL: IVP Academic, 2013), 247-48.

[32]Wes Howard-Brooke and Anthony Gwyther, *Unveiling Empire: Reading Revelation Then and Now* (Maryknoll, NY: Orbis, 2003), 188.

[33]Boring, *Hearing John's Voice*, 126.

New Jerusalem communities must extend their arms in a posture of embrace. We must welcome the poor and the powerful, the marginalized and the mainstream, the migrant and the citizen into spaces of security and reconciliation. As a multinational people of God, we will affirm the good and the beautiful in all the rich cultures and nations of the world. As one writer tersely states it: "Ethnocentrism is not an option in the new creation."[34]

Communities of holiness. New Jerusalem is a *holy* city (Rev 21:2), saturated with the sanctifying presence of a holy God. As we have seen, the whole city, shaped like a gigantic cube, becomes a sanctuary like the most holy place in Solomon's temple (Rev 21:16; cf. 1 Kgs 6:19-20). Only those who wash their robes may enter the gates of the city (Rev 22:14). Here clean clothes symbolize a holy character and lifestyle, made possible through the cleansing work of Christ (Rev 7:9). Those who are morally unclean cannot set foot in the holy city (Rev 21:27; 22:15; cf. Rev 21:8; 22:11). Andy Johnson comments that the whole cosmos becomes a place where God's name is hallowed, his rule unchallenged, and his holiness pervades everything and everyone.[35] This is no exclusive, skinny version of holiness. A new creation liberated from the presence and power of sin represents the wholeness and the flourishing life that God intended for his creation from the beginning.

Making this practical, our future in a city whose hallmark is holiness carries at least two implications for the church in mission today. First, only a holy people can embody and bear witness to the mission of a holy God. Second, our mission involves far more than getting people saved so that they can go to heaven someday. A new creation mission compels us to invite people into a life of wholeness, in which the Spirit transforms us, as persons and as a people, into the holy character of the God we serve.

Communities of justice. Injustice has no street address in the new Jerusalem. Babylon's wealth comes by the exploitation and greed of the powerful, but Jerusalem's opulent riches are shared by all (Rev 21:11-21). The future city harbors no depressed neighborhoods. No gated communities. No "haves" and "have nots." Malnutrition and food deserts are inconceivable

---

[34]Middleton, *A New Heaven and a New Earth*, 174.
[35]Johnson, *Holiness and the* Missio Dei, 175.

because everyone enjoys an abundance of food and water (Rev 21:6; 22:1-2). No one's economic, political, or legal status denies them access to the healing of the tree of life (Rev 22:2). Such future realities must energize God's people to call out and confront all forms of injustice, inequality, and exploitation in our world. We are called to make the costly choice to live differently, embodying new creation justice in our societies.

> *"The heavenly New Jerusalem breaks into present reality*
> *whenever people take seriously the Lord's Prayer,*
> *'Your will be done, on earth as it is in heaven.'"*[36]
>
> J. NELSON KRAYBILL

Communities of creation care. God's mission reaches its climax in new *creation* and a transformed *earth*. John pictures a garden city, with trees bearing a rich diversity of fruit (Rev 22:2). This amped up Eden represents ecological harmony and the flourishing of the whole created order. As we saw in chapter 2, God's purpose for a restored creation carries consequences for the church's mission now. God's people simply do not have the option of ignoring the massive threats to God's creation, which human irresponsibility and its role in a changing climate pose to all forms of life on this planet. A holistic understanding of the mission of God compels us to find concrete ways to become agents of restoration not only for the people God made and redeemed but *all* of God's creation.

FINAL REFLECTIONS

The Bible begins in a garden and ends in a city. But that city is unlike any city in the present world. For around a decade, I lived in an overcongested Majority World city. It shared much in common with many urban metropolises I have seen throughout the developing world. I offer these reflections on the stunning contrast between sections of these cities and the holy city of Revelation 21 and 22.

---

[36]J. Nelson Kraybill, *Imperial Cult and Commerce in John's Apocalypse*, JSNT Sup 132 (Sheffield: Sheffield Academic Press, 1996), 221.

Like New Jerusalem, a river runs through this city. But instead of a pure, life-giving stream, its water is undrinkable, stinking, a source of disease and sometimes death. The river's banks are lined not with fruit-bearing trees but makeshift shanties, where extended families live on top of each other in tiny, crowded rooms. Many neighborhoods in this city are made not out of precious jewels but discarded plywood and scrap metal. Instead of streets paved with gold, its roadways consist of rutted mud or pock-marked asphalt. When the rains come, they flood, leaving behind instant lakes of fetid, standing water. Rather than the ever-present light of God and the Lamb, the inhabitants of this city deal with frequent blackouts, if they can access electricity at all. In New Jerusalem, people of all nations walk securely and openly down the city's broad streets, but in parts of this city, residents venture down dangerous, narrow alleys in fear of criminal gangs.

The present city also boasts palatial dwellings and high-rise business districts, luxury hotels and sparkling shopping malls. Its resources, however, are not shared by everyone. An ecosystem of corruption and greed funnels wealth upward to the city's power brokers. Sheltered behind their high walls and security fences, the rich do not have to gaze on the city's poverty and suffering—except when pathetic-looking beggars approach their luxury cars at a traffic light, as they inevitably do. Not far away, thousands live on top of a smoldering city dump, eking out an existence by sorting through the population's garbage. Far from a place of healing, the city churns out toxic air, congested corridors, filthy water, feral dogs, sick children, and trafficked bodies. There is never a shortage of suffering, pain, and tears.

Yet signs of hope abound. Throughout the city, followers of the Lamb form small communities of redemption, justice, and healing. Congregations gather to sing praises to the slain Lamb, as they imagine the new world to come. A family of believers offers a street kid a first chance at a loving home. Christians join an array of other citizens to oppose corrupt officials and institutionalized injustice. Lamb-followers pick up mountains of trash and plant urban community gardens. If you know where to look, you can find previews of the city of God throughout the metropolis.

New Jerusalem is a city of hope. John shows us a better city, God's purpose for creation in full bloom. Three times Jesus extends his personal guarantee that it will happen: "See, I am coming soon!" (Rev 22:7, 12, 20). But for those living in the shadow of Babylon, it often seems like a distant, unreachable land. We join the churches in Roman Asia, crying, "Come, Lord Jesus!" (Rev 22:20).

> *"The help will come," said Trufflehunter.*
> *"I stand by Aslan. Have patience, like us beasts.*
> *The help will come. It may be even now at the door."*[37]
>
> C. S. LEWIS

We long for God's presence to soak the earth like an autumn fog. We yearn for genuine human community, for people from all nations, tribes, races, and cultures to surround the throne in a united song of praise to God and the Lamb. We ache for the healing of all the wounds of sin and selfishness: no generational poverty, no people trafficking, no racial profiling, no gun violence, no abused children, no on-demand abortions, no displaced peoples, no political corruption, no war or genocide. We long for God to wipe all tears from our eyes, to put an end, forever, to pain, pandemics, disease, and death. We yearn for a restored, flourishing earth that no longer bears the curse of changing climates and human greed. We can taste the Lamb's banquet feast. We thirst for the wholeness of new creation's life-giving streams.

As sojourners between the longing of "Come, Lord Jesus!" and the fullness of "everything made new" (Rev 21:5), here is our missional challenge: Are we willing to *live* what we long for?

---

[37]C. S. Lewis, *Prince Caspian: The Return to Narnia* (New York: Harper Collins, 1998 [1951]), 164.

CHAPTER TEN

READING REVELATION
MISSIONALLY TODAY

Blessed is the one who keeps the words of the prophecy of this book.

REVELATION 22:7

IT'S TIME TO WRAP THINGS UP. We began this book with a question: What does it mean to read the book of Revelation *missionally*? And we offered a tentative answer. A missional reading of the Apocalypse leads us to explore this book's understanding of what God is up to in the world (God's mission) and how God's people, both in John's time and our own, are called to be a part of that (our mission), in our various global settings. From different angles, we have discovered how Revelation addresses those questions. This chapter will summarize what we have learned. But it will also try to push us further by reflecting on what a missional reading of Revelation might mean practically for the church today.

1. *To read Revelation missionally, we must read it from the back*, in light of God's ultimate purpose for all people and for creation. John's magnificent vision of the new heaven and earth (Rev 21 and 22) reveals the goal of God's sweeping mission. Two statements in these chapters especially sum up that aim. One is spoken by God on the throne: "See, I am making all things new" (Rev 21:5). The other describes the abundant tree of life in the new Jerusalem, whose leaves "are for the healing of the nations" (Rev 22:2). Together, these

visions declare that God's project for the world is to bring about healing, abundance, restoration, and new creation at every level. It's important that we read the whole of Revelation—Christ's messages to the seven churches in chapters 2 and 3, the heavenly vision of God and the slain Lamb in Revelation 4 and 5, and, especially, the cycles of judgments on the powers of sin and evil in chapters 6 through 20—with the destination of God's mission in mind.

But that's not all. God's purpose to heal the nations and to make everything new gives us a perspective from which to read not only Revelation but the entire biblical story. God's desire to bring wholeness and abundance to the world he made, which goes back to Genesis 1, is finally realized in Revelation's transformed creation. God's purpose to redeem a humanity enslaved to sin and the worldly powers, a rescue mission that unfolds throughout Scripture and is accomplished by Jesus' cross and empty tomb, comes to ultimate fulfillment in John's vision. Satan and the powers of death are totally routed; sin's curse is reversed (Rev 22:3). Humans are lavished with the intimate presence of God (Rev 21:3-4; 22:3-5). Israel's call to be a people of blessing for the whole world (Gen 12:1-3) and a light to the nations (Is 42:6; 49:6) finds its goal in the redeemed community from every tribe and nation, standing in full harmony as they worship God and the Lamb. The nations are finally healed! (Rev 22:2). The ending gives meaning to the whole story the Bible tells.

2. *Reading Revelation missionally means reading it as a follower, not a forecaster.* Christians expend far too much time and effort trying to figure out the end-time script, either by decoding its symbols or using it as a template for predicting future events. Instead, John calls us not simply to hear but to *keep* the words of his prophecy, as disciples who "follow the Lamb wherever he goes" (Rev 14:4). That involves approaching Revelation as communities that are shaped by the mission of God and engaged in the mission of God. A missional reading liberates us from the burden of having to put on a prognosticator's hat and figure out the correspondences between Revelation's visions and the headline news. A faithful, missional interpretation involves reading Revelation "not as a script for the future but as a script for the church."[1]

---

[1]Michael J. Gorman, *Reading Revelation Responsibly: Uncivil Worship and Witness: Following the Lamb into the New Creation* (Eugene, OR: Cascade, 2011), 189.

3. *To read Revelation missionally, we must keep our focus on the God who owns the mission.* As we've seen, talking about the *church's* mission only has meaning if we understand that God is the true missionary and that the church is called to participate in the loving mission of God. Revelation offers an incomparable vision of the triune God, a God who reigns over all things, who seeks to redeem all people, who is present in the slaughtered Lamb, and whose Spirit enables the church's witness. This God-centered focus will shield us from thinking that mission is *primarily* about formulating strategies, executing programs, or engaging in evangelistic or service activities, as worthy as those may be. God by the Spirit is already at work in all the places where sin and evil hold sway, and God invites his people to join him in his patient project of making everything new.

4. *If we read Revelation missionally, we will read it as a people shaped by the story of the slaughtered Lamb.* Whatever struggles we face interpreting the book's strange symbols and perplexing visions, one thing remains constant: this is the revelation of *Jesus Christ.* Revelation tells the story of Christ—his awesome majesty, his final victory, his glorious return. But above all, it narrates the story of the Lamb who was slain to redeem people from every tribe, tongue, and nation to serve him as a kingdom people and as priests in the world (Rev 1:5-6; 5:9-10). The same Lamb who loves us, in effect, issues the invitation: "Follow me *wherever* I go, all the way to the cross" (Rev 14:4). The costly, cross-shaped mission of the Lamb not only provides people a way of salvation; it also affords the church a way of doing mission. We engage in God's mission as a *cruciform* community. When conventional wisdom says, You have to wield power and promote yourself to be successful, Revelation calls us to a mission that is vulnerable and Lamblike.

When I think of Lamblike mission, I think of my doctor friend Gary, who organized the Covid Care Force, a group of Christian medical professionals who traveled *to* New York City during the height of the early coronavirus emergency to relieve frontline medical personnel in overstretched hospitals. Later, they extended their volunteer efforts to the Navajo Nation in the American Southwest and to Tijuana, Mexico, to care for the sick and vulnerable in communities devastated by Covid-19.

In a less dramatic role, I think of my father.[2] He chose early retirement from a leadership role in his denomination so that he and my mother could focus on a ministry of speaking in churches and mission conferences. Soon opportunities came to travel and speak internationally. They were thrilled about how God had opened doors for ministry. Then my mother was afflicted with Alzheimer's disease and everything changed. All their speaking engagements abruptly ended, and my father shifted to caring for my mother full-time—for seven years. As the disease progressed, that service became increasingly difficult and degrading. But I never heard Dad complain.

Sometime later, after my mother's death, the subject came up. I said, "Dad, that must have been so hard!" He paused and then reflected, "When I had to stop preaching and doing any type of public ministry, I felt utterly useless to God. I was pouring out my heart to God one day and feeling extremely sorry for myself. Then the Spirit seemed to say to me, 'Floyd, *this* is your ministry.' In that moment, I realized that caring for your mother during her time of great need was just as significant as anything else I had done in Christian ministry. From then on, I viewed serving my wife day after day as my highest form of service to Christ."

5. *To read Revelation missionally, we must read it as communities of witness.* The stream of *witness* winds its way through every form of terrain in the Apocalypse. Churches in John's world and ours continue Jesus' Lamblike testimony, empowered by the prophetic Spirit. Today followers of the Lamb sometimes wrestle with the question, "What should be our *priority* in Christian witness: What we *say* or how we *live*?" But that is like asking, "Which wing of an airplane is more important?" Revelation reveals a way of witness that is both spoken and lived; it involves both telling and doing. Christian communities that are shaped by the "testimony of Jesus" bear public witness in this comprehensive way. Let me give you one example.

Philip, one of my former students from Germany returned from theological college to his home area and began the work of Church in Action (*Kirche in Aktion*) in the city of Mainz.[3] His vision was, "to see Heaven break into

---

[2] I have adapted the following account from my book *Self-Giving Love: The Book of Philippians* (Bellingham, WA: Lexham, 2021), 65-66.
[3] Church in Action, accessed June 19, 2020, www.churchinaction.com/.

our lives, our city, and our world." Two years later, his lawyer brother Cris started Church in Action in a pub in Frankfurt, and ultimately their combined ministry expanded throughout the Rhine-Main region of Germany. Church in Action's multifaceted approach to mission involves gathering for worship and the Word (often along with meals) in public places like cafés, theaters, pubs, restaurants, and homes for the elderly, nurturing the spiritual growth of their small group "communities on mission," and serving the marginalized in a whole range of ways. That includes providing housing for refugees from the Middle East, offering food deliveries and free movies to the homeless, playing soccer (football) with asylum seekers, conducting youth clubs for urban teenagers, giving refugee children the gift of play through mobile game stations, having conversations with senior citizens at "Granny's Coffee," and organizing international service trips. Recently, they intervened on behalf of Emanuela, a sex worker who has been in Germany for twenty-five years. They helped her fill out forms for the health insurance she desperately needed, connected her to a debt counselor, and offered her unconditional love and friendship. In all this, they bear witness to the slain Lamb. Through both their lips and their lives they invite others to take up their cross and follow.

Revelation assures us that the church's costly, public witness *will bear fruit*. God will use the faithfulness of his people, even when it appears that God's opponents have the upper hand, to draw people from every nation to himself. The question is, Are we willing to engage in such a witness, when it costs us time, money, comfort, security, relationships, or reputation? Sharing in "the testimony of Jesus" demands no less.

6. *Reading Revelation missionally means reading it as communities of worship.* One of Revelation's most undertold stories is the way it weds mission and worship. Worship in Revelation places God firmly in the center of everything. It celebrates God's loving acts of creation and redemption in the past, and it reveals the future goal of God's mission—people from every tribe and tongue uniting in worship of the triune God. In between those events, Revelation hollows out a place for Christian communities to participate in that heavenly worship even now. Designed to be heard in a worship context, Revelation invites us, through liturgy and song, to reimagine the way we see

the world. Revelation-style worship publicly declares that God sits on the universal throne, a reality that *dethrones* the idols and ideologies that compete for our allegiance. If God alone is worthy of worship, then the church's mission is defined by our calling to invite people of all cultures and religious backgrounds to join the chorus of worshipers. By announcing the way things really are, the church's worship broadcasts a bulletin to outsiders who are listening in: come and join the worship and mission of the living God!

Does worship still carry a missional impact? Let me tell you a story. My former student Alex left a good marketing job in Shanghai, China, to do a six-month language course in a village in Germany. It happened to be the location of the theological college where I used to teach. Several students from the college got jobs cleaning the building where Alex was staying. They spent time with him, and in the course of their conversations, began to tell him about the God they knew and how he had changed their lives. This language about "knowing God" sounded strange to Alex, but he was intrigued. Then his German teacher, a new believer, invited Alex and the other students to visit a worship service at the college, where they might have an opportunity to get to know more people. Alex was immediately attracted by the joy that he witnessed in the students as they worshiped. He reflects, "I felt like a wanderer who finally found his home after a long journey."

Following the service, Alex spoke with Josh, one of the students who had befriended him. Alex commented, "You know, I think I'd like to become a Christian someday." Josh replied, "Why don't you become a Christian now?" "I don't know how," Alex said. "Don't I have to take *classes* first?" Josh explained, "All you have to do is pray and ask God." Alex didn't know how to pray, so Josh led him through a simple prayer of repentance. That morning, Alex joined the chorus of worshipers of the Lamb. Within a month, he enrolled in the college, and I had the privilege of mentoring him for three years. In time he sensed a calling to Christian ministry, migrated to the United States to serve a Chinese congregation, graduated from seminary, and eventually became an ordained minister and a military chaplain. For Alex, the joyful worship of Christians became a pivotal milestone on his journey to faith. That's missional worship.

7. If we want to read Revelation missionally, we will read it as part of a global, multinational community.[4] Revelation stretches our vision of the kingdom to include others from every nation, tribe, ethnicity, race, culture, and social and economic status. John's vision moves us to stop "othering" others. Biases, especially implicit ones, run canyon deep. Revelation calls us to face them squarely, for they have no footprint in the new creation. The Bible's last word pushes us to think beyond purely national interests and consider what is good for those from every "tribe and language and people and nation" (Rev 5:9).

Reading Revelation well, then, means reading it not only out of our own GPS location, or with like-minded companions. We also must carefully listen to how others read this book, particularly people whose culture, race, gender, or economic circumstances are different from our own. Otherwise, we will too easily adopt the familiar interpretations of our own mainstream culture or group. Isolated from others, we might, for example, think the symbol of power-hungry Babylon (Rev 17–18) only applies to "somewhere else" and struggle to recognize Babylon's presence in our midst. J. Nelson Kraybill is surely right that for churches in relatively powerful and secure societies like the United States, "it may be difficult to hear or accept John's radical critique of imperial power, a critique that seems logical to many people in the two-thirds [majority] world."[5]

My own perspective has been strongly shaped by reading Scripture together with students and colleagues from cultures other than my own. I gained a deeper insight into the beastly nature of religious nationalism from students in Western Europe, whose societies have suffered its devastating effects. I learned to empathize more fully with the victims of Babylon's dehumanization through interacting with students in the Philippines and Africa who bear its wounds. My understanding of Revelation's images of the persecution of God's faithful was transformed through teaching Middle Eastern and Asian students, for whom that was a common life experience.

---

[4]Sections 7 to 10 borrow significantly from Dean Flemming, "Locating and Leaving Babylon: A Missional Reading of Revelation 17 and 18 in light of Ancient and Contemporary Political Contexts," *Missiology* 48 (2020): 122-24. Used with permission.

[5]J. Nelson Kraybill, *Imperial Cult and Commerce in John's Apocalypse*, JSNT Sup 132 (Sheffield: Sheffield Academic Press, 1996), 10.

Students from the East helped to expand my sensitivity to the *shame* borne by those who identify with the slaughtered Lamb. These were, and continue to be, humbling encounters. They force me to see what otherwise I couldn't see.

Certainly, we must bring questions to the text that arise out of our local circumstances. Revelation's message must be contextualized to be meaningful to people within their life situations. But the goal is not to splinter our interpretation of Scripture into a host of self-contained readings from isolated contexts. Done well, reading Scripture missionally enables each local or national church to hear how its own voice contributes to the multinational chorus in God's coming kingdom (Rev 7:9).

8. At the same time, *a missional reading of Revelation must prioritize God's truth.* John shows deep concern for bearing witness to the truth of the sovereign God and the slaughtered Lamb, and we must follow his lead (Rev 20:4; 21:5; 22:6). This suggests that we cannot accept every interpretation of Revelation as equally valid. Popular dispensationalist readings, for example, which see Revelation simply as an unfolding script for future events that has little to do with the church in the present, represent an *escape* from God's mission. They are as different from the story Revelation tells as kale is from cotton candy! Such readings too often have led to highly individualized interpretations of Revelation (making sure I'm transported to heaven before all the bad stuff happens on earth). They have blinded Christians to the church's mission of embodying heaven on earth *now.*

On the other side, readers who think that John's visions are about resisting empire and bringing about the transformation of society in present history *alone* miss John's prophetic already-but-not-yet perspective.[6] Ultimately, our missional readings of Revelation, however relevant to a specific context, must be rooted in "a vision of a God who reigns over history and the story of a victorious Lamb who has redeemed a people of all nations through his sacrificial death and will return bearing both judgment and salvation."[7] John's way of doing theology for his first-century context flows

---

[6]E.g., Pablo Richard, *Apocalypse: A People's Commentary on the Book of Revelation* (Maryknoll, NY: Orbis, 1994), 3-5; Howard-Brooke and Gwyther, *Unveiling Empire*, 158-59.

[7]Dean Flemming, *Contextualization in the New Testament: Patterns for Theology and Mission* (Downers Grove, IL: IVP Academic, 2005), 293.

out of this defining vision, and *our* readings of Revelation must as well. Particularly in contemporary settings where truth is a chameleon that changes its colors to fit personal preferences or political agendas, we must seek to anchor our readings of Scripture in the bedrock truth about God and Christ.

9. *If we are going to read Revelation missionally, we will read it* as a *prophetic community.* A missional reading of Revelation can't help but challenge the idolatry, immorality, injustice, and violence in our societies, since they directly oppose the loving purposes of God. The Bible isn't partisan, but it is profoundly political. God's people must discern and name sins like racism, nationalism, individualism, and consumerism, which are woven into the fabric of our systems of political and economic power. Many Western Christians hide behind a fig leaf of privatized piety, quoting prooftexts like "Render unto Caesar the things that are Caesar's" (Mt 22:21 ASV) and Romans 13 to absolve them from resisting the powers that challenge God's rule over the world.

> *"The African church continues to contribute substantially to bad governance . . . mostly by default, through silence and inaction. . . . Failure to resist evil means accepting evil, with all its consequences."*[8]
>
> GEORGE KINOTI

Whatever our setting, we can't merely point fingers. Revelation forces us to confess where *we* have participated in the arrogance and injustices of Babylon.

I write these words from the context of *both* the global pandemic of Covid-19 *and* the outcry spurred by recent cases of unspeakable violence against Black people in the United States. In my context, churches, particularly predominantly White churches, have been forced to reckon with

---

[8]George Kinoti, *Hope for Africa and What the Christian Can Do* (Nairobi: AISRED, 1994), 40. Cited in Gift Mtukwa, "Holiness, *Missio Dei* and the Church in Africa," in *African Contextual Realities*, ed. Rodney L. Reed (Carlisle, UK: Langham Global Library, 2018), 14.

our historic silence about the structures of injustice that dehumanize Black persons and create the conditions for a pandemic that disproportionately ravages communities of color. Too often the White American church has played the role of the priest and the Levite in Jesus' parable of the Good Samaritan, not the Samaritan, regarding the presence of systemic injustice. Like those pious religious leaders, we *see* the suffering of a neighbor but look away and continue our comfortable lives (Lk 10:31-32). We (which includes *me*) need the courage to *confess* our silence and indifference, to *listen* to others who have experienced injustice, and to *stand up* to evil and empire, whether it dresses in personal or structural clothes. I am encouraged that my local church joined many other congregations in entering into partnerships of conversation and service with Christian communities from a different cultural and social demographic than our own. I pray that such relationships will help us discover our blind spots and find ways to engage in practices that promote justice in our communities. I have so much to learn.[9]

> *"Action is the proper response to take with respect to a world that is not the way it should be, because, although human action does not bring about life in God (that is God's unconditional gift to us), human action of a certain sort is what life in God requires of us. Only one way of living in this world—living so as to counter suffering, oppression, and division—corresponds to life in God, achieved in Christ. Life in God is not inactive then. Life in God sets a task for us."*[10]

KATHRYN TANNER

---

[9]For seven concrete practices toward creating antiracist churches, see Drew Hart, *Trouble I've Seen: Changing the Way the Church Views Racism* (Harrisonburg, VA: Herald Press, 2016), 98-105.

[10]Kathryn Tanner, "Eschatology Without a Future?," in *The End of the World and the Ends of God: Science and Theology on Eschatology*, ed. John Polkinghorne and Michael Welker (Harrisburg, PA: Trinity Press International, 2000), 234.

10. It follows that *to read Revelation missionally, we must read it from below*, in solidarity with the weak and the marginalized. Babylon's violence targeted not only persecuted *Christians* but also "all who have been slaughtered on earth" (Rev 18:24). Interpreters such as Allan Boesak and Pablo Richard insist that Revelation's prophetic critique of Babylon calls God's people to get caught up in God's liberating, restoring work on behalf of powerless people.[11]

Reading from below doesn't require that we feel the scorpion sting of Babylon's injustice and exploitation personally. Revelation's audience, after all, included the Laodiceans, who famously boasted they were rich and needed nothing (Rev 3:17). What's more, Babylon hoodwinked not only the "big shots" but also the ordinary crew—"seafarers" and "sailors" (Rev 18:17), who profited from the city's wealth and protection. Today, the poor and the powerless also can buy into a "God and country" Christianity or a promise of wealth and security that degrades others. Bauckham wisely claims that a perspective from below "is the result of standing for God and his kingdom against the idolatries of the powerful." As a result, Revelation's message of prophetic resistance speaks to both the affluent and the oppressed.[12] Whatever our circumstances, we must read Revelation through the lens of the wounded Lamb.

11. *Reading Revelation missionally involves reading it as communities that care about God's creation.* Revelation extolls God as the Creator and sustainer of the world and unveils God's plan to reestablish his sovereign rule over all creation through the mission of the slaughtered Lamb. That plan reaches its goal in the new heaven and the new *earth*—a flourishing creation that is transformed by the loving presence of God. As Barbara Rossing quips, "God still loves the earth and comes to dwell in it. . . . God will never leave the world behind!"[13] In Revelation, God's purposes of healing and

---

[11] Allan Boesak, *Comfort and Protest: The Apocalypse from a South African Perspective* (Philadelphia: Westminster: 1987), esp. 118-22; Pablo Richard, "Reading the *Apocalypse*: Resistance, Hope, and Liberation in Central America," trans. C. M. Rodriguez and J. Rodriguez, in *From Every People and Nation: The Book of Revelation in Intercultural Perspective*, ed. David Rhoads (Minneapolis: Fortress, 2005), 146-64.

[12] Richard Bauckham, *The Theology of the Book of Revelation* (Cambridge: Cambridge University Press, 1993), 161.

[13] Barbara Rossing, "For the Healing of the World: Reading Revelation Ecologically," in Rhoads, *From Every People and Nation*, 171, 172.

redemption embrace humans, trees, rivers, and stars. It almost goes without saying that "God, humans, and creation are all entangled together."[14]

If we read Revelation well, it can help set an agenda for *Christian* environmental action and advocacy. That agenda includes at least six dimensions: First, we must *repent* of "our part in the destruction, waste and pollution of the earth's resources and our collusion in the toxic idolatry of consumerism."[15] We must recognize and lament that our lifestyles have contributed to the alarming loss of biodiversity that earth depends on and the increase of greenhouse gasses that contribute to a warming planet. Too often, the church has been tone-deaf to the groaning of creation (Rom 8:22).

Second, local congregations must begin to *teach* God's people the biblical mandate for creation care, including Revelation's vision of new creation, as part of their ongoing preaching and discipleship ministries. Leaders and teachers must help Christians understand and practice the full implications of the mission of God. As Douglas and Jonathan Moo put it, "We need . . . to put creation back into new creation."[16]

Third, we must *alter* our lifestyles, as persons and Christian communities. That includes rethinking everyday decisions in light of their effect on God's creation. It also means breaking our habits of unnecessary consumption, which contribute to environmental distress.[17]

> *"The right thing to do today, as always, is to stop, or start stopping, our habit of wasting and poisoning the good and beautiful things of the world which once were called 'divine gifts' and now are called 'natural resources.'"*[18]

WENDELL BERRY

---

[14]Micah D. Kiel, *Apocalyptic Ecology: The Book of Revelation, the Earth, and the Future* (Collegeville, MN: Liturgical, 2017), 116.

[15]*The Cape Town Commitment*, Lausanne Movement, I.7.A, www.lausanne.org/content/ctcom mitment.

[16]Douglas J. Moo and Jonathan A. Moo, *Creation Care: A Biblical Theology of the Natural World* (Grand Rapids, MI: Zondervan, 2018), 222.

[17]For concrete suggestions on practicing lifestyle creation care, see Moo and Moo, *Creation Care*, 225-35.

[18]Wendell Berry, *Our Only World* (Berkeley, CA: Counterpoint, 2015), 171.

Fourth, we must learn to *rejoice* in God's creation. Nothing renews my attentiveness to the task of biblical creation care more than the experience of inhaling a mountain vista, walking on a tree-lined bike path near my home, or listening to a cuckoo bird call in the spring. For me, these are moments of renewal and worship, but they also remind me of the fragility of God's earth in the present age.

Fifth, we must *encourage* "Christians whose particular missional calling is to environmental advocacy and action, as well as those committed to godly fulfilment of the mandate to provide for human welfare and needs by exercising responsible dominion and stewardship."[19] Can we begin to see creation care vocations, including scientific research, habitat conservation, partnering with communities and churches, and advocacy for creation at various levels, as legitimate mission work, deserving of our blessing, prayer, and support?

Sixth, we must appropriately *take action* to persuade governments, companies, and agencies to place the protection of the earth ahead of political and financial self-interests. *How* we go about that will depend on the local context and the opportunities available to us. Nevertheless, the scale of the problem demands that personal lifestyle changes alone aren't enough. Issues such as climate change and the destruction of ecosystems beg to be addressed at policy levels.

Even as Rome's greed and violence exploited both people and the earth's resources in John's world, today misuse of God's creation is soldered to economic and social injustice. The damaging effects of climate change, for example, disproportionately target the poor throughout the world. Micah Kiel points out that "changing climate will have an unbalanced impact on smallholder farms and those who practice subsistence agriculture. Poor countries do not have the infrastructure or income to deal with rising seas, air pollution, or water pollution."[20] Lack of care for God's creation cannot help but harm people. In one case, the greed of the multinational oil industry in collusion with political power brokers in Ogoniland in northern Nigeria over that past fifty years has left a legacy of poisoned water, denuded

---

[19]*Cape Town Commitment*, II.B.6.
[20]Kiel, *Apocalyptic Ecology*, 91.

mangrove forests, toxic soil, and smoke-filled air in that region, with devastating health and economic consequences for local people.[21] Although the options for Christians in modern democratic societies are quite different from those in John's world, Revelation's perspective surely invites us to speak truth to power, to advocate on behalf of both oppressed people and an exploited earth, to urge those with power to have the courage to envision and enact real change.

"The scriptures always promised that when the life of heaven came to earth through the work of Israel's Messiah, the weak and the vulnerable would receive special care and protection, and the desert would blossom like the rose. Care for the poor and the planet then becomes central, not peripheral, for those who intend to live in faith and hope, by the Spirit, between the resurrection of Jesus and the coming renewal of all things."[22]

N. T. WRIGHT

12. *If we read Revelation missionally, we will read it with a renewed imagination.* One of Revelation's greatest gifts to the church is its capacity to help, and sometimes, push God's people to reimagine their world. Richard Bauckham reminds us that the Apocalypse "recognizes the way a dominant culture, with its images and ideals, constructs the world for us, so that we perceive and respond to the world in its terms."[23] Revelation unmasks that world as a false story, one that seeks to maintain the power of the powerful and substitutes idols of various stripes for worship of the God who reigns. John calls us to resist counterfeit versions of reality, to see the world through

---

[21]"UNEP Ogoniland Oil Assessment Reveals Extent of Environmental Contamination and Threats to Human Health," UN Environment Programme, August 7, 2017, www.unenvironment.org /news-and-stories/story/unep-ogoniland-oil-assessment-reveals-extent-environmental -contamination-and.

[22]N. T. Wright, "The New Testament Doesn't Say What Most People Think It Does About Heaven," *Time*, December 16, 2019, https://time.com/5743505/new-testament-heaven/.

[23]Bauckham, *Theology*, 159.

Spirit-corrected lenses, to imagine a world in which God is on an unstoppable mission to make everything new. That's a vision worth following.

Such a transforming vision sculpts not only what we *see* but also how we *act* and *live*. In 1963, Martin Luther King Jr. had the audacity to reimagine his world. He narrated a God-given vision, a *dream* that resisted the bitter state of inequality and systemic racism in his world. He dreamed of a day when places that sweltered with the heat of oppression would be changed into oases of freedom and justice, when the Lord's glory would be revealed and all flesh would see it together (Is 40:5).[24] That vision determined the character of his active witness in the world and the direction of the community he represented. In many ways, King's dream visualized Revelation's new creation, a vision whose full realization still lies in the future. But John's vision continues to urge us to actively bear witness, through our words and our lives, to the dream of New Jerusalem in the very midst of Babylon.

> *"We are perhaps most true to [Revelation] when we . . . engage in constructing visions true to the ideals represented by God. Those who are able to dream—to visualize a state of affairs where war, violence, prejudice, and poverty are no more—can never again devote their gifts and services to anything but bringing that vision into reality."*[25]
>
> DAVID deSILVA

In the movie *Contact*, scientist Dr. Ellie Arroway journeys through a wormhole and becomes the first human to see a part of the universe never seen before. Awestruck by its beauty, she barely manages to utter, "They should have sent a poet."[26] To grasp, teach, and embody John's vision of

---

[24]Martin Luther King Jr., "I Have a Dream," speech, Lincoln Memorial, Washington, DC, August 28, 1963.
[25]David deSilva, *An Introduction to the New Testament: Contexts, Methods and Ministry Formation*, 2nd ed. (Downers Grove, IL: IVP Academic, 2018), 829.
[26]I owe this illustration to Kiel, *Apocalyptic Ecology*, 94.

God's mission in Revelation takes more than scientists. It calls for poets, *re*imaginers, people who, by the Spirit's eye surgery, "see visions" and "dream dreams" (Joel 2:28).

Revelation unveils the power of symbols and images to express God's truth. This connects well with many people in the Majority World, where symbols, oral storytelling, and drama often communicate the good news better than reasoned arguments. But the imaginations of Westerners today are also shaped largely by media, music, images, and sensory experiences. Fantasy flicks enjoy massive popularity. Might John's poetic and imaginative way of doing theology suggest a pattern for helping our neighbors and fellow Christians to revision their understanding of God's work in the world?[27]

13. *To read Revelation missionally, we must read it as people whose present is shaped by God's future.* Throughout this book we've seen that everything in Revelation leans toward the future, when God's purpose reaches its goal. At the same time, that future provides the key to how we perceive and practice our present mission in the world. Jim Belcher offers a helpful analogy:

> Imagine . . . that you can't be present to watch your favorite team on TV in the Super Bowl. So you DVR it. On the way home to watch it, you stop at the 7-Eleven for some chips and salsa and overhear, to your chagrin, the final score of the game. Your team has won, but you are ticked at the spoiler. You go home and start watching the game anyway. Right away your team falls behind by two and then three touchdowns. Normally, you would be losing your mind and your temper, throwing things at the TV, full of anxiety and anger. But this time you aren't. Why? Because you know the end of the story, and your team wins. This knowledge transforms how you see the sporting world on that day. . . . And when the end of the game comes, the feeling is fantastic. Knowing the end beforehand changes everything.[28]

Helpful. But the analogy only goes so far. Knowing how the game ends *does* change my whole perspective, but not simply so that I can kick back in my recliner and watch things play out. For John, grasping the story's outcome *draws us into the game* as players, not spectators. *We* become part of

---

[27]Flemming, "Locating and Leaving Babylon," 122.

[28]Jim Belcher, *In Search of Deep Faith: A Pilgrimage into the Beauty, Goodness and Heart of Christianity* (Downers Grove, IL: IVP Books, 2013), 246-47.

the Lamb's team! The mighty Lambs! That means actively playing a position on a unified squad, giving it utmost effort, never losing sight of the triumph that we know lies ahead. In the process, we risk getting injured, suffering a broken leg or a bloody nose. But when the final whistle blows, we can share in the Lamb's victory in a way we never could have from the comfort of an easy chair.

"If we cannot join our beginning to our end, we will live scattered and incoherent lives. The expectation of Jesus' coming provides a goal that shapes and unifies life in accordance with its origins in Christ, in patterns that are consonant with its completion in Christ."[29]

EUGENE PETERSON

Revelation assures us that the victory that changes everything has already been accomplished in the slaughter and resurrection of the Lamb. But that triumph can't reach its fulfillment until God has driven every droplet of evil from his world. Until "the kingdom of the world" has truly become "the kingdom of our Lord" (Rev 11:15). Until the world's nations are wholly healed (Rev 22:2). That's the magnificent goal of God's mission. Yet *until* that happens, we are called to live as outposts of New Jerusalem, in who we *are*, what we *do*, and what we *say*. We are granted the task and the privilege of showing a world that's watching over the fence what it looks like for God to make *everything* new, in a partial but very real way. And when that happens, in small ways, new creation breaks through in this world.

Whenever a Chinese student encounters the joy of a worshiping community and embraces the God they glorify, new creation breaks through. Whenever a team of medical personnel walks into the crucible of a viral pandemic ward in the name of Jesus to offer hope and healing, new creation breaks through. Whenever a community of Christians in secular Europe brings the loving presence of Christ into the bars, brothels, and refugee

---

[29]Eugene H. Peterson, *Reversed Thunder: The Revelation of John and the Praying Imagination* (San Francisco: HarperSanFrancisco, 1988), 191.

camps of their city, new creation breaks through. Whenever small gatherings of believers, in forgotten places, doggedly bear witness to their neighbors in the face of persecution and suffering, new creation breaks through. Whenever privileged Christians dare to break their silence, when they work side by side with sisters and brothers of color to dismantle the fortresses of injustice, new creation breaks through. Whenever Christians reprioritize their overconsuming lifestyles or work with local communities to restore a stripped forest in Africa out of love for God and God's world, new creation breaks through. Whenever believers from different cultures, nationalities, and income levels join to truly listen to one another and to worship the Lamb together, new creation breaks through.

> *"Revelation sings of God's power and intent to renew God's world, and in this sense it is gospel. . . . Revelation is important to Africans because it nurtures this vision of the future and inspires them to action to bring the vision about."*[30]
>
> JAMES CHUKWUMA OKOYE

I write these closing words from a context of uncertainty, fear, and upheaval in the world. A global pandemic rages, cries for justice for all reverberate, national economies reel. Creation groans as ancient rainforests are leveled at unprecedented rates. As in many times and places, the world feels broken and the future insecure. It is a good time to *reimagine*.

My local church has a vision statement, part of which reads like this: "Imagine a place where . . . the lost are found, the hurting are healed, the young are nurtured, the old are cherished, where all are welcomed and Christ is adored." Let me expand that vision. Imagine a place where . . . the disabled are valued, every culture is celebrated, racial hierarchies are demolished, ethnocentrism ends, human trafficking dissolves, persecution disintegrates, refugee camps disappear, and underserved neighborhoods become

---

[30]James Chukwuma Okoye, "Power and Worship: *Revelation* in African Perspective," in Rhoads, *From Every People and Nation*, 121.

extinct. Imagine a place where every species of tree, insect, or amphibian can flourish, where justice flows like a river, where God's presence fills the earth, and where people of every language group join with all creation in perfect worship of God and the Lamb.

Revelation implores us to imagine such a place. This isn't John Lennon's humanistic dream of people living only for today. It is *God's* vision for a new creation. But a missional reading of Revelation also teaches us to let the future cast its light into the present to guide our way. When outsiders see our Christian communities, do they see concrete evidence of God's loving purpose to make everything new? May we who have ears truly hear what the Spirit continues to say to the churches today.

QUESTIONS FOR REFLECTION
OR DISCUSSION

INTRODUCTION: REIMAGINING REVELATION

1. What is the first thing that comes to your mind when you think of the book of Revelation? How would you characterize your experience with Revelation in the past?

2. How would you describe the basic approach to interpreting Revelation for you and your Christian community? Has reading this chapter caused you to rethink that approach?

3. Does the way *mission* is defined in this chapter agree with or challenge your previous understandings of *mission* in the Bible?

1. WHAT IS REVELATION TRYING TO DO?

1. Does a *literal* or an *imaginative* reading of Revelation come more naturally to you? Why do you think that is the case?

2. How might Revelation's character as a "word on target" for real churches in ancient Asia Minor influence how your Christian community interprets and applies Revelation today?

3. Following the lead of first-century congregations in Asia, try reading or listening to Revelation as a whole in one sitting. How did that experience change your perspective on the book?

4. Can you think of any cultural images, stories, or values that Christians today could draw on to communicate God's transforming good news to people in your setting?

2. The God of Mission

1. In your own words, summarize how Revelation might answer the question, "What is God like?" How does this compare with how you would typically answer that question?

2. How do you respond to the idea that caring for God's creation is a vital aspect of our participation in God's mission in the world? What might that mean for you personally or for your Christian community?

3. How does Revelation's witness that God seated on the throne is the one and only source of salvation, healing, and restoration for the world speak into your culture? In light of this, how should we respond to people of other religious traditions or belief systems?

3. The Mission of the Slaughtered Lamb

1. Does your Christian community or tradition tend to give more emphasis to Jesus as the conquering Lion or the vulnerable Lamb? Practically, how has that influenced your understanding of Christ's mission in the world?

2. What difference does it make that the slaughtered Lamb is not only the source of our salvation but also the pattern for *how* we engage in God's mission? Give some practical examples of what a Lamblike mission might look like in your context.

3. Revelation shows us a God who conquers his enemies not by power and force but by the weakness and self-giving love of the slain Lamb. How does that picture challenge common ways of thinking and living in your culture?

4. The Mission of God's People

1. Which of the attitudes that we find among the congregations addressed in Revelation 2 and 3 do you think best fits the church in your context and why?

   - Faithfulness in persecution

   - Compromise

   - Loss of first love

   - Complacency

2. Practically, what would it mean for your Christian community to stand in the middle, mediating between God and the world today?

3. How does Revelation's picture of the church as a unified worshiping community from every nation, people, and language (Rev 7:9) speak into your church context? What barriers might hinder that from becoming a reality?

4. Can you think of any ways that the character and conduct of God's people might either advance or detract from your congregation's participation in the mission of God?

5. Mission as Witness

1. Do you think that a witness of word or of lifestyle is more needed today in your context? Explain.

2. Do you feel that you have ever had to endure suffering because of your costly witness to Christ? If so, what form did that take and how might it compare with some of the examples in this chapter?

3. What might a public, prophetic witness before a watching world look like in your Christian community's setting?

6. MISSION AND JUDGMENT

1. After reading this chapter, how would you describe the relationship between God's judgment on the wicked and God's loving purpose for all nations in Revelation?

2. Have you ever struggled with the violent images in the book of Revelation? How has this chapter informed your view of those passages?

3. How do you think Revelation's message of God's judgment and God's salvation might speak to people who are suffering and oppressed today? What specific groups of people in your community might need to hear that word?

7. MISSIONAL WORSHIP

1. On a scale of 1 to 10, where does the worship music in your local Christian community fall between declaring the truth about God and his restoring mission (1) and offering adoration and praise to God (10)? Can you think of ways to reach a better balance between the two?

2. In a world that is often a broken and fearful place, how might our worship help us to reimagine the way things really are, in light of God's loving purposes for the world?

3. Revelation's worship invites us to declare publicly that God alone is worthy of our loyalty and the idols of our culture are not. What are some of the idols that compete for peoples' loyalty and worship in your congregation and culture?

4. In what ways might your congregation's worship serve as a catalyst for mission in your context?

8. MISSIONAL POLITICS

1. Is the idolatry of "civil religion" ever a temptation in your church context? How might your local congregation concretely respond to this issue?

2. Can you think of any cases in which Christians might need to push back against political or government powers that act in "beast-like" ways by aligning themselves with injustice or demanding ultimate loyalty?

3. How would you answer the question, "Where is Babylon today?"

4. What might it mean for God's people to leave Babylon behind in your life situation? Specifically, what are the implications of that for economic practices and the treatment of "outsiders"?

9. A NEW JERUSALEM MISSION

1. What is the popular view of heaven in your church context? How does it compare to Revelation's picture of New Jerusalem in chapters 21 and 22?

2. Practically, what might it look like for God's future purpose to make everything new (Rev 21:5) to be embodied now by God's people in your setting?

3. What would it mean to live as a community of hospitality that embraces the "other" in your context?

4. How do the cities in your setting compare to Revelation's picture of New Jerusalem? Practically, how can we enable our longing for the future city to shape how we respond to the realities of the cities and towns in which we live?

10. READING REVELATION MISSIONALLY TODAY

1. Is the book of Revelation seen as a resource for guiding the church's participation in the mission of God in your context? If not, why do you think that is so?

2. Which dimensions of a missional reading of Revelation discussed in this chapter especially seem to target you and the Christian community where you live?

3. Have you ever read Scripture in conversation with people from a different culture, race, or economic situation? If so, what fresh insights or perspectives did that experience provide? If not, what might make that practice possible?

4. What are some specific ways that your understanding of Revelation and its message for the church have changed while reading this book?

FURTHER READING

Bauckham, Richard. *The Theology of the Book of Revelation*. Cambridge: Cambridge University Press, 1993.

Beale, G. K. *The Book of Revelation: A Commentary on the Greek Text*. Grand Rapids, MI: Eerdmans, 1999.

Boesak, Alan. *Comfort and Protest: Reflections on the Apocalypse of John of Patmos*. Philadelphia: Westminster, 1987.

Boring, M. Eugene. *Hearing John's Voice: Insights for Teaching and Preaching*. Grand Rapids, MI: Eerdmans, 2019.

———. *Revelation*. Louisville, KY: John Knox, 1989.

Blount, Brian K. *Revelation: A Commentary*. Louisville, KY: Westminster John Knox, 2009.

deSilva, David A. *An Introduction to the New Testament: Contexts, Methods and Ministry Formation*, 2nd ed. Downers Grove, IL: IVP Academic, 2018, chapter 24.

Flemming, Dean. *Contextualization in the New Testament: Patterns for Theology and Mission*. Downers Grove, IL: IVP Academic, 2005.

———. "Revelation." In *Wesley One Volume Commentary*, edited by Kenneth J. Collins and Robert W. Wall, 908-34. Nashville, TN: Abingdon, 2020.

———. *Why Mission?* Nashville: Abingdon, 2015.

Goheen, Michael W., ed. *Reading the Bible Missionally*. Grand Rapids: Eerdmans, 2016.

Gorman, Michael J. *Reading Revelation Responsibly: Uncivil Worship and Witness: Following the Lamb into the New Creation*. Eugene, OR: Cascade, 2011.

Hansen, Ryan L. *Silence and Praise: Rhetorical Cosmology and Political Theology in the Book of Revelation*. Minneapolis: Fortress, 2014.

Hays, Richard B., and Stefan Alkier, eds. *Revelation and the Politics of Apocalyptic Interpretation*. Waco, TX: Baylor University Press, 2012.

Howard-Brooke, Wes, and Anthony Gwyther. *Unveiling Empire: Reading Revelation Then and Now*. Maryknoll, NY: Orbis, 2003.

Johnson, Andy. *Holiness and the* Missio Dei. Eugene, OR: Cascade, 2016, chapter 9.

Kiel, Micah D. *Apocalyptic Ecology: The Book of Revelation, the Earth, and the Future*. Collegeville, MN: Liturgical, 2017.

Kovacs, Judith, and Christopher Rowland. *Revelation: The Apocalypse of Jesus Christ*. Malden, MA: Blackwell, 2004.

Koester, Craig R. *Revelation: A New Translation with Introduction and Commentary*. New Haven, CT: Yale University Press, 2014.

———. *Revelation and the End of All Things*, 2nd ed. Grand Rapids, MI: Eerdmans, 2018.

Mangina, Joseph L. *Revelation*. Grand Rapids, MI: Brazos, 2010.

McCaulley, Esau. *Reading While Black: African American Biblical Interpretation as an Exercise in Hope*. Downers Grove, IL: IVP Academic, 2020.

Middleton, J. Richard. *A New Heaven and a New Earth: Reclaiming Biblical Eschatology*. Grand Rapids, MI: Baker, 2014.

Ngundu, Onesimus. "Revelation." In *Africa Bible Commentary*, ed. Tokunboh Adeyemo, 1543-79. Grand Rapids, MI: Zondervan, 2006.

Okoye, James Chukwuma. "Power and Worship: *Revelation* in African Perspective." In *From Every People and Nation: The Book of Revelation in Intercultural Perspective*, edited by David Rhoads, 110-26. Minneapolis: Fortress, 2005.

Paul, Ian. *Revelation: An Introduction and Commentary*. Downers Grove, IL: IVP Academic, 2018.

Peterson, Eugene H. *Reversed Thunder: The Revelation of John and the Praying Imagination*. San Francisco: HarperSanFrancisco, 1988.

Reddish, Mitchell G. *Revelation*. Macon, GA: Smyth and Helwys, 2001.

Rhoads, David, ed. *From Every People and Nation: The Book of Revelation in Intercultural Perspective*. Minneapolis: Fortress, 2005.

Rossing, Barbara R. "For the Healing of the World: Reading Revelation Ecologically." In *From Every People and Nation: The Book of Revelation in Intercultural Perspective*, edited by David Rhoads, 165-82. Minneapolis: Fortress, 2005.

Thomas, John Christopher, and Frank D. Macchia. *Revelation*. Grand Rapids, MI: Eerdmans, 2016.

Weinrich, William C. ed., *Revelation*. Ancient Christian Commentary on Scripture, New Testament 12. Downers Grove, IL: IVP Academic, 2005.

Wright, Christopher J. H. *The Mission of God: Unlocking the Bible's Grand Narrative*. Downers Grove, IL: IVP Academic, 2006.

———. *The Mission of God's People: A Biblical Theology of the Church's Mission*. Grand Rapids, MI: Zondervan, 2010.

Wright, N. T. "Revelation and Christian Hope: Political Implications of the Revelation to John." In *Revelation and the Politics of Apocalyptic Interpretation*, edited by Richard B. Hays and Stefan Alkier, 69-83. Waco, TX: Baylor University Press, 2012.

IMAGE CREDITS

Figure 1.1. Pietro Perugino (c. 1448-1523). St. John the Evangelist on Patmos. Monastery of San Benedetto (Sacro Speco), Subiaco, Italy. Fresco. Photo by Livioandronico2013, Oct. 4, 2015. CC BY-SA 4.0 license / Wikimedia Commons (https://creativecommons.org/licenses/by-sa/4.0/deed.en)

Figure 1.2. The seven churches in Asia/ Wikimedia Commons

Figure 1.3. Bust of emperor Domitian (AD 81–96). Marble statue. Ephesus Museum, Selçuk, Turkey, 1st C. AD. Photo by Carole Raddato, April 8, 2015. CC BY-SA 2.0 license / Wikimedia Commons

Figure 2.1. The river of life in the new Jerusalem (Rev 22:1-2). Anonymous illustration from *The Apocalypse with Commentaries from Andrew of Caesarea*, c. 1800, Russia. Illuminated manuscript / Wikimedia Commons

Figure 2.2. Albrecht Dürer. *St. John Before God in the Heavenly Throne Room* from *The Apocalypse of St. John*, 1496-1498. Woodcut. Cleveland Museum of Art / Wikimedia Commons

Figure 2.3. Emperor Nero (54-68) and *Salus* (Salvation) with a libation dish, 65-66 AD. Roman coin. Classical Numismatic Group, LLC., www.cngcoins .com. CC BY-SA 2.5 license / Wikimedia Commons

Figure 3.1. Jan van Eyck, *Adoration of the Mystic Lamb* from the Ghent Altarpiece, 1432. St. Bavo Cathedral, Ghent, Belgium. Oil on panel / Wikimedia Commons

Figure 3.2. The Lamb Defeating the Ten Kings. From *Commentary on the Apocalypse,* Beatus of Liébana, 1220-35, Spain. Illuminated manuscript. J. Paul Getty Museum / Wikimedia Commons

Figure 3.3. Procession of the Black Nazarene, Quiapo, Manila, Philippines. *Get Real Post*, Jan. 8, 2019. CC BY-SA 3.0 license / Wikimedia Commons

Figure 4.1. Seven Churches of Asia. Trier Apocalypse, 800-850. Illuminated manuscript. Stadtsbibliothek, Trier, Germany / Wikimedia Commons

Figure 4.2. Columned street in ancient Ephesus. Turkey. Photo by author

Figure 4.3. Ruins of the temple of Artemis, Sardis. Turkey. Photo by author

Figure 4.4. Adoration of the Lamb on Mount Zion (Rev 14:1-5). Facundus Beatus, 1047. Illuminated manuscript. Biblioteca Nacional, Madrid, Spain / Wikimedia Commons

Figure 5.1. Statues of twentieth-century martyrs, west façade of Westminster Abbey, London, UK. Photo by Cephoto, Uwe Aranas, Oct. 3, 2013 / Wikimedia Commons

Figure 5.2. Rejoicing over the bodies of the two witnesses (Rev 11:9-10). Dyson Perrins Apocalypse, 1255-60, England. Illuminated manuscript. J. Paul Getty Museum, Los Angeles / Wikimedia Commons

Figure 5.3. The two witnesses ascending to heaven (Rev 11:12). Great East Window, York Minster, 1405-1408. Stained glass. York, UK / Wikimedia Commons

Figure 6.1. Albrecht Dürer. *The Four Horsemen* (Rev 6:1-8) from *The Apocalypse of St. John*, 1496-1498. Woodcut /Wikimedia Commons

Figure 6.2. The Eternal Gospel (Rev 14:6-7). The Cloisters Apocalypse, c. 1330, France. Illuminated manuscript. Metropolitan Museum of Art, New York / Wikimedia Commons

Figure 6.3. The Eschatological Harvest (Rev 14:14-20). Escorial Beatus, 950-55, Spain. Illuminated manuscript. Real Biblioteca de San Lorenzo / Wikimedia Commons

Figure 6.4. Pieter Bruegel the Elder. *The Last Judgment* (Rev 20), from *The Seven Vices*, 1558. Woodcut. Bibliothèque Royale, Cabinet Estampes, Brussels, Belgium / Wikimedia Commons

Figure 7.1. Adoration of the Lamb on Mount Zion (Rev 14:1-5). The Cloisters Apocalypse, c. 1330, France. Illuminated manuscript. Metropolitan Museum of Art, New York / Wikimedia Commons

Figure 7.2. John Bale. The beast worshiped by the nations (Rev 13) from *The Image of Both Churches*, 1535. Woodcut / Wikimedia Commons

Figure 7.3. Temple of emperor Domitian, Ephesus. Turkey. Photo by author.

Figure 8.1. The dragon giving a scepter to the beast from the sea (Rev 13:2-4). *The Apocalypse of Angers*, 1375-1380. Musée de Tapisseries, Angers, France Tapestry. Photo by Jean-Pierre Dalbéra, July 30, 2012. C BY-SA 2.0 license / Wikimedia Commons

Figure 8.2. William Blake, *The Number of the Beast Is 666* (Rev 13:18), c. 1805. Watercolor. Rosenbach Museum and Library, Philadelphia / Wikimedia Commons

Figure 8.3. Harlot of Babylon (Rev 17:1-8). Polyptych of the Apocalypse, 1360-90. Gallerie dell'Accademia. Venice, Italy. Photo by José Luis Bernardes Ribeiro, September 13, 2016. CC BY-SA 4.0 license / Wikimedia Commons

Figure 8.4. Emperor Nero (AD 54-68) and the goddess Roma holding the image of victory, 64-65 AD. Roman coin. Photo by Siren-Com, May 30, 2016. CC BY-SA 4.0 license / Wikimedia Commons

Figure 8.5. The goddess Roma sits on the armaments of defeated enemies. Relief on the exterior of the *Ara Pacis* (Altar of Peace), 1st century BC. Museo dell'Ara Pacis, Rome. Photo by Miguel Hermosa Cuesta, March 2, 2014. CC BY-SA 3.0 license / Wikimedia Commons

Figure 9.1. John sees the new Jerusalem descending, from *The Apocalypse of Angers*, c. 1375-1380. Musée de Tapisseries, Angers, France. Tapestry. Photo by Kimon Berlin, May 23, 2006 / Wikimedia Commons

Figure 9.2. The river of life (Rev 22:1-2). Facundus Beatus, 1047. Illuminated manuscript. Biblioteca Nacional, Madrid, Spain / Wikimedia Commons

SUBJECT INDEX

SCRIPTURE INDEX